The Ethics of Community

NEW DIMENSIONS TO RELIGIOUS ETHICS

Series Editors: Frank G. Kirkpatrick and Susan F. Parsons
Trinity College, Hartford, US, and Margaret Beaufort Institute of Theology, Cambridge, UK

The aim of this series is to offer high quality materials for use in the study of ethics at the undergraduate or seminary level, by means of engagement in the interdisciplinary debate about significant moral questions with a distinctive theological voice. Each volume investigates a dimension of religious ethics that has become problematic, not least due to the wider climate of reappraisal of Enlightenment thought. More especially, it is understood that these are dimensions which run through a number of contemporary moral dilemmas that trouble the postmodern world. It is hoped that an analysis of basic assumptions will provide students with a good grounding in ethical thought, and will open windows onto new features of the moral landscape that require further attention. The series thus looks forward to a most challenging renewal of thinking in religious ethics and to the serious engagement of theologians in what are most poignant questions of our time.

Published

1. *The Ethics of Community*
Frank G. Kirkpatrick

Forthcoming

The Ethics of Gender
Susan F. Parsons

The Ethics of Sex
Mark D. Jordan

The Ethics of Nature
Celia Deane Drummond

The Ethics of Race
Shawn Copeland

The Ethics of Community

Frank G. Kirkpatrick

Trinity College
Hartford, Conn.

First published 2001

2 4 6 8 10 9 7 5 3 1

Blackwell Publishers Ltd
108 Cowley Road
Oxford OX4 1JF
UK

Blackwell Publishers Inc.
350 Main Street
Malden, Massachusetts 02148
USA

British Library Cataloguing in Publication Data

A CIP catalogue record for this book is available from the
British Library.

Library of Congress Cataloging-in-Publication Data

Kirkpatrick, Frank G.
  The ethics of community / Frank G. Kirkpatrick.
    p. cm. — (Blackwell religious ethics)
Includes bibliographical references and index.
  ISBN 0–631–21682–0 (alk. paper) — ISBN 0–631–21683–9 (pbk. : alk. paper)
  1. Christian ethics. 2. Community—Moral and ethical aspects. 3.
Social ethics. I. Title. II. Series.
  BJ1251 K52 2001
  241′.62—dc21
                      00–009969

Typeset in 10.5 on 12.5 pt Bembo
by Graphicraft Limited, Hong Kong
Printed in Great Britain by MPG Books, Bodmin, Cornwall.
This book is printed on acid-free paper.

Contents

Acknowledgments

I would like to acknowledge the continuing support of colleagues both at Trinity College and elsewhere who have discussed with me the ideas in this book over many years. They include: Patricia Byrne, Maurice Wade, Jim Jones, Richard Nolan, Jack Costello, the Dean of the Faculty and the Dana Research Professors at Trinity who selected me to become one of their own, which gave me the time a few years ago to start the research that made this possible, the students who explored with me many of the ideas found herein, Alex Wright, and especially Susan Parsons, former colleague in the Religion Department at Trinity, and now for many years a long-distance colleague without whose support and encouragement this book would not have been undertaken.

For Liz, Amy, and Daniel: the community that is my immediate family.

Introduction

Together met, together bound: these words from a hymn by Brian Wren capture one of the most basic Christian themes: God intends persons to live in community with each other and with God as a condition for their fulfillment, well-being, and flourishing. Christians over the centuries have articulated (if not always practiced) variations on a philosophy of community in which the intention to live together with others in bonds of mutual love, compassion, and service has figured prominently. In most cases, they have also tried to live responsibly in political societies that, by their nature, are not communities of love, but rather, at best, associations characterized by principles of justice. The tension between the sometimes conflicting, sometimes complementary, allegiances to community and society have created an underlying problematic for a Christian ethics of community.

Today we live in a world in which there is both dominance of most human life by large political, economic, and social institutions and a continuing yearning for the intimacy of smaller, more directly personal communities. Especially in the cultures shaped by modern European history, there is an abiding tension between the ideologies that stress individual self-sufficiency and independence ("individualism") and those that speak a rhetoric of social belonging and fellowship. That tension (when stretched to the point of polarization) may well be the single most difficult obstacle that an ethics of community must attempt to overcome.

The task for a Christian ethic in the modern world is figuring out how to navigate responsibly between the political/economic societies in which we make our economic livings and struggle politically to bring justice to the oppressed, and the personal/mutual communities in which we hope to find a greater, more intense measure of personal meaning and fulfillment. The larger societies help us to give concrete expression to the demands of justice, especially for those with whom we are not intimately bound, and the smaller communities help us to express and to receive the gifts of love in more direct and personal ways. The complex orderings of an institutional and highly structured society also bring with them the promise of greater efficiency in the production, distribution, and consumption of the material goods that we have found are necessary to a life of well-being and flourishing in a created material order that we know to be "good" by God's design. This claim remains uncontested even when one goes on to say that not by bread alone is one's life fulfilled. Without bread, life is less full and the dignity of the human person less respected. The economic and political structures of society are necessary for getting that bread from the seed in the ground to the loaf on the table. The longing for the mutual intimacy of community alone will not produce bread on the scale necessary to feed all the members of all societies that share a common earth.

To complicate the picture, there are numerous "bridging" associations that stand between the individual and the larger society that offer a little bit of community and a little bit of society. These associations include more forms of human linkage than one could easily enumerate. They are neither wholly instrumental formal structures nor exclusively intimate personal communities encompassing the deepest dimensions of the human spirit. There are many different but often overlapping ways in which human beings live and work together. They include such things as bridge clubs, professional associations, recreational groups, fraternities, labor unions, fellowship groups, civic organizations, institutions, networks, fraternities and sororities, support groups, assemblies, congregations, leagues, neighborhoods, villages, unions, businesses, corporations, and so forth. Professional commonalities, geographic proximity, religious affiliation, business objectives, political goals, and common recreational pursuits, among other things, unify them. In much of the literature written by and about persons in them, the term "community" is used indiscriminately to refer to all of them at one time or another.

A Christian ethic of community must find a way to account for this whole range of forms of human association without eliding the significant differences between them. Nor must it confuse them with that form of community that is more distinctly rooted in a Christian understanding of what constitutes the fulfillment of human life under God. Today the claim that there is "a" Christian understanding of community is immediately contestable. Historically, of course, there have been many different understandings of community found under a Christian rubric. The community of the monastic order, of the Brudherhoff, of the inner-city Roman Catholic congregation, of the sprawling suburban megachurch, of the house church, the mainline suburban congregation, of the base community in

Latin America: each is a form of Christian community. Wherever two or
three are gathered together in Christ's name a community of some kind
has come into being.

One task for an ethics of community, therefore, is to establish the
ground on which claims can be made for a Christian understanding of
reality, in which community will take its rightful place. Or, to put it more
precisely, Christians need to understand reality as it is (both as created by
God and as intended for transformation and fulfillment by God. Reality is
what it is, including what it is capable of becoming. A Christian ethics of
community has as much of an obligation to grasp what reality is as any
non-Christian worldview does).

A Christian ethic must also articulate a notion of community/society
that without sacrificing the intimacies of smaller communal groupings is,
in some way, also inclusive (at least by design) of all human persons. God's
intention seems to be for some kind of universal community even while
the delights of lived community inevitably take place in historically vari-
able, contingent gatherings of fellowship that are, perforce, much more
restricted in size and inclusivity. How this divine intention is related to
a notion of human nature that is neither completely static (frozen in
the essentialities of the transtemporal) nor completely elastic (having no
essence that together binds all human persons in some commonalities),
must be worked out.

The thesis that will drive this study of the ethics of community is that
a viable Christian ethic must not only understand what it is about communities writ small that evokes something essential in our very nature as
human beings, but also what it is about communities writ large that
demands our attention and responsible social actions. We may be made for
community but we also live in societies that meet needs that communities
so far have not been able to meet.

A conversation is therefore imperative with the work of political philosophers, especially with those whose work provides a philosophy of society
hospitable to a Christian ethic of community. Much of the discourse presently available on Christian community focuses on the internal dynamics
of those communities that attempt to model or exemplify biblically
grounded visions of *koinonia* (the early Christian fellowships). As a result
they often avoid or take for granted the political and economic policies
and practices of the societies in which these communities find themselves.
These policies, however, are themselves highly contested within the field
of political philosophy and, as such, open up possibilities of conversation
with Christian moral philosophers. A viable Christian ethics of community
must find a way to bring its insights into community into conversation

with philosophers of society. The unity of the world and God's intention for an inclusive community do not permit the option of refusing such conversation. We cannot live fully (until the Kingdom comes) either in community or society.

However the link between community and society is worked out, it will mean a return to one of the most basic themes in Christian ethics: the relation between love and justice. I want to update that relation by reference to some of the most recent and influential work in political philosophy.

An adequate Christian ethics of community must have at least the following: an understanding of human nature, an awareness of the historical development of human beings enacting community in a variety of ways, a grounding in a biblical construal of nature and history, and a coherent understanding of the complexities of the relationship between community and society.

A preliminary distinction between community and society might be put this way:

1) *Community* is the locus of ultimate personal fulfillment: communion, fellowship, mutuality, and intimacy. The relationships that constitute a Christian communion are between human persons and between them and the divine Person. Personal relations in the community are generally direct, intimate, loving, and mutual. Friendship or fellowship among equals characterizes such gatherings.

2) *Society* is the locus for the impersonal distribution of power among large groups of people for attaining political and economic ends according to principles of justice. In the western liberal traditions these normally aim at greater equality of power and equal access to economic resources and political decision-making. The relationships that constitute a society are normally indirect, impersonal, and determined primarily by law and contractual obligations. Culture tends to straddle the two forms of association. Societies can reflect culture but so, at a more intimate level, can communities. And culture is necessary for both.

Outline

In chapter 1, "Foundations," I will develop and then build on the foundation of a Christian moral ontology that informs an ethics of community. That ontology will be informed by a reading of the biblical material, focusing primarily on the earliest forms of Christian community, or *koinonia*. These will be rooted in earlier Hebraic notions of what God was up to in the world in the calling of Israel to be God's people. The tension between a community as inclusive as the nation of Israel and the much narrower confines of the Christian *koinonia* will be explored.

In chapter 2, I want to look at some salient historical experiments in the building of Christian community as they occurred in European and American history. If history is the locus of human beings working out their construal of God's intention for history, then there are lessons that can be drawn from the success or failure of various communal and societal endeavors and their interrelationship. Their successes and failures can help to inform contemporary efforts at community, both as more narrowly intentional as well as more broadly societal. History cannot foreclose future options, but a purely abstract study of the philosophy of community runs the risk of foreclosing the insights and possibilities for community found in the myriad attempts to work out an ethics of community in practice over the course of the last 2000 years. There is much more in western history that gives credibility to community building than many traditional historical studies have acknowledged.

I will then turn to a philosophical grounding of community in the nature of human persons. If the moral ontology on which I am basing my ethics of community is correct, then, given God's intention and creative acts, there is some commonality and "essence" to human nature that can find fulfillment only in community. Drawing upon the work of the twentieth-century philosopher John Macmurray, I will develop a "philosophy of the personal." The philosophy of Macmurray provides essential and comprehensive metaphysical principles for establishing both a Christian concept of community and a secular (natural) understanding of society without segregating them from each other. The philosophy of community just established will then guide us as we work our way through recent philosophical and political visions, centering on liberalism and communitarianism, of what a good society and a fulfilling community ought to be, and what their relationship to each other might be today.

A theological caution against losing the authenticity of the church community in indiscriminate engagement with the secular world will also be explored. I will be attempting to build an argument that such engagement is theologically legitimate, even imperative, even though it ought not to lead to the loss of the distinctive contributions church communities can make.

It will then be time to explore the problematic and dangers of community. I want to balance the appeal of community with the need for individual "space" and rights protected from the overweening intrusions of too much community. This is the problem, in part, of respecting individual "otherness" or diversity and how to preserve it within community

without either subsuming it into a homogenous controlling ethos or de-
stroying the bonds of community in order to protect it.

Finally, I want to suggest some directions for communities as they
confront the structures of contemporary society around specific flashpoints
of social injustice. I will focus this discussion around the issue of economic
justice. What negotiations with society are required from within a Christian ethic of community in addressing this issue will be explored. What
political philosophies of society are more congruent with that ethic will be
developed.

The thread that holds all this material together is the notion of the
intention of God, working with and through human beings, to bring
God's vision of community to fruition. God's intention, according to the
ontology I lay out, is reflected in the creation of human beings such that
they, too, want community and will only be fulfilled by it. But it is also an
intention that works itself out historically. It weaves in and out of smaller
intentional groups and larger formal institutions and societal structures. It
holds in tension justice and love, community and the nation-state, the
dynamics of mutuality and the realities of power politics. But it will not let
go of the overarching commitment to the building of a community that is
intentionally if not always in practice universal and inclusive. This is what
is meant, I believe, by the last verses of the Christian canon in the Book
of Revelation when the writer declares "Then I saw a new heaven and
a new earth, . . . and I saw the holy city, new Jerusalem, coming down
out of heaven from God . . . Behold, the dwelling of God is with men"
(Rev. 21:1–3).

Chapter 1

Moral and Scriptural Foundations

Scripture and the Ethics of Community

When the postmodern "hermeneutic of suspicion" is trained upon the use of Scripture by ethical theory, it often leaves one drained of hope that anything can be salvaged from that text. Nevertheless, Scripture has been and remains one of the sources of authority for Christian ethics. Contemporary scholars can admit the contextuality of the text without abandoning its deep insights into the relationship between God and the human community as they developed historically.

Shaping a text is the work of human beings and, as such, it is a series of intentional acts. The biblical writers develop a narrative that constitutes testimony to what they took to be their encounter by and engagement with Someone whom they believed to be the most decisive influence in their individual and collective lives. They called that Someone Yahweh (as well as other names) and understood Yahweh to have acted with overwhelming force in their lives and the lives of their ancestors, whose stories they are narrating.

Old Testament scholar Walter Brueggemann has argued that the Bible is human speech (sometimes reporting what it takes to be divine speech) about (some) human beings' encounter with God over the course of a long period of history. Biblical scholarship is focused on what is said in the text about God, not upon what God is in Godself. We get at God today, he claims, through the text as uttered testimony to what the witnesses took God to be up to in their lives and in the world about them. Testimony through speech, of course, "shapes, enjoins, or constitutes" the reality to which it is a witness.[1] Eventually, that testimony becomes revelation when it is taken by later communities to be a "reliable disclosure about the true character of God."[2] The truth of scripture is precisely its reliability in disclosing the reality of a Being whose actions made and continue to make a difference in the world. If scripture has gotten its "take" on God's action and purposes wrong, then it will not prove reliable in the long run in guiding human action. When it fails the test of reliability it loses authority.[3] This suggests that no use of scripture for ethics can proceed until it comes to grips with the testimony to Yahweh by the people of Israel, and later of the Christian community that took Jesus to be significantly (even decisively) related to Yahweh. Unless the major part of that testimony has resonance today, it can be of interest only to antiquarians. If we are to find scripture "relevant" or "meaningful" to us, the experiences narrated in the text must somehow echo or illuminate our own experiences in the present. That is the basic presumption that must give force to any authority the Bible has for ethics. This is especially true for an ethics of community which, by the nature of its subject-matter, is grounded in a belief that it has truly discerned that one of the things God is up to in God's actions in the world is creating the conditions, often through trial and error, for a cooperative venture in creating a universal community for all persons characterized by peace, love, and justice. Community is both fact and intention in the Bible and an ethics of community is committed to the conviction that only by aligning or conforming one's actions with the direction of God's actions, can true community come into being. To use H. Richard Niebuhr's words, we must try to figure out through the text "what God is up to" in the world as God's actions are described in the text.[4] Getting a purchase on what God is up to is the foundation on which a viable ethics of community is to be established (assuming, as I will argue, that what God is up to is the creation of community).

[1]   Walter Brueggemann, *Theology of the Old Testament* (Minneapolis: Fortress Press, 1997), 121. Brueggemann, as I argue elsewhere, often confuses the proper relation between text and reality, as the phrase in this quotation indicates, when he says that speech "constitutes" reality. The point I want to make here is simply that testimony by others is our way into getting hold of their understanding of what they take to be reality.

[2]   Brueggemann, 121.

[3]   How long the "test" of one's construal of God's purposes and actions is to go on is a serious problem. But there has to be some kind of historical test because the text, in and of itself, cannot be its own authority.

[4]   See H. Richard Niebuhr, *The Responsible Self* (New York: Harper and Row, 1963).

Those who work within the boundaries of a religious community find that the texts that constitute the testimony of the shaping events and experiences of those who have constituted that community in the past yield a generally plausible picture of reality to which they intend to conform their lives. At the heart of that picture is a construal of God as the central dynamic Agent whose actions have been powerful enough to change lives and to have done so over and over again through a very long period of time. The picture one has of such a God is the result of a series of inferences drawn from the testimony of others in the past. This makes it less than absolutely certain knowledge but more than a wildly fictive construction made out of whole cloth (or merely imaginary material). Inferences are always tentative. They can be overturned or qualified by future experiences. They are also risky, especially if we commit ourselves to actions based upon them. The heart of the use of the biblical testimony for ethics is the inference that God is doing things that generally enact some overarching divine intentions that are coherent and consistent with one another and with human life. Ethics then becomes the intention of the human person who is grabbed by the power of the testimony to conform his life to what he has discerned to be the divine intention(s). Ethics is the active response to the inference or construal of what God is up to in the world. It is aligning one's life with what one thinks is the direction of history under the guiding purpose of the divine Agent.

The risky inferential nature of our knowledge of God is compounded by the biblical claim that God is a God of history. Things would be a lot easier if God were only the God of classical theology. In the classical view God is conceived as so ontologically transcendent of time, space, and matter that God has no direct engagement with history. The classical God is not an Agent, does not act, and is "beyond" all the contingencies of history. Believing in such a God is not risky, inferential, tentative or subject to historical confirmation or disconfirmation. To believe in the God of classical theology requires only a willing suspension of belief that knowledge (of some kind) is restricted to the temporal world of contingent experiences. A God who transcends that world totally, absolutely, ontologically is not subject to its limitations nor to its thought categories. But for ethics the bottom line is that this classical God can have no purposes or intentions, and can perform no actions to put them into effect in the world. Such a God, therefore, would have precious little to provide to an ethics of response to what God is doing in the world.

It is only a God who acts in the world according to intentions and purposes, and whose acts have the power to shape the world according to those purposes, who must be taken into account by a full ethics of response and intentionality. A full defense of the notion of God as personal Agent who acts in history is taken up elsewhere.[5]

The ontological foundations of the Christian ethic I am presuming in this study yields the following basic claims:

1) Christian ethics is founded on the ontological reality of a personal supreme divine Agent.

2) That Agent (God), expresses or manifests God's reality through historical actions, including but not restricted to the original act of creating the basic and essential conditions of life itself and the on-going acts of sustaining these conditions of creation; metaphysical systems that have no place for an acting, loving, relational, community-building God are not adequate to a Christian ethic. This means that such an ethic is committed to the further belief that:

3) The historical acts of the personal agent God are guided by a divine intention to fulfill, nourish, enhance, and bring to completion all life, but most especially human life; human beings may not be the sole end of God's intention, but they are special within the created order because, like God, and (to our present knowledge) unlike any other part of creation, they have the ability to act freely and in accord with moral principles and values;

4) The overarching divine intention requires that human life be lived in some particular ways if it is to be in conformity with the divine intention that persons be enabled to experience fully what it means to be fulfilled as persons. It is not compatible with every conceivable form of human behavior or with every possible notion of human nature; this means that a Christian ethic has a shape and content that specify it, concretize it, and differentiate it from other "life-plans" that are live options in the world today; this means that;

5) Morality is the actual living of human life in conformity with the conditions God has laid down for fulfillment; a Christian ethics is the reflection of this morality in thought; but the ethics is "proven" by the morality, and the morality is proven by its actual contribution to the working out of the divine intention, and this intention "doubles-back" and implicates as well as fulfills the life of the moral agent; this fact gives Christian ethics a strong teleological orientation (even though this does not obviate the need for principles, rules-of-thumb, attention to personal virtues, etc.);

6) The basis for human choices regarding values, therefore, is their willingness to conform to values that a more powerful agent has set forth, *provided that they want at some deep level to live in accord with the kind of life*

---

[5] See my *Together Bound: God, History, and the Religious Community* (New York: Oxford University Press, 1994).

those divine values promise and support (i.e., a life of flourishing and exquisite well-being); this means that at one level God is an "external" or heteronomous authority: God has structured reality in particular ways (i.e., it is not completely "open-ended") and complete human fulfillment is not possible unless it conforms to those ways, though human beings retain the freedom to reject the way of life God has determined to be the most fulfilling (but not to escape from the consequences of such a rejection);

7) The exercise of values in the shaping and living of a human life in interdependent relation with both human and non-human others (as opposed to a life of self-sufficiency or radical individualism) is the most distinctive form of human response to the divine intention;

8) If the divine intention includes the fulfillment of human persons, and human persons can be fulfilled only when their freedom is respected, then the divine intention cannot, logically, be fulfilled unless human beings freely choose to cooperate or align themselves with it;

9) Human life can be expressed in a variety of different cultural and personal ways (i.e., in diverse communities and societies) without violating or undermining the overarching divine intention that life is to be fulfilling: diversity in the expression of humanly fulfilling ways of life is a good that God intends and it does not need to conflict with universal, underlying structures of reality common to all life that intends to be in conformity with God's values;

10) The condition that holds together both universal human fulfillment in accord with God's intention and the diversity of human life that is also part of that intention is that fulfilling life, ultimately, can only be lived *in and through particular communities that are themselves oriented toward a universal human community bound together by God's love for it and the members' love for each other as empowered by God's love for them.* Mutual community is the singular locus that creates and reconciles diversity, particularity, fulfillment, and universality; the conditions of human community set the limits to diversity but at the same time provide the basis for its expression since no community can be satisfactory unless it nourishes the particularities of its members;

11) In practice, given the realities of the world, Christian ethics cannot be thought or done except in the context of particular, historically conditioned communities informed by and experiencing God's will as they are led by and intend to work toward a universal inclusive community as envisioned and intended by God. Christians cannot make adequate moral judgments completely outside the context of communal life lived in conformity with God's will. It cannot be stressed strongly enough that the origin of Christian ethics is in the life and work of Christians living together in community. It is their experience, prayers, convictions, and commitments, that constitute

the basis of theological reflection which, in turn, yields notions of the God who acts in their lives and who grounds the ethics by which they live.

Not all communities that express the intention to live together in love are necessarily conscious of their relation to the work of God as construed by Christian theology. If God's intention is truly hard-wired into the fundamental structures of the world, it should not be surprising if many persons have found the clue to reality (communal life together) without having found it through the Christian or biblical framework.

Holding all these claims together is the moral ontology reflected in a set of convictions that reality has been structured in a certain way by the acts of a particular decisive individual that we call God. The realities of God and the world that God has created cannot be ignored either in practice or in theory if one is to do Christian ethics for community in an adequate and persuasive way.

Moral Principles

Given the moral ontology I've laid out, it should be clear that I am placing the ethics of community primarily within a teleological framework. Moral action contributes to and is informed by a vision of the telos of divine activity in the world.

Because its goal is community, however, it is also an ethics of relationality. At the heart of community is the fulfillment that comes to persons only when they are in the most complete and satisfying relationships possible. Those relationships reach their culmination in bonds of intimacy and love with other persons, including, of course, God. As Charles Curran has said, "morality should never be seen primarily in terms of a legal model but rather in terms of a relationality-responsibility model which sees the individual human person in multiple relationships with God, neighbour, world and self."[6]

I would also suggest that this ethics is congruent with, if not identical to, a natural law ethic in the sense that it is grounded in an understanding of human nature as "essentially" relational and communal. Ironically, the "essence" of relationality is the opposite of a frozen or static essentiality: instead it is characterized as openness to change, growth, maturation, and freedom. As such the essence of the human is not a timeless, oppressive, imprisoning fact. We should not be misled by the traditional criticism of "essence" that it necessarily confines us to some transhistorical/ahistorical

---

[6]   Charles Curran, "Absolute Moral Norms," in Bernard Hoose, ed., *Christian Ethics: An Introduction* (London: Cassell, 1998), 79.

condition that severely constrains our freedom to develop as persons in a variety of ways and under different historical conditions.

Given the centrality of relationality and responsibility, the ethics of community will be guided by moral principles that encourage actions that contribute to the building of relationships of trust, love, compassion, and justice. These qualities or virtues constitute the fully human and are the core of any fulfilling community.

Moral actions that intend the construction of community also have a strongly pragmatic dimension to them. Moral action is not simply reduplication of present prevailing patterns of behavior. It also looks toward the future, toward that which has not yet come fully into being and which will not come into being without the concerted efforts of human persons acting morally to achieve the telos of community. The evaluation of action intending community is, at least in part, dependent upon the actual results of such action. If the biblical narrative is right, then not even God's own actions are finally complete until, in practice, the community God intends has come fully into being.

In a relational ethic actions are always dependent upon the response of the Other. Thus there is a certain uncertainty, contingency, and precariousness (even risk) in the undertaking of ventures that intend community. Experiments in community will come and go, succeed and fail in various ways and to different degrees. These ventures in community have a pragmatic quality to them: if evaluation of them is appropriate it ought to be based on their relative success (or failure) in attaining the goals of community. Pragmatism, however, is not to be saddled with notions of short-run gain for private or selfish reasons, or focused primarily on superficial objects or ends. Pragmatism, as I am using the term, simply means paying attention to the results of action and not just to the actions themselves or the purity of their motives. I am situating the ethics of community, therefore, in the context of a teleological ethic that intends community, grounded in the primacy of relationality, as it takes shape over the course of time in the contingencies and pragmatics of history.

It should also be clear that I am developing "an," not "the" ethics of community. I have construed from the biblical text and from history a particular way in which the sources of Christian ethics can be deployed in the service of community-building. I do not claim that this way trumps all the other forms of Christian ethics that have been developed over the ages. I would claim that the ethics of community I have developed is consistent with the core of Christian ethical thinking, but given the historical contingency in which we all exist, and the limited nature of human knowledge, I can only present my take on an ethics of community as one among many.

Scripture and Community

It is now a commonplace of biblical scholarship that the narrative of scripture reveals a deep and abiding interest in the construction of human community (always lived in relation to God). What community means for the biblical writers turns out to include a great deal of diversity but also some common threads. At the heart of the biblical ethic is a conviction that what is appropriate and good for the creation and maintenance of community remains always under the ministering agency of God.

Within the biblical testimony there were in the historical experiences of the biblical people emergent and shifting senses of community. At the beginning of the narrative, community was virtually synonymous with the "nation" or the "people" of Israel. Later a sense of a more universal and inclusive community of all the gathered nations of the earth began to take shape. Nevertheless, much of the prophetic literature is still focused on the problems of justice within the people of Israel. When we reach the New Testament, there seems to be a dual emphasis on the universality of Christ's redemption of all people (the Kingdom of God on earth) and, in the between-times, on much smaller, more intentional communities (or *koinonia*) that stood apart or withdrawn from larger social entities. Nevertheless, even the *koinonia* model practiced by the early Christians never entirely replaced the vision of a universal community of persons that was anticipated sometime in the future. An ethics of community lives in the tension between the aspiration toward an end-of-history universal, inclusive community of all persons and the historical reality of living now in a complex relation between intentional communities and larger, increasingly global, societies.

Whatever else God was inferred to be "up to" in God's actions in the world, the growth of community was always taken to be central to God's intentions.[7] One assumption that Paul Hanson and other biblical scholars make is that community is part of what God has intended from the beginning for the fulfillment or completion of all human beings. It is therefore both an historically enacted purpose of God and, through God's original creative act, a fact that human nature is fulfilled only in community. Biblical scholar Robin Scroggs has said: "God has created persons *for*

---

[7] I will draw heavily on the work of New Testament scholar Paul Hanson in my treatment of community in the Bible. His book *The People Called: The Growth of Community in the Bible* (San Francisco: Harper and Row, 1986) is a major text dealing with the subject.

community, and only within this sustaining community is his [sic] creation of authentic humanity complete."[8] (For a nonbiblical accounting of the necessity of community for human fulfillment see the later chapter on John Macmurray and the metaphysical grounding of community.) Hanson has also claimed that both social science and our own experiences have verified the truth of our need for community.[9]

The importance of this claim cannot be overlooked. If it is true then the biblical construal of attempts to build and sustain community is not just one myth set over against others having little more than relative truth. The biblical narrative would have to be seen as grounded in a claim to truth about human reality as such, no matter how many different historical *variations* of communities there are. So what God is up to can be tracked by narratives drawn from historical human experience, by stories told about experiences in the present, and by philosophical reflection on the deeper nature of human beings and their world. These trackings of God's work should all converge at some point in an understanding of community that, at some level of abstraction, unifies, complements, and completes them. In short, community is not a will-'o-the-wisp dream but a well-justified hope built into the very foundations of reality itself as that reality has been constructed decisively (but not entirely) by divine action. An ethics of community would, therefore, necessarily have to conform to that reality if it wishes to complete itself by reference to reality. An ethic that flies in the face of "what is the case" (or what *will be* the case if God's intentions prevail) is an ethic that can ultimately only lead to frustration and failure. This does not mean that an ethic cannot seek to *transform* the *present* structures of reality as they have been devised and revised by human hands. The direction of change, however, must be guided by some sense of which structures are, in fact, ultimately most appropriate for the relational, communal nature of persons.[10]

---

[8]   From Robin Scroggs, *Paul for a New Day* (Philadelphia: Fortress Press, 1977), 39. Quoted in Hanson, 1.

[9]   Hanson, 1.

[10]   It will be obvious that throughout this treatment of the Bible and community I am presupposing the moral ontology previously laid out. I assume the reality of God as a personal Agent who acts in history to accomplish God's intentions. I assume the reality of human persons who are free, to various degrees, to respond to, challenge, refuse, or accept God's intentions (as best they have construed them) for the building of community as that which will fulfill their nature. I also assume the continuing necessity of construing and inferring from the text certain conclusions that never quite reach the status of absolute certainty.

The Hebrew Scriptures: Deliverance from Egypt

Clearly the originating event in the growth of community in the Bible was the exodus from Egypt. By God's decisive actions, a people was created and brought from oppression into freedom. (Later, stories would be imagined or remembered about ancestors of this people such as Abraham who had been called by God to go forth so that God could, in time, make of him a "great nation." By Abraham all the families of the earth would eventually bless themselves (Gen. 12:1–3).) This clearly suggests a vision of a universal community bound together by God's power and covenant. What the biblical writers seem to have in mind here is a sense of community first as a nation, and, ultimately, of all nations gathered together under the lordship of one God. There are virtually no references in these particular biblical texts to what today we would call smaller, more intentional face-to-face communities, though these, presumably, had their place in the overall intention of God. The biblical picture of community never entirely abandons the notion of community as a larger, sometimes even tribal or national association of persons that goes beyond direct and intimately personal relations. This point underscores the importance of larger, less directly personal forms of association even as the ethics of community focuses on more intimate models of relationality that now seem to predominate in the contemporary literature on community. What writers often refer to as "community" in the Bible really is what we will call "society," suggesting that the lines between the two are much more blurry than some treatments might suggest. This will reinforce my claim that communities and societies must be in constant negotiation with each other over their respective contributions to the full development of the human person both socially and individually.

The exodus experience itself reveals a direct confrontation by God with the structures of political and economic power in a nation. God does not restrict God's actions to direct personal relationships. In the actions of the exodus event the personal characteristics of the Pharaoh, while adding color to the narrative, never subsume the importance of the Pharaoh's office as a political institution. In truth, it was the undermining of many of the structural privileges of the Egyptian "state" that constituted the heart of God's liberating action on behalf of a "people," not simply of discrete, individual persons taken separately. In particular the assumption that the wealthy as a "class" could presume to control the lives of the poor by virtue of their wealth was fundamentally challenged. Later, as the nation of Israel came into being, a special concern for the poor as a class and not just as individuals denuded of class or economic status permeated its sense of covenant and was the oft-repeated message of the social prophets.

As Hanson puts it, "within this community [Israel as it emerged from the exodus], every individual was equally precious to God, regardless of social standing, and thus to be protected from exploitation and oppression by the structures intrinsic to the covenant between God and people."[11] The text, however, makes fewer references to God's personal relationship with specific individual persons, such as Moses and Aaron, than to the people as a whole. When God's love for the people is highlighted it has less of the sense of mutual intimacy between persons (of the kind normally associated with community) than of a sense of the choseness of a group for God's special purposes.

God's love brings Israel into being and sustains her. Love in this context is primarily fidelity, commitment, and trustworthiness, not intimate passion. "I have loved you with an everlasting love; therefore I have continued my faithfulness to you" (Jer. 31:3). Brueggemann has said of the term love (of the people for Yahweh) in this context that it is a "covenant word that means to acknowledge sovereignty and to keep one's oath of loyalty."[12] From Israel's side this love does not "rule out an affective dimension" but the emphasis remains on keeping one's promises to the Other, not necessarily on deep affection for the Other. From God's side, this sense of love as faithfulness and choice of the Other is not incompatible with a sense of love as rejoicing in the presence of the Other or as delight in mutuality. But the passionate desire for intimacy with the Other is not highlighted in the more common references to God's love for Israel. It is not clear, in short, what God gets out of the love relationship God establishes. (That is part of the wonder expressed in the notion of choseness.) It is also one of the themes that later gets expressed in the concept of God's *agape* love. For reasons having more to do, perhaps, with assumptions regarding God's radical Otherness in relation to the world, later theologians would insist on *agape* love as having no element of divine self-regard or reciprocal attachment. This lack of reciprocity on God's part to the feelings toward God of the people God has chosen limits (but does not fatally undercut) the relevance of a notion of God's love for the people set forth in the testimony of the Exodus experience for a notion of an intimate loving community of mutual delight.

The community that came into being as a result of the exodus was a nation, not a *koinonia*, a society, not strictly speaking a community. It was

[11]   Hanson, 23.
[12]   Brueggemann, 420.

to be structured by social, political and economic policies grounded in a notion of justice. This particular "community" meant persons "bound in membership to each other, so that each person-as-member is to be treated well enough to be sustained as a full member of the community."[13] The elements of that sense of justice were recalled vigorously by the prophets as they chastised the political and economic practices of the people, especially with respect to their treatment of the poor and marginalized, the outcasts, the aliens, and the strangers. Justice is to be the foundational public policy of the nation. It is a "mandate to order public policy, public practice, and public institutions for the common good and in resistance to the kind of greedy initiative that damages the community."[14] Even when the most intimately personal metaphors are employed to describe God's relationship to Israel (such as the husband and his wayward bride by the prophet Hosea), they are directed to justice in the nation, not to individuals in limited direct personal relations with God. It is the people, as a collective whole, who are to be the recipients and bearers of the responsibility of covenant action.

One implication of this claim is that community is an historical phenomenon: it grows and changes over time; the goal of community will be expressed in a variety of forms; it is subject to human intervention and alteration; it does not or ought not to reify structures and institutions when they have outlived their usefulness; and usefulness is always determined, within a theistic framework, by reference to the intention of God for the fulfillment of human being. Hanson puts it this way: "every new generation was afforded the opportunity of gaining a deeper insight into God's righteousness on the basis of new chapters in God's involvement with this world." This explains the community's ability to "adopt profound changes" and "experience new lessons in righteousness and compassion."[15] This openness to change did, as Hanson admits, lead to a sense of historical "precariousness" that many other ancient communities tried to avoid by retreating to timeless myths. But the Yahwistic community was able to be open to the future and to new ways of being in community precisely because it trusted in the overarching power of God's purpose to bring about a universal kingdom of love, peace and justice out of the tentative and historically contingent experiments in community.

The universal thrust of the mission of the people of Israel becomes pronounced in the prophet known as Second Isaiah. In his rendering of

[13]   Brueggemann, 421.
[14]   Brueggemann, 423.
[15]   Hanson, 76.

the idea of the Servant whom God will raise up, the notes of extending God's love to the whole earth are played more strongly than before. God now declares that "it is too light a thing that you should be my servant to raise up the tribes of Jacob and to restore the preserved of Israel; I will give you as a light to the nations, that my salvation may reach to the end of the earth" (Isa. 49:6). Israel is reminded that she remains central to God's intentions but is not the sole object of God's love or faithfulness.

This universal vision articulated by Second Isaiah did not, of course, immediately supplant the life of community/society within the Israelite nation itself. As Hanson points out, it would be historically irresponsible to fail to notice that in the restoration of the people after exile in the Second Temple tradition, the universal vision often gave way to the practicalities of getting the particular community of faith, Israel, reestablished. That community would lead over time to Judaism as it developed under Hillel and the Rabbinic teachers. Christians and the anti-Semitism that arose from some interpretations of their teachings bear no small part of the responsibility for having kept that community from expressing the more universal vision found in Second Isaiah. Judaism remains today one of the many experiments in community that emerges from the biblical tradition and is well-grounded in it. "If Christians expect religious Jews to take seriously their interpretation of Second Isaiah's vision, they dare not neglect the carefully developed exposition of how God's righteousness and compassion can find embodiment in the everyday life of the faithful community that was developing within the stream of tradition reaching from Ezra and Nehemiah to Hillel and Judah the Patriarch."[16] As we will see, other experiments in human community would arise in the Christian tradition. They, too, would exhibit a tension between the particularities of a close-knit community and the universalities of a community that at least intended to be inclusive of all people. That tension constitutes the problematic within any genuine ethic of community for the modern and postmodern age.

New Testament and Community

It would be difficult to find a more central or exemplary expression of community in Christian literature than that which appears in the New Testament descriptions of the church. These communities of believers

[16] Hanson, 251.

were called *ekklesia* or *koinonia*. *Ekklesia* meant simply a public assembly, often the popular assembly of the political community. In the Hebrew Bible the most significant such assembly was that of the people of Israel called together by God at Mount Sinai to receive the covenant. The term was taken over by the Christian church to refer to the assemblies of fellow Christians also understood as the people of God. *Koinonia* meant a community of sharing, having all things common (*koina*), and referred primarily to the practices of the early Christian gatherings. It also seems to have referred to some kind of "fellowship" of sharing, some sense of participation in a common task.

In a sense these gatherings were a kind of condensed or compressed people of God, the nation of Israel squeezed into small, usually face-to-face, communities scattered across the Middle East and the Mediterranean basin. What they were not were socioeconomic political states or nations in the modern sense (comprising a large number of people who share a civic commonality but not necessarily a religious one). They did not have the same contours or structures as had the nation of Israel in both its pre- or post-exilic life.

The *koinonia* were primarily withdrawn from the larger, often hostile or indifferent political societies in which they were precariously located. Those whose lives were shaped and even consumed by the *koinonia* had little to contribute to the "secular" society around them. Using the early Christian *koinonia* as the only reference point for all other communal expressions clearly skews an understanding of community away from engagement and negotiation with social-political societies and towards the more personal, direct, intimate communities of love. The problems, dynamics, and promises of the latter do not always transfer easily to the former. The underlying thesis of this study is that some kind of transfer is necessary but not sufficient for an ethics that wants to come to grips with living with political and economic power responsibly in a world that is heavily structured by societal, not just communal, arrangements. The early Christian *koinonia* are vital for understanding what Christians understood as the fullness of life, but their potential for illuminating contemporary questions about the proper economic, social, and political institutions that determine the structures of societal justice has to be carefully parsed. A limited potential is not no potential, however. The difficulty will be to find how to utilize the potential of the *koinonia* for life in a complex, highly institutionalized world without either collapsing them into each other or making unwarranted claims for the power of *koinonia* as the complete answer to the inadequacies and ambiguities of society.

Pauline Communities of Faith

It is clear from Paul's letters that the ministry of the early Christians in their *koinonia* was first to each other. They were to build each other up and love each other as brothers and sisters. There is far more emphasis on this intramural devotion than there is on ministry to the world around them, except in the broad sense of making Jesus' message of salvation known to all the peoples of the earth.

Numerous references are made throughout Paul's letters to the churches as the new Israel, the Israel of God, and the people of God. But the complex social, economic, and political dimensions of the older Israel are either removed from this new Israel or brought within the confines of the *koinonia* itself. Like the first Israel, the Christians understood that they too had been delivered, not from political/economic bondage in Egypt but from bondage to sin and had now been bound together by the power of God through a new covenant in a community of common faith and life.

Gerhard Lohfink insists that the public life of Israel as a people was always at the center of Jesus' concerns. His calling of the twelve apostles exemplified his eschatological hope for the eventual restoration of the people of Israel as a prelude to the rule of God universally applied to all the nations or peoples of the earth.[17] But Jesus understood God's rule as first taking concrete shape in a community of persons claimed immediately and directly by God as a foreshadowing of the Kingdom to come. Jesus' "goal was that the rule of God be fully established, that it come *visibly* into appearance . . . in the people of God"[18] as found in the church. Robert Banks has argued that while Paul's communities were small voluntary associations of "like-minded" people, he taught them to "regard themselves as the visible manifestation of a universal and eternal commonwealth in which men [*sic*] could become citizens."[19] Neither wholly as a universal society nor simply as segregated enclaves of intimacy alone would the developing Christian understanding of community be constituted.

Nevertheless, without abandoning the universal thrust, Paul's letters deal almost exclusively with the internal dynamics of the ekklesial life of the people of God. The ethics of community for these congregations was almost entirely inward-looking. How could they live together responsibly,

[17] Gerhard Lohfink, *Jesus and Community: The Social Dimension of Christian Faith* (Philadelphia: Fortress Press, 1984), 10.
[18] Lohfink, 27.
[19] Robert Banks, *Paul's Idea of Community* (Grand Rapids: Eerdmans, 1980), 49.

in the Spirit, making themselves a people worthy of the salvation God had granted them? An essential part of that worthiness consisted in making themselves as different from the pagan world around them as possible. They were to put on the new nature God had given them. They must structure their communities so that this new life could be lived most fully. This meant separating as much as possible from "the world." As Wayne Meeks points out, conversion to a life in Christ meant one faced a fork in the road: the one (back into the world) led to vice; the other (more deeply into the church) led to virtue.[20] Only in relationships with like-minded and like-inspired persons could life in Christ be fully manifested.

In its inner life the community of Christians will be characterized by mutual love and compassion. But between it and the world beyond there will be enmity and strife. So much so that while new unities are being forged among the believers, new divisions will tear up previous bonds of attachment in the outer world. Jesus says he came to bring division even among such "sacred" unities as the family. "Do you think that I have come to give peace on earth? No, I have come to bring division." Jesus' attack on the traditional understanding of family relations is replaced by a new understanding of the family as that community which does God's will.

The church exists in the tension between its responsibility to model life in the kingdom within its *koinonia* bound together by mutual love and the Spirit of God, and its awareness that the kingdom has not yet come for all persons. It has a vision of the ultimate unity of all people under God according to the divine plan "set forth in Christ" in which God will "unite all things in him, things in heaven and things on earth" (Eph. 1:9–10). But the day of unification is not yet and life in the here and now for these early Christians was to be led inside their communities, not between them and the world beyond.

Its internal life was not entirely divorced from its vision of the whole world living eventually in community with God and each other. Nevertheless, the day-to-day practicalities of ecclesial life as described in the New Testament are clearly not suitable for a worldwide community as such, at least not until the kingdom comes in all its fullness transforming all the structures and institutions of the world.

The *koinonia* brought together a variety of individual gifts, as Paul notes on more than one occasion. But these gifts are to be exercised for the community itself, for its common good (Acts 4:32 and 1 Cor. 12:7). To convey the unity of the community Paul invokes the image of the body

[20] Wayne Meeks, *The Origins of Christian Morality* (New Haven: Yale University Press, 1993), 69–70.

with its many organs or functions. The body is one, the members are many, but together they comprise a unified integrated whole. The members are to have the same care for each other, so that if one suffers they all suffer; if one is honored they are all honored.

Love recurs again and again as the unifying element in the community of faith. It should be noted that when Paul speaks so eloquently about love it is always with reference to what the members of the *koinonia* owe each other, not what they owe those outside their faith communities. This does not suggest necessarily that they were unconcerned about the "others" beyond their circle. It simply means that relations in the world "out there" were either to be characterized by something other than love, e.g., by justice, or were understood to be potential recipients of God's transforming power that would be fully realized when the Kingdom came in all its fullness.

But concretely, what did love entail for the actual practices of these ecclesia? For one thing, love broke down the social (and artificial) boundaries that civil societies had drawn around certain classes of people. Women and slaves, for example, are to be treated as full members of the religious ecclesia. How far the community went in actually living up to this radical egalitarianism is, of course, debatable. But the principle was clear.

Notions of the absoluteness of private property were seriously qualified if not abolished in these early koinonia. Not only did they hold possessions in common, but they were to be used for meeting human need, not primarily for individual pursuits. "There was not a needy person among them, for as many as were possessors of lands or houses sold them, and brought the proceeds of what was sold and laid it at the apostles' feet; and distribution was made to each as any had need" (Acts 4:34–5). This distribution also extended to the need of other churches (e.g., from the Church in Corinth to the church in Jerusalem: 1 Cor. 16:1–4).

It is true that this practice of an early form of communism did not survive intact much beyond the first few centuries, especially after the church was finally given toleration and eventually a privileged position in the Roman empire. Nevertheless, the principle of the stewardship of possessions would remain for many Christians one that they could eventually carry over into the socio-political arena once they occupied positions of power within it, and by which they would be able to critique various ideologies that extolled the supremacy and absoluteness of private property without reference to the needs of the poor. How that principle is made operative in a pluralistic, liberal society is one of the most crucial issues that presently faces an ethics of community that wants to negotiate the relationship between communities of love and societies of justice. We will take this issue up more fully in a later chapter.

The radical experimentation in trying to live without reliance on social distinctions or the unlimited ownership of goods has led Lohfink to call these early *koinonia* "contrast-societies."[21] They were eschatological communities, waiting actively for the Kingdom in its fullness to manifest itself. They tried to live by principles not generally honored in the world around them. Lohfink claims that while Jesus preached an ethic of nonviolence to his disciples (and by extension to the communities that would emerge in his name after the Resurrection), he intended it to be an ethic "directly related to society; it had public character."[22] Just how that application to society was to take place is not clear, however, (though it led, in fact, to some Christians refusing military service) and continues to be one of the most trying problems facing Christians today who are usually torn between the nonviolent ethic of the early church and the just war principles that evolved during the middle ages.

Lohfink also notes that the early church practiced a kind of internal non-domination in its contrast mode of existence. If the Son of Man came not to be served but to serve (Mark 10:42–5), then in the church the mark of leadership is service to others. This service will build up the community for the common good through the ministries of love. Implicitly, of course, this model of authority through service could be used to critique the tyrannical forms of authority prominent in the world beyond the ecclesia. But again, given the eschatological mindset of these early Christians, it is not surprising that that critique was, in practice, much muted.

Paul willingly acknowledges the power of the state (though he severely limits the use Christians are to make of it). Given the reality of sin, Paul understands the need for order (which in turn requires the "sword" as the vehicle by which the non-Christian will be intimidated into obeying the law (the civil authority "is the servant of God to execute his wrath on the wrongdoer")). This in turn justifies the role of the sovereign, magistrate, or the "governing authorities." Their justification is ultimately, of course, God who provides them as a "terror" to bad conduct (of which Christians would presumably never be guilty) (Rom. 13:1–7).

Despite this acceptance of secular power and its use of violence, the early *koinonia* tried, as "contrast-societies," to live by very different moral principles. Nevertheless, if R. Riesner is right then the contrast dimension

[21] Lohfink. See especially the section on "The Church as Contrast-Society," pp. 122–32.
[22] Lohfink, 55.

of the church, its radical "otherness," was ultimately a means to the renewal of the whole world. "The decision to prefer to remain a minority with an unambiguous identity (rather than to secularize the church) is the presupposition of activity which will change the world."[23] This means that while the church is "separated to a different style of life and to new forms of life which realize what God wants society [sic] to be" it is also to make disciples of all nations.[24] Lohfink takes this to mean that there should be an increase in the number of Christian communities in the world "until one day all nations have become church."[25] Lohfink admits that Matthew has no idea how this is to happen, and neither does he. Nevertheless he is convinced that "*Jesus' complete concentration on Israel is thus not a lack of universalism, not a limited horizon, not retreat from the world; on the contrary, it is the essential presupposition for the possibility of the reign of God reaching all peoples.*"[26]

Lohfink has stated both the intentionality of the New Testament communities and their problematic. They clearly outline a way of life, lived in and through the Spirit of God, that promises fullness of life to all. Their chief marks are *agape* love, mutual service for the common good and the most needy, nonviolence, non-discrimination, and non-domination. These marks will presumably characterize the Kingdom of God. But what are those who understand these marks and look forward to the Kingdom to do in the meantime?

As the *koinonia* communities began to lose their separated status, as they spread into more of the "secular" world, and especially as they came under the privileged protection of the state, how were they to maintain their "contrast" character while embracing the opportunity to realize their universalizing "mission" character? Could they be communities in society or would they become institutional agents for administering and controlling society?

These became the key questions that would carry over into the middle ages, the Reformation, and eventually into the modern and postmodern world of today.

---

[23]   R. Riesner (from *Apostolischer Gemeindebau*) as quoted in Lohfink, 131.
[24]   Lohfink, 135–6.
[25]   Lohfink, 136.
[26]   Lohfink, 137. Emphasis in the original.

Chapter 2

Community in the Monastic Tradition

Any study of the ethics of community has to take into account monastic movements that, at least in part, attempted to form communities of persons devoted to the religious life lived before God. However, the monastic experience is ambiguous in terms of what can be retrieved from it for an ethics of community that is rooted in the primacy of mutual love between persons *and at the same time* wants to intersect in multiple complex ways with the larger societies in which such communities exist.

The problematic of monastic communities is their dual ambivalence regarding the importance of fraternal, communal feelings in relation to the individual's striving for a solitary relationship with God, and their ambivalence regarding their relationship to the larger society in which they existed.

The very word "monasticism" reveals the ambiguity of the monastic experience. Mono means solitary while a monastery is a community of persons. By design many of the monastic communities recalled the life of the earliest Christian *koinonia*. They built their communities around common worship, a common discipline (summed up in a "Rule" for each order), and communal possession of property. Many of them even cultivated a sense of common love and respect among the members.

Nevertheless, there is a strong emphasis in many of these monastic congregations on the community as a necessary scaffolding for each individual's attempt to rise above human attachments in order to achieve personal spiritual perfection and communion with God. There was, therefore, an abiding tension (more or less successfully reconciled depending on the particular monastic community one considers) between what is called the cenobitic (communal) impulse and the eremetic (or reclusive) aspiration.

The earliest model for the monastic life was the eremetic Anthony of Egypt in the third century who exemplified the retreat into the literal Egyptian desert, away from the world, to develop a solitary relation with

God. Persons following the model of Anthony often lived in caves devoting themselves to prayer, meditation, and the reading of scripture with little or no contact with other persons.

In the middle of the fourth century another Egyptian, Pachomius, introduced the cenobitic or common life dimension to eremetic monasticism. Those seeking spiritual perfection would live together under rules of chastity, poverty, and obedience. They were to be bound together as in the early *koinonia* in "one heart and one soul." But the intrinsic delight of simply sharing fellowship with each other was not mentioned as one of the goals of the community. Pachomius himself wanted a combination of strict asceticism and a sense of the monk's obligation to other people.[1] Nevertheless he saw his common life monasteries as extensions of the early *koinonia*.

In the medieval period the attempt to reconcile the cenobitic and eremetic traditions continued. On the one hand individuals entered these communities in order, as one writer put it, "to follow naked the naked Christ."[2] The community of fellow seekers for the solitary relationship with God was necessary, almost as a means to an end, because without communal support it would have been nearly impossible to maintain the intensity and rigor of an individual spiritual discipline. But within the communal setting the individual monk often experienced a "loneliness amid the crowd."[3]

The relation of the medieval monasteries to the world around them was itself often ambiguous. On the one hand they were retreats from that world. On the other hand they relied upon the world for their very existence. Most monasteries were endowed by wealthy patrons in the hope that the monks would pray for their souls. As one nobleman put it in the tenth century, while he cannot himself "despise all things," nevertheless, "by receiving those who do despise the world . . . I may receive the reward of the righteous."[4]

It is clear that most of these monastic communities were not interested in confronting or challenging the economic or political structures of the medieval world, at least frontally. Even internally they modeled much of the hierarchical authority pattern of the feudal society around them. Abbots

---

[1] See Philip Rousseau, *Pachomius: The Making of a Community in Fourth-Century Egypt* (Berkeley: University of California Press, 1985), 65.
[2] Ludo J. R. Milis, *Angelic Monks and Earthly Men* (Woodbridge, UK: Boydell Press, 1992), 29.
[3] Milis, 138.
[4] C. H. Lawrence, *Medieval Monasticisn* (London: Longman, 1984), p. 89.

and monasteries absorbed the hierarchical authority structures of the feudal world such that they generally admitted to their membership only the sons and daughters of the nobility. Even their commitment to hospitality to strangers rarely went beyond hosting the nobility or members of other monastic communities. While the monastic orders followed the *koinonia* in practicing hospitality, it was not always clear even in the early church that this was to extend beyond the community of faith itself as we saw earlier.

Many of those to whom hospitality was shown were Christians journeying from one place to another, often on pilgrimages. Thus monasteries looked outward toward the stranger but he was usually the Christian stranger, as well as inward toward the brothers already bound in communion with each other.

The feudal relationship between the monastery and the secular powers surrounding it also determined its form of engagement with the world. Princes and kings could call upon abbeys to supply them with soldiers just as feudal lords could demand such filial obedience from those dependent upon their authority and largesse. On occasion monks themselves donned the sword and went to fight for their prince. In such a climate, it was rare for a monastic order to challenge the political and economic practices of the feudal society around them on which they so clearly depended.

One exception to the tendency of most monastic communities to live harmoniously with their societies were some dissident Franciscans. They challenged some of the prevailing notions about the accumulation of wealth and the right to private property. However, this challenge was directed primarily at the Church, not at society at large. The so-called Spiritual Franciscans, drawing upon the practice of the earliest *koinonia*, claimed that since Christ had not instructed the disciples to own property, it was not appropriate for members of their order to do so. They could have, at most, what they called "poor use" (*usus pauper*) of material goods.[5]

In an important document from the period, the Franciscan St. Bonaventure wrote of the difference between two forms of poverty. The first requires a person to renounce all "private and personal dominion over temporal goods." Such a person is sustained by things he does not own but are shared with a community. The second requires him to make the same renunciation but he is sustained only by an outsider, not by the community. Bonaventure claims the first form of poverty prevailed in the early

---

[5]   See Edward Peters, ed., *Heresy and Authority in Medieval Europe* (Philadelphia: University of Pennsylvania Press, 1980), 235.

koinonia while the second came directly from Christ as an injunction to his apostles. Thus, he concludes, the more rigorous form of poverty is closer to Christ's command. It is "to be observed by renouncing not only material possessions, but even money and other things by which a community's life is generally sustained and held together."[6] Bonaventure's claims for the more demanding form of poverty were eventually rejected by Pope John XXII who declared it heretical because holy Scripture "expressly states in some places that they [Christ and the Apostles] did possess some things."[7]

While this dispute was ostensibly internal to the Franciscan order, it does suggest that the Spirituals' reading of poverty could be seen as having negative implications not only for the Church but also, albeit in an attenuated form, for society. Possession of property was dangerous because "the vice of covetousness [a deadly sin] and its disorder find their root in a disposition of the mind and their occasion and fuel in things possessed externally, [and therefore] extirpation of it must apply to both in order that the damaging passion of greed and alluring possession of earthly wealth may be given up both spiritually and materially."[8] A morally serious layperson could not help but feel the sting of this indictment even though, as the tenth-century noble referred to earlier said, he might not be able to live at the highest moral level enjoined by Bonaventure. The problem of wealth, in short, was not restricted to the monastery. To this extent the Christian monastic communities had an implicit critique of the larger society's economic practices even though they rarely developed it or applied it consistently or systematically either within or outside the monastery or the church at large.

While not suggesting that the monastic movement of the medieval period is irrelevant to an ethics of community for the present day, its understanding of community has limited potential for seeing community as something more than a vehicle for individual spiritual formation which does not challenge the structures and assumptions of the society that sustains it. While it certainly had a place for the brotherly (and sisterly) feelings of belonging and fellowship for the other members, the medieval monasteries were always tinged with a sense that community was ultimately a means to a greater end: the union of the self with God in which the communal dimension of the Kingdom is somewhat muted.

---

6 "St. Bonaventure: On *dominium* and *usus*," in Peters, 243.
7 "Pope John XXII: The Decretal *Cum inter nonullas*, 1323," in Peters, 247.
8 "St. Bonaventure: On *dominium* and *usus*," in Peters, 241.

Medieval Society

It might be argued that medieval society represented the "high water mark" of the Christian attempt to turn society into a large, comprehensive community incorporating essentially Christian principles and practices. Whether this society was a community in any meaningful sense remains an open question. It is true that under the influence of Church teaching and the administration of church officials, a common culture and a common set of religious convictions characterized most of western Europe. The lessons for an ethics of community from the medieval period are, at best, ambiguous and not easily transferable to a highly diverse, pluralistic, multi-cultural society typical of most western countries today. At the same time, the Christian conviction that somehow God's kingdom must embrace not only all people but all aspects of their lives, the universalizing dimension of the Christian faith, does explain to an extent the reach and sweep of Christian intentions that undergirded western medieval society.

At the heart of the attempt to structure all regnant societies around ostensibly Christian principles was a vision of a single organic whole of human life comprising religious, political, economic, military, and other social structures. The belief that moral principles derived from God ought to influence all private and public life was common throughout all divisions of society. Divisions common in a highly secularized culture such as our own between "church" and "state" were not configured in the same way, if at all, in the medieval period. It was, in a way, a true theocracy. God ("theos") was the source of government (from *kratein* = to rule, or *kratos* = authority), the foundation of society, and the ground of "community."

The problematic of thinking of medieval society as a single organic community did not center on its grounding in God's will, but on how that will was understood to be deployed across the religious–political spectrum. And the deployment was in turn grounded in a fundamental sense of the need for order imposed on a sinful humanity and an evil world. This order reflected itself in the hierarchical structures of medieval institutions, both secular and religious.

Paul's and Peter's references to the obligation of Christians to honor the governing authorities (see Romans 13 and Peter 2:13) provided a smooth transition into the medieval notion of "orders" by which church and state were placed in a functional relationship of hierarchical control and authority over the society in which each subpart had its own distinct role to play. In a preamble to a letter sent by Pope Gregory the Great to some bishops in 595 the organization of this Christian organism is set forth clearly.[9] Gregory says:

> Providence has established various degrees and distinct orders so that, if the lesser show deference to the greater, and if the greater bestow love [*dilectio*] on the lesser, then concord and conjunction [*contextio*: the word evokes a fabric or weave in a very concrete way] will arise out of diversity. Indeed the community [*universitas*] could not subsist at all if the total order [*magnus ordo*] of disparity [*differentia*] did not preserve it.

The three orders that emerge from this understanding of the deployment of *potestas* or power were the clergy, the nobility, and the "third" estate, or farmers. Ideally, they were to work together for the good of the whole society in which both body and soul cooperated to a single end: subjugation of evil in this world, salvation of the soul in the next. The clergy were to ensure salvation, the emperors to ensure peace on earth by establishing and maintaining order through hierarchical and coercive administration of law. The same hierarchical administration also characterized authority structures in the church, but this simply reflects the common assumption that power devolves from God downward in ranks of ordered hierarchical subordination. The papacy had received from God "plentitudo potestatis" (fullness of power) according Pope Leo I in the middle of the fifth century.

Thus was established what Colin Morris calls the "papal monarchy" which extended not just over the church but over the society as well. This monarchy would, of course, be contested by the secular powers throughout the medieval period, with various degrees of success,[10] but the claim of supreme papal power meant that, in principle, the "community" of the church now extended as widely as its power could reach and that reach was as broad as the whole of medieval society. To think of all the nations,

---

[9] See Georges Duby, *The Three Orders: Feudal Society Imagined*, trans. Arthur Goldhammer (Chicago: University of Chicago Press, 1980), 3–4, for a full rendering of this important text. I have left out some of the Latin terms Duby keeps in the quoted text, but I have kept his editorial comments intact.

[10] See Colin Morris, *The Papal Monarchy* (Oxford: Clarendon Press, 1989). Pope Leo III could place the Roman imperial crown on Charlemagne's head in 800 as a sign of the superior power of the papacy, and Gregory VII could make Henry IV wait outside his winter palace for the lifting of excommunication in 1077, but Henry also invested bishops with authority in his kingdom and, in the greatest blow against papal power, Philip of France could have Pope Boniface kidnapped and held in captivity in Avignon in the fourteenth century, leading to the eventual election of two more popes, each excommunicating the others. Claims to power are one thing: facts on the ground are quite another.

cultures, and kingdoms of "Christendom" as a single community completely obscures any relevant differences between the *koinonia* of the first
century and the whole of organized societal human life. It effectively
eliminates any tension between the one and the other, a tension that many
would contend is essential to the Church having a prophetic voice that
can cut against the corrupt, unjust, and dehumanizing practices of society.

The virtual identity of Church and society could mean one of two
things: one, that the Church, under the conditions of Christendom, could
bring into being a civilizing, humane, and just moral order in all spheres of
human life, from the private to the public. Or, two, that the Church would
succumb to the temptations of worldly power such that it holds back the
critical sting of its moral standards from worldly practices and "realpolitik."
That the second alternative was the road most taken is no surprise. The
church, after all, had to establish "diplomatic" relations with secular powers
and had to instruct them on how to provide the appropriate protection for
the church, it having no military legions of its own. It had to demarcate
the divisions between arenas in which secular power could function without direct church intervention and those in which it could not (e.g., the
investment of sacerdotal power for clergy could not be a secular privilege).

It cannot be denied that something like the life of *koinonia* could still be
found in this society, but it was usually *within* the church, not coterminous
with the church. One obvious locale for such intimate communal fellowship were the monastic communities. (See pp. 20–3 for a fuller examination
of monastic life.)

Churches and clergy soon became deeply implicated in the economic
affairs of the areas in which they existed. They not only owned property
(it has been claimed that by the sixth century the Church was the single
largest property owner in all of Europe), but to them were often assigned,
by secular powers, the right to collect monies in the form of tolls, fines,
and tithes levied on the inhabitants of the region. Morris argues that the
source of many of the moral complexities in the relation between clerical
and lay power was the emergence of private ownership of property. Laity
as well as religious officials could own property that included church
buildings as well as such things as mills, ovens, and land. He points out
that by the eleventh century "the idea of the church as a local community
or even as a body capable of possessing rights, had been largely lost. *Ecclesia*
meant a building."[11] The advance of privatization, according to Morris,
meant the "collapse of clerical communities."[12]

---

[11]   Morris, 25–6.
[12]   Morris, 27.

Privatization is closely linked to the growth of a money economy. The days of the early *koinonia* in which all wealth, including money, was to be shared for the good of the whole and in particular for the relief of the most needy, were gone. The church was too closely tied to the fortunes of the secular world and spread too thin across it to return to the withdrawn world of the *koinonia* communities. Nevertheless, concern over the corruption of the church never died and from time to time reformers tried to reinstill in church teaching a sense of a radical difference between it and the world beyond it. These reformers, many of whom were monks, were driven by a kind of "contemptus mundi" or hostility toward the world, which was often defined as "kings and dukes, marquises and counts, fleshly bishops and every one who is given up to fleshly desires."[13] For the reformers, the solution to the problem of too much intercourse with the world was to turn back to what they took to be the "innocence of the primitive church."[14] Clergy were encouraged to return to segregated communities where simony, marriage, and monetary temptation would not exist, or at least could be controlled. The clergy would not interfere in worldly affairs, and the laity would not try to run the church. "Laymen should arrange and provide for their own business, which is secular, and clergy for theirs, which is ecclesiastical."[15]

Under these conditions a search for community in the more ancient *koinonia* sense could culminate only in the monastic life. The attempt to make Christendom as a whole conform to the principles of *koinonia* was a lost cause as the church's intertwinement with social norms and mores made it virtually incapable of challenging society on issues of fundamental social justice, especially those having to do with economic justice.

Nevertheless, there were some attempts to develop an economic ethic that challenged growing notions of private property. No effort was more important in this regard than the development of a natural law moral theory under the skillful hands of St. Thomas Aquinas in the thirteenth century. His use of natural law to establish the basis for an economic ethic provided then (and, I would argue, can still provide) a point of linkage between an ethic of community and an ethic of society. Thomas gives us an excellent example of how moral principles developed in community can be used to negotiate a morally realistic relationship with a larger society, without obscuring the essential differences between community and society. In this way Thomas opens up an avenue of practical ethics

---

[13] Morris, 98. Quote is from Abbot John of Fecamp.
[14] Morris, 98. Quote is from Peter Damian.
[15] Morris, 99. Quote is from Humbert's work *Adversus Simoniacos*.

that can still be useful in the modern age. His argument for natural law provides both a common foundation for social ethics and a flexibility in applying moral principles to the complex realities of social life.

The natural law, as Aquinas developed it, assumes that under God's eternal law there are fundamental commonalities in the nature of all persons and insofar as they reflect the eternal law they are morally binding and informative (through the use of human reason to which they are transparent). Thomas admits that the natural law can be added to in certain respects "for the benefit of human life." Two examples he gives of such "additions" are the distinction of possessions and slavery, which were not brought in by nature, but devised by human reason for the benefit of human life, even though "*the possession of all things in common and universal freedom*" are strictly speaking more reflective of the natural law. And second, a precept may be changed "in some particular cases of rare occurrence, through some special causes hindering the observance of such precepts."[16]

Thomas accepts Aristotle's view that man is "naturally a social and political animal."[17] Every man, he says, is "part of the community" and that which he "is and possesses belongs to the community, just as any part belongs to the whole." There is need, therefore, for human government to oversee this organic whole. The human law that is created by such government, as long as it does not violate the natural law, is morally binding on the citizens of that society. And the end of human law (as natural law) is "the common good" or the general welfare of all citizens. "Human law is justified only insofar as it benefits the public interest."[18] This common good includes all the particular goods of individuals within the society and must respect the customs of any given country.[19]

Thomas is enough of a realist to recognize that what might work in a truly communal setting, such as the monastery, cannot be expected to work in the larger society. The private possession of external things is necessary for human life because "everyone is more careful to procure something that concerns himself alone than something that is common to all or to many others," and, second, "because human affairs are handled in

[16] Thomas Aquinas, *The Summa Theologica*, in Anton Pegis, First Part of the Second Part, XIII, Law, Question 94, Article Five in *Basic Writings of Saint Thomas Aquinas*, vol. 2 (New York: Random House, 1945), 780.

[17] Thomas Aquinas, *Summa of Theology*, I–II, q. 72, a. 4, in Mary T. Clark, ed., *An Aquinas Reader* (New York: Image Books, Doubleday, 1972), 367.

[18] Thomas Aquinas, *Summa of Theology*, I–II, q. 97, a. 1, in Clark, ed., *An Aquinas Reader*, 376.

[19] Thomas Aquinas, *Summa of Theology*, I–II, q. 72, a. 4, in Clark, ed., *An Aquinas Reader*, 372.

a more orderly fashion when each one goes about his own business," and, third, "because this leads to a more peaceful condition for man, while everyone is content with what he has. Hence we see that among those possessing something in common, disputes arise more often."[20]

Having established the legitimacy of private possession, however, Thomas immediately adds that, as to the use of external things, "man should not hold external things for his own use but for the common benefit, so that each one should readily share material things with others in their needs." And, he adds (implicitly recalling the *koinonia*), the communal possession of things is "attributed to natural law" because according to natural law "there is no distinction of property." Where then does such distinction arise? From human or positive law. As such, private property or ownership is not opposed to the natural law but is "an addition to natural law devised by human reason" for the three reasons cited above.[21]

Nevertheless, the justification of private property is always subordinate to the use to which such property is to be put, namely, "the alleviation of human needs. Therefore, the division and ownership of things that proceed from human law must not interfere with the alleviation of human needs by those things. Likewise, whatever a man has in superabundance is owed of natural right to the poor for their sustenance." What counts as "superabundance" or superfluity is determined pretty much according to one's station in society. Thomas is no economic egalitarian or democrat even as he recognizes the legitimate demands of the poor on the rich.

Whether Thomas's economic ethic was instructive to the economic society of his time, or whether it works today in all respects is not as important as his attempt, on the basis of natural law, to find a point of connection between an ethic that worked more purely in a religious community and an ethic that could inform the economic practices of the larger society. The distinction in natural law between human law and natural law made this linkage possible. While natural law regarding communal ownership of property might be easier to follow in a monastic community (one of which Thomas belonged to), it could be adapted with qualification in the secular world, at least in theory. The common point of reference would remain the needs of the most needy. Finding the most effective way to meet those needs (whether privately or corporately) would be a strategic question, but the overriding moral principle would remain

[20] Thomas Aquinas, *Summa of Theology* II–II, q. 66, a. 2, c and ad. 1, in Clark, ed., *An Aquinas Reader*, 383.
[21] Thomas Aquinas, *Summa of Theology* II–III, q. 66, a. 2, c and ad. 1, in Clark, ed., *An Aquinas Reader*, 383–4.

the same: that human need and the common good always trump justifications for private property that rest upon private good and private benefit over and above basic human needs. One of the great contributions of this religious thinker in the medieval period is his claim that society is subject to moral law and by virtue of this fact an absolute distinction between community and society cannot be drawn.

Calvin and the Experiment in Geneva

The hegemony that the papal monarchy had over medieval European Christendom began to crumble with the Reformation of the sixteenth century. While none of the "magisterial" reformers challenged the essential elements in the prevailing understanding of the relationship between Church and State, some, such as John Calvin, tried to build something more closely akin to the early *koinonia* that would be neither monastery nor universal Christian society. Calvin's experiment of a Christian commonwealth in Geneva exposed a new way of thinking about how Christians could live together without abandoning society and its structures of power, identifying them exclusively and exhaustively with the *koinonia*, or seeking to extend them universally and indiscriminately.

Calvin agreed with his predecessors that the State (which he variously referred to as the "politia," the "magistratus," and "res publica") exists because of human sin and God's grace in combating it, and because it is necessary for the preservation of the human race. It is an "order" that gives sinful human beings the necessary structures and restraints to conduct their public business without anarchy or chaos and with a modicum of justice and care for each other. But the State is not simply the Church writ large, which is a community of faithful persons who have been elect by God for salvation. As "saints" gathered in the church they are bound by a common worship, a common baptism and ordered discipline, a common participation in a sacred supper, and a unity of belief or doctrine.[22]

The church is also the place in which Christian love is most fully expressed. "Nothing," Calvin claims, "fosters mutual love more fittingly than for men to be bound together with this bond. . . . For if anyone were sufficient to himself and needed no one's help (such is the pride of human nature), each man would despise the rest and be despised by them."[23]

---

[22] John Calvin, *Institutes of the Christian Religion*, ed. John T. McNeill, trans. Ford Lewis Battles (Philadelphia: The Westminster Press, 1960), Bk. IV, ch. I, 9, p. 1023.
[23] Calvin, *Institutes*, Bk. IV, ch. III, 1, p. 1054.

The State is the instrument of law and order for all persons who share a common territory under a common magistrate according to common rules of justice. Civil government "pertains only to the establishment of civil justice and outward morality."[24] In addition, however, the State is mandated to "adjust our life to the society of men, to form our social behavior to civil righteousness, to reconcile us with one another, and to promote general peace and tranquility."[25] These more positive functions of the State seem to echo, at the societal level, some of what is to take place within the *koinonia* or the church. Thus the state and its rulers are divinely willed [*pace* Romans 13] and, as such, are to be obeyed for the *function* they perform and the *office* they hold.

Since both Church and State are creatures of divine providence, they should work together in this world as complementary forces. The point of overlap between them has to do with fostering the quality of life together with others in that which we call (often indiscriminately) community or society. Within the church that life will be intensely focused upon worship of God among fellow believers. Within civil society social life will be focused not only upon a negative kind of justice with respect to maintaining order and to "providing that each man may keep his property safe and sound," but also upon a more positive sense of working to establish social relationships of reconciliation and order.

Calvin can be seen as negotiating a relationship between community and society that preserves their differences without separating them in practice from one another. In particular their relationship permits, even demands, that the church be vigilant that the state not enact laws that are inimical to worship or that transgress the basic social needs of human beings. This even leads, in some instances, to the right of the minister to "remonstrate" with the magistrate over issues of social justice.

Using its positive power, the government must be particularly attentive to the needs of the society as a whole. This would include, for Calvin, the establishment of an educational system to prepare people "not only for ministry but [also] for civil government."[26] These schools were to be free to the poor (and even compulsory, because they would be seedbeds of civic virtue). Calvin also continues the line of thought begun with Augustine that would give to the government the right to wage war provided it

[24]   Calvin, *Institutes*, Bk. IV, ch. XX, 1, p. 1485.

[25]   Calvin, *Institutes*, Bk. IV, ch. XX, 2, p. 1487.

[26]   John Calvin, "Ecclesiastical Ordinances," in Hans J. Hillerbrand, *The Reformation: A Narrative History Related by Contemporary Observers and Participants* (New York: Harper and Row, 1964), 192–3.

meets the criteria of justice, especially that of defense of the public good for which the State serves as steward.

In the area of economics, Calvin was not unaffected by the Thomist teaching regarding the priority of the public good over private good. Property and wealth remain firmly under the moral auspices of the civil and religious community working together. Calvin seems, in fact, to have a particular concern with the poor and urges his Christian commonwealth to take up the plight of the poor as a clear moral obligation. Those who were blessed with wealth are to consider that their abundance "was not intended to be laid out in intemperance or excess, but in [using language reminiscent of Acts] relieving the necessities of the brethren."[27] This relief will sometimes need to go beyond what one can easily afford. Here Calvin echoes Aquinas's notion of the obligation to give whatever is required to meet the need. Calvin, in referring to Jesus' injunction in Matthew to the wealthy young man to give all that he owns to the poor, rejects the Spiritual Franciscan idea that property in and of itself is morally impure. He does say, however, that "we must not be satisfied with bestowing on the poor what we can easily spare, but that we must not refuse to part with our estates, if their revenue does not supply the wants of the poor."[28]

Calvin was informed by a notion of community, which often carried over to the Christian society as a whole, in which we are members of a single body. "When we regard each other in this way, each will then conclude: 'I see my neighbor who has need of me and if I were in such extremity, I would wish to be helped; I must therefore do just that.'" Calvin goes on to say, "here is the fraternal affection which proceeds from the regard that we have when God has joined us together and united us in one body, because he wants each to employ himself for his neighbors, so that no one is addicted to his own person, but that we serve all in common."[29] This sense of common service means that for Calvin commitment to the common good determined the virtue and validity of the society as a whole, and thus justified civil interventionist measures in its economic life when that good was threatened by inappropriate private economic behavior. The line between community and society was never drawn by Calvinists with great conceptual clarity and challenges most of our contemporary notions of how churches and states should be radically differentiated from each other. It must be remembered, however, that this

[27] Calvin, quoted in Fred Graham, *Jean Calvin: The Constructive Revolutionary* (Richmond: John Knox Press, 1964), 68.
[28] Calvin, quoted in Graham, 69.
[29] Calvin, quoted in Graham, 70.

lack of differentiation occurred, for all practical purposes, at a level that extended no further than the small town or city. It was not based on an understanding of ecclesial community and civic society that was meant to encompass the entire culture or Christen*dom* as a whole (if any such thing still existed). Nevertheless, the fundamental point is that Calvinists regarded their civic life as "an organic Christian hierarchy" or "organic Christian community bound together by mutual concerns."[30] Parker believes that this notion of the community was clearly rooted in the medieval understanding of a Christian society[31] that we have already covered.

Calvin understood that the mutual love characteristic (at least ideally) of the church did have a role to play in modifying behavior in the larger society. Calvin never made the mistake of assuming that love could be the only principle of social policy, but nor did he rule out the possibility that the State could craft laws and policies that worked to reconcile persons with each other. He did not abandon the medieval and early Christian notion that social bonds were necessary to human well-being and that those bonds carried a special obligation to the poor. Like his medieval predecessors, Calvin refused to render the Christian values born in and of the *koinonia* entirely inoperative at the societal level. Economic, political, and even military issues were not immune to values derived from an ethics of community.

Anabaptism and Community

At one extreme of the Reformation (sometimes called the "left-wing" or "radical" reformation) were those Christian groups that are somewhat indiscriminately called Anabaptists.[32] Their vision of the ethics of community drove them into opposition not just to both Roman Catholics and mainstream Reformers, but also to the State itself.

This opposition to the State did not question its legitimacy, only its relevance to the Christian community. The magistrate was still recognized as an institution of God, but not for them. The Anabaptists did not see

---

[30] Charles H. Parker, *The Reformation of Community: Social Welfare and Calvinist Charity in Holland, 1572–1620* (Cambridge: Cambridge University Press, 1998), 32.

[31] Parker, 18, 31.

[32] I am using the term "Anabaptist" to refer to those groups at the time of the Reformation whom G. H. Williams calls the Anabaptists "proper," sometimes the evangelical Anabaptists. See "Introduction," by G. H. Williams, ed., *Spiritual and Anabaptist Writers*, The Library of Christian Classics, vol. XXV (Philadelphia: The Westminster Press, 1957).

themselves as needing such an institution. It belonged to the worldlings, the "knaves and rascals or children of the world who pursue no Christian piety" who "must yet have a worldly and gallows-piety."[33]

The Anabaptists regarded the medieval experiment of a *corpus christianum* as an utter failure corruptly mixing the *koinonia* of true believers with the secular world that had fallen into depravity because it failed to embody fully in its life the teachings of Christ. Only separation between world and *koinonia* could provide the appropriate conditions for true Christian community (Gemeinde). "We should plainly not have community with them [the worldlings] and run with them in the mass of their strife."[34] Instead they were to follow the injunction of II Corinthians 6:17 to "come out from them, and be separate from them."

The only authority they would recognize for themselves was that which they believed was exercised by the early church, the authority of the spirit, not of the sword. As Franklin Littell has argued "the dominant theme in the thinking of the main-line Anabaptists was the recovery of the life and virtue of the Early Church."[35] In fact, they did not recognize the legitimacy of the institutional "church" after its alliance with the State under the rule of Constantine. For them the church did not need reforming (it was too hopelessly corrupt for that); it needed "restitution." The true church had simply failed to exist from the time Constantine fatally embraced it in the fourth century to their own time in the sixteenth century. Anabaptism emerged in the wake of the Reformation to restore the heart and soul of Christianity, namely a number of covenanted communities of persons trying to live Christ-like and Christ-inspired lives in a hostile world. (Rarely, if ever, did the Anabaptists talk about a "universal" or single global Christian community.)

Everything they taught and practiced flowed from this basic belief: the insular covenanted community of faith and life was the essence of Christianity. Their practice of communism and pacifism, for example, was not intended first and foremost as an attack upon the secular culture but rather as an attempt to model the virtues of Christian living, even to hope for spiritual and moral perfection within their covenanted communities. That the world would not accept their model of true life did lead, as they expected it would, to the same kind of persecution and martyrdom that had greeted Jesus and the early Christians. In their martyr deaths at the

---

[33] Quoted in Franklin H. Littell, *The Origins of Sectarian Protestantism* (New York: Macmillan, 1964), 106.

[34] Littell, 89.

[35] Littell, 79.

hands of both reformers and the State many of the Anabaptists saw vindication of the truth of their beliefs and practices.

They acknowledged the legitimacy of the sword (the remedy for sin) in the "world," but substituted for it within their communities the spiritual discipline of the Ban, shunning, or excommunication. Understood as a form of "fraternal discipline," the Ban was an "exclusion and separation to such an extent that no fellowship is held with such a person by Christians." Fellowship with others was so central to the identity of each believer that to be denied it was to be denied life itself. Loss of material goods, or status in the world, or even of bodily life was of no account compared with loss of belonging to the true community of faith. The ban was more powerful than the gun or the sword.

One implication of the Anabaptist idea, exemplified by their contemporary descendants, is that the true community of Christians is invariably local or congregational. The further away the brother or sister lives, the further from genuine fellowship they are. Christian life in community, they insisted, is lived in direct, personal, face-to-face relations. In this sense the Anabaptists are repeating, in their own way, the life of the *koinonia* and the monastic communities. What they reject is the larger ecclesial structure within which the monastery was set. For the Anabaptists, community could not exist at abstract, institutional levels: it existed only when brother and sister in Christ met and lived in direct relationships with each other. They embodied the full meaning of community in the narrow and proper sense of the term.

This kind of spiritual intimacy and fellowship accounts in part for how the Anabaptists were able to implement both the pacifism and communism of the early *koinonia*. As separated from the State they had no reason to contribute to its defense or governance in matters military or political. Communism, as an economic practice, was not only consistent with the notion of community as a sharing of goods for the benefit of the most needy, it was also a real possibility since such communities were relatively small, even parochial. As Littell observes, "individualism was a sin against God. Union with others in economic affairs was not an act of religious romanticism; neither was it an optimistic expression of social hope. It was the result of an inescapable religious mandate."[36]

Anabaptism, in the end, failed to provide any lasting direct influence on the structures of society or of the institutional church. They embody, even today, an ethics of community in its most withdrawn, secluded, even exclusionary, form. In many cases their embodiment of the meaning of the

---

[36]   Littell, 97.

New Testament *koinonia* has become enmeshed with cultural manifestations of seventeenth-, eighteenth-, and nineteenth-century rural European life. Nevertheless, they represent a sense of community that will not, at least by design, make compromises with the "worldlings."

The Bruderhoff

A contemporary example of Anabaptist life together experienced as intrinsically satisfying is the Bruderhoff community. Described by one writer as the "joyful community,"[37] the Bruderhoff see themselves as a living witness to what life can be if lived communally in the Spirit of God. At the heart of the Bruderhoff community is the centrality of interpersonal relations. These are to be "governed" by the "First Law of Sannerz" which states explicitly that "There is no law but that of love. Love is joy in others. Passing on the joy that the presence of others brings us means words of love."[38] The attitudes they seek to foster are those of commitment to the community, and the attitudes that run counter to that are pride and selfishness. The Bruderhoff believe that "the collective self is an absolute good. The individual self is an absolute evil," according to Zablocki. While this tends to put the difference between individual and community perhaps too starkly, what the Bruderhoff value most in their communal lives is joy. Joy is the "payoff" for subordinating one's individualistic tendencies to the group. Joy is felt by the individual but made possible by the community. In this respect the Bruderhoff (as well as other contemporary Anabaptist-type communities such as the Amish and the Mennonites) have rightly identified a key element in the original Christian meaning of community. Unless there is a "payoff" for communal life in the experience of mutual delight, pleasure, love, and joy living in and with and through other persons, one would have to judge communities solely by their functionality in serving other, presumably, societal needs. What is often left out of such functional studies of community is the *intrinsic* meaning they have for the emotional fulfillment of their members. And if the moral ontology on which this study is based is correct, then the full emotional enjoyment in interpersonal relations of the nature God has given us must, of necessity, constitute the heart of any divinely intended community. Societies, by their nature, serve many important and vital functions. But rarely do they constitute the emotional fulfillment of their

[37] Benjamin David Zablocki, *The Joyful Community* (Baltimore: Penguin Books, 1971).
[38] Quoted in Zablocki, 58.

members. This is one thing a genuine community of persons can be expected to do and which the Bruderhoff, among others, explicitly claim that they do in fact, at least from time to time.

All of these Anabaptist-type communities are living testimony to the struggle to find a way to lead what is, to them, the Christian life in withdrawn communities of faith. While perhaps untenable and non-paradigmatic for an ethics of community that seeks to work out a realistic relationship with the structures of state and society, the Anabaptists and their descendants nevertheless remind us of what living by an almost literal inter-pretation of Jesus' words and deeds can amount to, especially what it means to live in love and joy with one another. They do have problems, accord-ing to those who left them, with the suppression of individual freedom and of too close an identification with the mores of an older European way of life. Nevertheless, they remind the ethicist of community of the dangers of too much compromise with the power brokers of the world even while they also manifest to some degree the dangers of self-righteousness and a failure to take the world (that God so loved that God gave God's only son to it) seriously enough to learn to work with and in it. The trick is to find ways to lift up the intrinsic joy of community to which they point without restricting all life just to those communities in which it is felt most intensely. Until the Kingdom comes there is much work to be done in the complex and multiform structures of society that can point to community and draw from the strengths of community but which are not to be confused with community. It may well turn out that the greatest gift of an intensely intimate, loving and mutually joyful community can make to the societies around it is to point forward to what the intention of history is. It may remind society-builders that society is not an end in itself but must contain "pockets of community" within it which live out in practice what fulfillment of human life is as intended by God. These experiments in community will not perhaps fully and always embody the fullness of life, but their experience of a kind of foretaste or first fruits of it are necessary if society is not to glorify itself as the final end of human purpose and completion.

Chapter 3

Historical Experiments in Community: America

I now want to explore some selected attempts in the United States to bring Christian notions of community into dialogue with the practices and philosophies of American society. These American "experiments" in community will reveal the complex relationship an ethics of community has had in negotiating its place in social, economic, and political structures that outrun the more limited boundaries of community, despite the uncritical use of the term "community" to cover everything from the nation to a small group of recovering addicts.

I am focusing this exploration upon the United States because it is the country I know best, having taught courses in the religious histories of America for over thirty years. The experiments in community I have chosen are illustrative, not exhaustive, of how community and society have danced together in complicated and multifarious ways for nearly 300 years in the United States.

The Puritans

The Calvinist experiment in Geneva foreshadowed and provided a model for further experiments in Christian community in America. Calvinists from England in the early decades of the seventeenth century brought with them to colonial America the zeal to establish communities in which the line between Church and State would not exactly be erased but would, in practice, lose many of its hard edges.

The utopian ideal of a civil community composed exclusively of persons who had already been converted and belonged to the covenanted church or "communion of the saints" had, at least for many Puritans, some hope of being realized in the wilderness of North America. At the heart of the

Puritan "errand into the wilderness" was the intent to establish communities that would model Christian love and fellowship, again very much on
the pattern of the early Christian *koinonia*. Unlike the Anabaptists, however,
the Puritan communities took the crasser elements of "secular" political
power seriously and tried, as had Calvin, to bring them under the control
of the "saints" who willingly lived in (not withdrawn from but also not
quite "of") the world. The legacy of these Puritans, especially their ideal of
community, has remained an important part of the American imagination
and experience.

H. Richard Niebuhr has argued that the motif of the Kingdom of God
has informed nearly all types of the relationship between religious community and society in America. The Kingdom to which Niebuhr refers was
a kingdom "prior to America and to which this nation, in its politics and
economics, was required to conform."[1] It stood, and still stands, as a form
of transcendent critique, as well as aspiration, for an ethics of community
that seeks to engage the larger society in the name of reconstructive, even
from time to time radical, but always transforming principles and values.
Even when these were being domesticated and converted into instruments
of secular self-justification and glory, they continued to haunt the American
sense of what kind of community it could become. (That Americans still
talk of themselves as "a community" is itself indicative of this Puritan legacy.)

The seminal document laying out the Puritan vision for community
is John Winthrop's 1630 "A Model of Christian Charity."[2] Originally
addressed to early Puritans settlers of New England while still aboard ship,
it is so powerful that its rhetoric and symbols continue to be drawn upon
by contemporary politicians, signifying perhaps that it still has some political
potential even though Puritanism itself is long gone. Its vision of a people
bound to each other in bonds of mutual support remains firmly embedded
in the American consciousness, not the European, and, as such, has become
part of the American historical memory. It lays out the principles of the
common good and the obligations they create for a moral relationship
between individual wealth and the needs of the poor. Even when those
principles tend to disappear from view as the fast-flowing waters of individualism and a competitive free-market sweep most Americans along,

---

[1] H. Richard Niebuhr, *The Kingdom of God in America* (Hamden, Conn.: The Shoe
String Press, 1956), 10.
[2] See John Winthrop, "A Modell of Christian Charity," in Robert N. Bellah et al.,
eds., *Individualism and Commitment in American Life: Readings on the Themes of Habits of
the Heart* (New York: Harper & Row, 1988), 22. The following selections from that
document are all taken from this source.

they have not been entirely forgotten as communities seek to address in a just and compassionate way the plight of the poor and needy.

Winthrop articulates an understanding of community that brings into harmony both religious and political concerns. While refusing to abolish the economic distinctions between rich and poor, Winthrop argues that they must brought into harmony within a single overarching community. The glue to holding them together is mutual love, mercy, and justice under the rubric of a common good to which individual interests must be subordinated. The economic differences between rich and poor are not simply the result of natural inequalities. They are due, ultimately, to God's concern that the "good of the whole" be shown by the "variety and difference [sic] of the Creatures," and by the opportunity for God to manifest the working of his Spirit "that the riche and mighty should not eate upp the poore, nor the poore and dispised rise upp against their superiors and shake off thiere yoke."

Here Winthrop echoes the medieval as well as Calvinist view that the structures of society require some kind of hierarchical ordering principle so that chaos and anarchy might not arise. But hierarchy is not a license for the rich and powerful to exploit those who depend upon them. Instead, he argues, the relation of dependence reminds everyone who is party to it that "every man might have need of other, and from hence they might be all knitt more nearly together in the Bond of brotherly affeccion."

In this regard, Winthrop acknowledges the importance of both mercy as well as justice. Mercy requires "that every man afford his help to another in every want or distress" and that this be done with "affeccion." Winthrop recalls in this context the practice of the early *koinonia*. "There is a tyme when the Christian must sell all and give to the poore, as they did in Apostolic times. There is a tyme allsoe when a Christian (though they give not all yet) must give beyond their ability. . . Likewise a community of perills calls for extraordinary liberallity and soe doth Community in some speciall service for the Churche." Winthrop shifts his audience throughout the document from "a Company professing our selves fellow members of Christ . . . knitt together by this bond of love" to "a place of Cohabitation and Consorteshipp under a due forme of Government both civill and ecclesiasticall." His refusal to clearly distinguish between the close-knit company bound by love (the church) and the civil society (bound by law) allows him to suggest that the principles of *koinonia* life can be brought to bear upon civic life. The chief example of linkage is the covenant principle that "the care of the publique must oversway all private respects" because "wee must love one another with a pure hearte fervently, we must beare one anothers burthens." These obligations are not to be restricted to the church community alone, but are to guide the whole life of this community, political, economic, social, and religious. Winthrop reminds his hearers that doing justice and loving mercy are always tightly linked under God's providence (Micah).

"For this end wee must be knitt together in this worke as one man, wee must entertaine each other in brotherly Affeccion, wee must be willing to abridge our selves of our superfluities, for the supply of others necessities . . . we must delight in each other, make others Condicions our owne, rejoyce together, mourne together, labour and suffer together, allwayes haveing before our eyes our Commission and Community in the worke, our Community as members of the same body . . . " He ends his speech by introducing what was to become one of the most influential images in American religious and political history: "wee shall be as a Citty upon a Hill, the eies of all people are uppon us."

Clearly conscious of the earth-shaking gravity of what they are embarking upon, these Puritans took into their understanding of community many of the principles both of the early church as well as of the medieval development of communal obligation to the needy (for instance, the Thomistic notion that one must give up one's "superfluities" and give beyond one's ability if the distressed neighbor is truly in need). The Puritan community was not self-consciously egalitarian, but under the auspices of a providential hierarchy it did place the needs of the poor and of the whole community ahead of what we might call the "rights" of the individual, a concept that at the time had yet to be fully articulated by European political philosophers.

One historian has described the early Puritan communities in America as "Christian Utopian Closed Corporate Communit[ies]."[3] Focusing on the town of Dedham, Massachusetts, Kenneth Lockridge observes that united as the town was it did not presume to practice radical equality, communism of goods, or pacifism. As he comments, "the settlers did not see any necessary contradiction between their emphasis on mutuality to the point of a form of collectivism, and a frank recognition that a certain hierarchy of wealth and status was as desirable as it was inevitable, for in their view of their culture each tended in its own way to ensure social harmony."[4] The town constituted a kind of organic unity in which all the members participated so that what we today call individualism was only incipiently present. The organic model of society inherent in this

---

[3] See Kenneth Lockridge, *A New England Town: The First Hundred Years* (New York: Norton, 1970), 16.

[4] Lockridge, 11.

understanding was pervasive in the Puritan mentality. It "portrayed the harmony and control the rulers sought when they hedged men about with law and authority, bound people to their stations, and stopped trespasses on the rights of others."[5]

But the Puritan-enforced organic unity did not hold. By the beginning of the eighteenth century wealth distribution in Dedham had already created two rather different economic classes. The town meeting became "the arena of a new politics based on their [the townsmen] contending interests . . . they were gradually turning Dedham into an open society where diversity prevailed and the majority truly ruled. More, they were moving toward an age in which the free individual would move among a vast array of choices – legal, political, religious, occupational, geographic – and would be enshrined as a new kind of god. The logical next step in this process was for men to begin breaking free of the last ties of the old community."[6] What they were buying into was nothing less than "opportunistic individualism" and "republican pluralism."[7] They had "shattered the old politics of Christian corporatism" and replaced it with a politics "of diverse, frank, and contending interests . . . Whether they liked it or not pluralistic democracy was replacing the democracy of homogeneity, freeing the individual from the dictates of the social order, and laying the experiential foundations of the ideology which was to become America's pride."[8]

The American Revolution and Community

Even while the Puritan communities were fragmenting in practice as they came up against the corrosive acids of factionalism, dissent, and emergent individualism, the dream of community for the American people as organically whole, cohesive, and united did not die. Although many interpretations of the American Revolution stress the importance of the "rights" of man and of independence, the idea of an American community in which individual interests were subordinated to the common good played a significant if not dominating role in shaping the ideology of the American Revolution. That idea, while not ultimately victorious in defining

---

[5]   Richard L. Bushman, *From Puritan to Yankee* (Cambridge: Harvard University Press, 1967), 3.

[6]   Lockridge, 159.

[7]   For the latter phrase see Bushman, p. ix.

[8]   Lockridge, 172–4.

the America that would emerge from the Revolution, provided a resonance that, as we enter a new millennium, is being heard by an increasing
number of people who have had to deal with the alienation and fragmentation the triumphant ideology of possessive individualism brought in its
wake.

The power of the older Puritan vision of community was revitalized for
a time by the evangelical revivals known collectively as the Great Awakening that swept across America in the 1740s. Many of these evangelical
"new lights" looked toward the possibility of restoring the sense of unity
and organic wholeness that had gotten lost in the bitter factional debates
between colonies, individuals, parties, interests, and towns.

At the heart of this evangelical passion for the renewal of American
society was the ideal of community under the guiding principles of Christianity. The fulfillment of this passion would require an America with a
renewed and transformed set of "attitudes and institutions appropriate to
the promise of the New World."[9] The attitude that most needed transforming was the spirit of personal acquisitiveness. Many evangelicals wanted
to return to a society much more firmly embedded in the principle of the
common good, but without the religious intolerance that had accompanied
it in most of the Puritan villages of seventeenth- and early eighteenth-
century New England.

Jonathan Edwards made clear for many of these evangelicals the political
implication of their theology: the public good is superior to the private
good. "As it is with selfishness, or when a man is governed by a regard to
his own private interest; independent of regard to the public good, such a
temper exposes a man to act the part of an enemy to the public."[10] This is
clearly an attitude that only a community built on a foundation of love can
sustain and nurture. Whether it could become the basis for an entire social
order was the question Edwards and his evangelical cohorts never answered.

Benevolence or true virtue was also associated by Edwards and the
evangelicals with "true" freedom. Their understanding of that oft-used
revolutionary-era term "liberty" was not the freedom of the individual to
be left alone by others or to chart his own course in life unimpeded.
Instead, freedom was always freedom in community with others. Heimert
draws upon the sermons of a number of late eighteenth-century New

---

[9]   Alan Heimert, *Religion and the American Mind: From the Great Awakening to the
Revolution* (Cambridge, Mass.: Harvard University Press, 1966), as quoted in John
Mulder and John Wilson, eds., *Religion in American History: Interpretive Essays* (Englewood
Cliffs, NJ: Prentice Hall, 1978), 141.
[10]   Edwards, 19.

England evangelical clergymen who, like Nathaniel Niles, expounded on the evangelical meaning of freedom. Liberty is the joyful experience of living in a community in which the members "unite in the same grand pursuit, the highest good of the whole."[11]

The primary obstacle to the attainment of this felicity and brotherhood were the sins of "selfishness, avarice, and extortion," all of which were "opposite to public spiritedness and general benevolence."[12]

For most evangelical clergy, castigation of selfishness found its readiest target in the insatiable desire for wealth and the consequent neglect of the poor. "It seems as if our rich men, like so many hard millstones, had got the poor people between them, and had agreed to grind them to death."[13] Some clergy pointed out that this hunger for wealth was absolutely contrary to the early *koinonia*. "Selfish acquisition," said one clergyman was a "shameful reverse of the example of the primitive christians [*sic*] at Jerusalem, who sold their estates, and distributed the money arising from the sales, to supply the wants of their distressed brethren."[14]

Some of the evangelicals argued explicitly for restrictions on the acquisition of wealth and property. Some were proponents of a "radical democracy . . . They urged free tenure of land, no large landed estates, equable distribution of property, perfect religious liberty, and an America the refuge of all distressed people the world over," and some even urged the abolition of slavery.[15]

Heimert summarizes this evangelical view simply: "society and government are one. Both as community and as polity, the ideal was that of a mutually interdependent commonwealth, governed and sustained by the virtue and energy of the multitude."[16]

While these evangelical clergy tried to make the Christian view of community relevant to the political struggles over the future of an America separated from Great Britain, they failed in many respects to appreciate the complexities of human nature, especially when it was in the business of building a nation and a form of government that would have to reconcile many competing and divergent interests, many of which had no grounding in a Christian moral ontology. Nevertheless, the evangelical desire for a new nation committed to the principle of building society as community

[11] Heimert, 456.
[12] Jacob Green, in a 1778 sermon, quoted in Heimert, 495.
[13] Quoted in Heimert, 497.
[14] Quoted in Heimert, 497. The quote is from Abraham Keteltas in 1777.
[15] Alice Baldwin, *The Clergy of Connecticut in Revolutionary Days*, Published for the Tercentenary Commission by the Yale University Press, 1936, V.LVI, 24–5.
[16] Heimert, 513.

was not entirely absent from the thinking of the more secular advocates of Revolution.

The Creation of the American Republic and the Struggle for the Common Good

The evangelicals' appeal to the will of the people of the community as the authorizing agency for societal action was echoed in the more secular arguments that began to take their place alongside the religious ones in the years prior to 1776. These constituted what has been called the republican vision of a new American society that shed itself of governmental control by the monarchy and parliament of England. Not unlike the evangelicals' hope, there was for these more secular Whig political philosophers a sense of promise and an as yet unrealized possibility for America.[17] "Republicanism" for them meant "a real and radical revolution, a change of society, not just of government . . . [It] assumed very different sorts of human relationships from that of a monarchy."[18] These expectations paralleled if not overlapped those of the evangelicals. Gordon S. Wood has gone so far as to claim that

> the republican revolution was the greatest utopian movement in American history. The revolutionaries aimed at nothing less than a reconstitution of American society. [This language is reminiscent of the Anabaptist attitude to the established Church.] They hoped to destroy the bonds holding together the older monarchical society – kinship, patriarchy, and patronage – and to put in their place new social bonds of love, respect and consent. They sought to construct a society and government based on virtue and disinterested public leadership and to set in motion a moral movement that would eventually be felt around the globe. People "begin to know one another, and that knowledge begets a love for each other, and a desire to procure happiness for themselves, and the great family of mankind."[19]

---

[17]   In a society that was so filled with the influence of Christian rhetoric and values, it is difficult to make a hard-and-fast distinction between a "religious" and a "secular" individual in eighteenth-century America. Clergy had a distinct office to fulfill but they read political philosophy and political leaders were often committed members of the church. Nevertheless, some of the rhetoric of the revolution appeared in literature that was written for more or less political purposes as compared to sermons composed for somewhat different, but not necessarily incompatible, reasons.

[18]   Gordon S. Wood, *The Radicalism of the American Revolution* (New York: Alfred Knopf, 1992), 169.

[19]   Wood, *Radicalism*, 229.

This utopian vision of what America could become, while not explicitly grounded in a Christian theology, reverberates with the tonalities of earlier Christian attempts at community. Here, however, the community would be, it was hoped, as large as America herself erasing colonial lines of division and sectional suspicion and animosity.

The promise and perils of trying to carry out this extended ethic of community in America can be instructive for contemporary movements in community life and practice. If part of an ethics of community is recalling and retelling the history of that community, then reminding Americans that there is deeply embedded in their history a story of community that seeks to overcome hostile divisions and the supremacy of private self-interest can only contribute to the possibility of rebuilding community (or at least a society receptive to communities) in America, and, by extension to other democracies.

"The participation of common people in government became the essence of American democracy."[20] The people within a community were to be "linked organically to everyone else, [and therefore] what was good for the whole community was ultimately good for all the parts. The people were in fact a single organic piece . . . with a unitary concern that was the only legitimate objective of governmental policy. This common interest was . . . an entity in itself, prior to and distinct from the various private interests of groups and individuals."[21] Here we see the convergence of neo-Calvinist evangelical thinking with Whig political philosophy, at least in 1776.

The language of rights so often in evidence during the struggle to articulate the patriot cause always assumed a communal context. The rights language of the eighteenth century in America was "generally regarded as defenses designed to protect a united people against their rulers and not as devices intended to set off parts of the people against the majority. Few Whigs in 1776 were yet theoretically prepared to repudiate the belief in the corporate welfare as the goal of politics or to accept divisiveness and selfishness as the normative behavior of men. The ideal which republican-ism was beautifully designed to express was still a harmonious integration of all parts of the community."[22]

Benevolence and the public good were the primary virtues that would temper and domesticate the vice of self-interest. The completely free and

---

[20]   Wood, *Radicalism*, 243.
[21]   Gordon S. Wood, *The Creation of the American Republic 1776–1787* (Chapel Hill: University of North Carolina Press, 1969), 58.
[22]   Wood, *Creation*, 60.

autonomous self was deeply suspect because it was prone to "rootlessness, immaturity, or sacrilege."[23] Even property rights, which would become by the nineteenth century the emblem of the individual's freedom *from* communal obligations, were not, during the eighteenth century, regarded as "absolute." They were subject to oversight by the community. Property ownership was "a right of stewardship that the public entrusted to an individual, for both private and public benefit. It was a right the public could withdraw if necessary,"[24] as in cases of eminent domain.

But successful government by the people required a level of mutual trust and virtuous character that proved as hard to establish as the inordinate desires of the self were to quench. The willingness of the individual to "sacrifice his private interests for the good of the community" was called simply "public virtue" and it "demanded an extraordinary moral character in the people."[25] The source of this public virtue was, without embarrassment, identified as love or charity formed in the character of each individual who would give himself to the good of the whole. It would be cultivated in bonds of relationality with others. Even when de Tocqueville described individualism as a feeling that "disposes each member of the community to sever himself from the mass of his fellows and to draw apart with his family and his friends"[26] he is affirming the importance of some kind of relationality, not the naked self in autonomous seclusion from others. The virtue of local communities vied with the specter of an impersonal national society. But the common assumption of the time was that community, in some form, was not antithetical to the good of the individual, but the condition for its completion and fulfillment. This did not mean the eradication of a social hierarchy (provided it was earned by individual merit, not inherited or bought). But it did mean that all social and economic differences were ultimately justified by their contribution to the good of the community as a whole.

The fact that Americans, or at least those who comprised much of the religious fraternity and the Whig political philosophers, could talk openly and without embarrassment about creating a democratic republic in which the common good would prevail should make us somewhat less reluctant to dismiss appeals to community as so much useless rhetoric in the face of

---

[23] Barry Alan Shain, *The Myth of American Individualism: The Protestant Origins of American Political Thought* (Princeton: Princeton University Press, 1994), 98.

[24] Shain, 183.

[25] Wood, *Creation*, 68.

[26] See Robert Bellah et al., *Habits of the Heart* (Berkeley: University of California Press, 1985), 37.

what today is taken to be a smug kind of worldly realism built on the principles of self-interest and individualism. As Gordon Wood has stated, the fact that America was not always steeped in philosophies of liberalism, self-interest or capitalism means that "maybe we're not destined to remain what we had become."[27] The reintroduction of an ethics of community drawn from the Christian vision and experiments in community might not, if selectively and carefully appropriated, be entirely out of place in attempts to craft a vision of society that attempts to embody, without embarrassment, the virtues of justice and compassion.

From Madison to Communalism

The divisions that remained among Americans, despite the radical democratic rhetoric of the public good and the need for a virtue than transcended self-interest, eventually led the new nation to adopt a political philosophy tempered by a new realism about human nature (which had not demonstrably changed to the degree hoped for by the republican idealists). In arguing for ratification of the United States Constitution, James Madison put forth the new view in defense of the new government that candidly acknowledged the factions and interests now constituting American society. Madison and his cohorts did not abandon the notion of a public good, but they accepted the persistence of various and clashing private and local interests out of which this good would have to emerge. These interests needed to be regulated (they could not be transcended) at a national level. A "well-constructed nation," Madison said, requires the ability to "break and control the violence of faction."[28] Madison concedes that "mutual animosities" are part of a strong and apparently ineradicable propensity of humankind. They lead to factions which are driven by "some common impulse of passion, or of interest, adverse to the rights of other citizens, or to the permanent and aggregate interests of the community."

The only answer to this clash of individual and sectional interests is a representative republic. Elected representatives will approximate the kind of wisdom necessary to keep the public good in view, particularly if they

[27]   Gordon S. Wood, "Hellfire Politics," Review of *The Lost Soul of American Politics*, by J. P. Diggins, *New York Review of Books*, 28 Feb. 1985, 29.
[28]   James Madison, *The Federalist Papers*, no. 10, in Russell B. Nye and Norman S. Grabo, eds., *American Thought and Writing*, vol. 2, *The Revolution and the Early Republic* (Boston: Houghton Mifflin, 1965), pp. 110–20, *passim*.

are chosen for their virtuous character. A representative form of government will actually function more effectively than a direct democracy. "It may well happen that the public voice, pronounced by the representatives of the people, will be more consonant to the public good than if pronounced by the people themselves, convened for the purpose."

America had now moved from an ideal of community as a single organic whole to a view in which it saw itself as a society broken, fragmented, divisive. "Once the people were thought to be composed of various interests in opposition to one another, all sense of a graduated organic chain in the social hierarchy became irrelevant, symbolized by the increasing emphasis on the image of a social contract. The people were not an order organically tied together by their unity of interests but rather an agglomeration of hostile individuals coming together for their mutual benefit to construct a society."[29]

From this point forward, with some notable exceptions, America saw herself and her government as having the chief aim of protecting the private interests of individuals, especially their interests in property, *from* the will of the majority, even *against* the public good which increasingly was seen as vague, abstract, even despotic. Individual and society, especially government, were now seen as having hostile interests because, while protecting each individual's rights, government must also seek to protect the rights of other individuals so that the rights of one did not run roughshod over the rights of others. Wood somewhat pessimistically concludes his analysis of this period in American history by lamenting that "America would remain free not because of any quality in its citizens of Spartan self-sacrifice to some nebulous public good, but in the last analysis because of the concern each individual would have in his own self-interest and personal freedom."[30]

The Second Great Awakening and Social Reform

While political philosophers may have conceded much to the self-interest of Americans, religious revivalists keep alive the vision of a united America morally reformed throughout by the fires of evangelicalism. At the beginning of the antebellum period the Second Great Awakening brought about a renewal of interest among many evangelical Christians in reforming American society. In two particular ways the negotiation between religion and

[29] Wood, *Creation*, 607.
[30] Wood, *Creation*, 612.

society evoked by this evangelical revivalism cut harder and sharper than was the case for the more moderate and accommodating relation between the churches and the larger American culture. In one way, some of those converted in the Awakening drew conclusions about the need for more radical reform of American institutions and practices than the mainstream was comfortable with, and in the other way some felt compelled to withdraw from what they saw as an increasingly corrupt and unchristian society into smaller, purer, versions of the early Christian *koinonia*.

The more radical readings of religion's relation to society stemmed for the most part from a religious conviction that if one was converted, then one had to work for the moral and spiritual perfection both of oneself, and by extension, of one's society. This led many evangelicals to embrace the causes of antislavery, women's rights, temperance, even communism, pacifism, and celibacy in some of the communal movements.

The work of the evangelically inspired abolitionists (and later of the suffragists, many of whom were drawn into radical reform by abolitionism) stands as an example of how one reading of Christian community has the potential to impact the whole society. Many evangelicals (by no means all) came to believe that slavery was an affront to the moral laws of God and threw themselves into the antislavery movement. At the core of the evangelical abolitionist experience was "a demanding inner spiritual discipline and an equally compelling need for continuing moral activism. Rebirth had broken their bondage to sin, but continuing triumph over it could only come if their striving toward perfect holiness – a frame free of sin and filled with evangelical concern to redeem the world – was unrelenting."[31] Some even proclaimed that "nothing short of the general renewal of society ought to satisfy any soldier of Christ . . . To destroy all national holds of evil; to root sin out of institutions; to hold up to view the gospel ideal of a righteous nation"[32] are the imperatives for a reborn Christian as he confronts the immorality of his society. The impact of this redemptive activity was generally limited to attempts to change the social and political practices of America and did not intend to turn America into a "Christian" society as a whole. In this respect the work of the reform-minded evangelicals in the antebellum period may be a more relevant model for

---

[31] Donald M. Scott, *From Office to Profession: The New England Ministry 1750–1850* (Philadelphia: University of Pennsylvania Press, 1978), 86.

[32] William Arthur, *The Tongue of Fire* (1854), quoted in Ronald C. White, Jr. and C. Howard Hopkins, eds., *The Social Gospel: Religion and Reform in Changing America* (Philadelphia: Temple University Press, 1976), 11.

contemporary options for the engagement of religion and society, informed by an ethics of community, than ones that would seek some new form of Christian America.

Communalism in America

In addition to the way of transforming American society there was also the way of retreat and separation, the way of seeking community by withdrawing, at least temporarily in some cases, from a hopelessly corrupt society. This was the way of communalism, which flourished alongside evangelical reform movements in America during the antebellum years. Most of these communal experiments drew upon a belief that one could approach moral or spiritual perfection in this life under the inspiration of the Holy Spirit. A community of like-minded persons was seen as the ideal context for living the truly Christian life. But separated communes generally had an ambiguous relation with the larger society, ranging from indifference, to hostility, to seeing themselves as laboratories for modeling true human life for the world around them.

All communal experiments in antebellum America shared a common belief that they were in the vanguard of the millennium or the imminent arrival of the Kingdom of God. Like the Puritans before them, they saw their experiments in community to be foretastes of the Kingdom. Unlike the Puritans, their attempts to bring life together into a single integrated whole did not extend to imposing the laws and government of their communities upon people who were not willing members of them. In their withdrawn or separated lives, they did not suffer, for the most part, from the Puritan dilemma of justifying repressive rule on unwilling subjects while acknowledging their own radical sinfulness. Repression there may have been, but it was internal to the commune and willingly accepted: if it became too harsh for some, they could always leave and return to "the world."

Most the communes, or what Mark Holloway has called "heavens on earth," tried to model themselves on the early Christian *koinonia*. Most remained fairly small. If they grew at all, they did so by hiving off different communities in different geographical locations. Most, for a time, practiced a form of communal sharing of all property and goods. Most adopted pacifistic stances toward violence and war. Many challenged traditional sexual relationships: some embraced celibacy, some polygamy, some group marriage, though monogamy remained the norm in most. Some practiced equality of the genders in leadership positions and nearly all proclaimed such equality. Most used some form of communal child-rearing.[33]

These communal experiments ran the gamut from Shakers (who practiced an equality of gender leadership, communism, pacifism, and celibacy), to the Mormons (who attempted to revive Winthrop's model of community), to the followers of John Humphrey Noyes and the Oneida community (which practiced a form of plural marriage). All were based on the belief that it was possible to achieve a degree of moral and spiritual perfection, or closeness to God and each other, only in separated communal settings. At best these might serve as models for other Americans, but they would not frontally engage American society in efforts of political or economic reform.

The Mormons, for example, tried to practice a form of economic sharing in which (according the Law of Consecration and the Law of Stewardship) each entering member would consecrate his property to the community. These communal goods would then be redistributed to each according to his ability to put it to successful use in a vocation. All surplus resources garnered from the vocation would be used to take care of the needs of the poor within the community as it strove for economic self-sufficiency. This practice (though it eventually was modified) was an attempt to bring into being the principles of the Kingdom of God on earth, albeit a Kingdom withdrawn from the larger society (often because of the hostile reception accorded the Mormons by their gentile neighbors).

The essential point that all these communal experiments reflect is that under what they took to be the guidance and inspiration of God, the communalists felt called to build the Kingdom on earth through concrete political and economic policies. Most of these approximated some form of socialism, as had the early *koinonia*. John Humphrey Noyes, founder of the Oneida community, put it best for all his fellow communalists:

> It is evident from what we have seen that Revivals breed social revolutions . . . Revivals are theocratic in their very nature; they introduce God into human affairs . . . [T]his power . . . tends to go into all the affairs of life . . . And the theocratic tendency, if it goes beyond religion, naturally runs first into some form of Socialism . . . Revivals, because they are divine, require for their complement a divine organization of society.[34]

---

[33] For a systematic chart of similarities and differences among a select number of communal experiments, see Dolores Hayden, *Seven American Utopias: The Architecture of Communitarian Socialism 1790–1975* (Cambridge, Mass.: MIT Press, 1976), 358–61.

[34] This long quote is taken from Alice Felt Tyler, *Freedom's Ferment* (New York: Harper and Row, 1944), 193–4.

This suggests that there is something in human nature and in God's plan for it that can reach fulfillment only when it is universalized to all persons, even in their "secular" lives. Ultimately God's intention for humankind knows no boundaries between secular and "religious" life. Human nature has been created such that it requires completion (flourishing and well-being) in and through the complex relations of the world as a whole. There is no secluded home, away from the world, into which the human person can *permanently* retreat and hope for fulfillment and the realization of all her divinely-created potential. The separated communes continued to believe that their way would eventually be the way of all people, even though they would refrain from direct engagement with the society for the time being.

It is a strategic or tactical question of how to negotiate the transition from life in smaller, intentional communities to larger, more inclusive universal society. But a tactic still presupposes the goal of the endeavor: and that goal, at least for a Christian ethic of community, must intend the human community as a whole, universally and inclusively.

The Social Gospel

Following the American Civil War some Protestant clergy became convinced that American social institutions had now been virtually sanctified by the blood shed on both sides during that conflict. As a result they believed that America's political and economic institutions needed no major moral reformation. But their uncritical defense of those institutions eventually evoked a reaction that called once again on the transformative potential of a vision of community for the society as a whole. Acceptance of American institutions as they were was reflected in a sermon by Horace Bushnell reflecting on the late conflict: "In these rivers of blood we have now bathed our institutions, and they are henceforth to be hallowed in our sight. Government is now become providential, – no more a mere creature of our human will, but a grandly moral affair."[35]

It was clear to many of the more prominent clergy like Bushnell (sometimes called the "princes of the pulpit") that God had so blessed America's political and economic institutions that major social reform was no longer necessary. The Kingdom of God (the great community of Christian hope) had finally found its true home in a post-Civil War America that had

[35]   Horace Bushnell, "Our Obligations to the Dead," in William McLoughlin, ed., *The American Evangelicals 1800–1900* (New York: Harper Torchbooks, 1968), 152–3.

beaten the demons of secession and stoked the fires of industry to the point where unheard-of wealth was now possible for virtually all ambitious persons as long as they adhered to the principles of the free market and individualism. America could be the great community/society in which individual moral virtue would coalesce with national destiny. The only real sin was failure and the only agent of virtue was the individual.

The Gospel of Wealth that summarized the alliance between America as God's blessed nation and the Christian Gospel was not without its critics, however. As it extolled the virtues of personal stewardship to the "worthy poor" made possible by the unprecedented accumulation of wealth, there was another religious voice struggling to be heard: the voice of the Social Gospel.

At the heart of the Social Gospel was the belief that social justice was of equal if not greater importance than individual virtue. The Social Gospel attempted to restore to Christian ethics a vision of society as a collective community in which just economic and social relations would prevail over the inadequacies of a purely individualistic ethic. Walter Rauschenbusch tried to reclaim this social vision from the uncritical acceptance of the individualistic ethic of the Gospel of Wealth he believed had undermined it. Christianity, he argued, should learn from its prophetic tradition that its essential purpose "was to transform human society into the Kingdom of God by regenerating all human relations and reconstituting them in accordance with the will of God."[36] It was from the prophets that Jesus caught the message that righteousness was not just an imperative for personal conduct but was also "the public morality on which national life is founded."[37] That public morality in ancient Israel was particularly concerned with the plight of the poor.

The importance of community as society is reaffirmed by Jesus who preached the Kingdom of God, which he saw as the "organic growth of the new society," not an otherworldly or completely spiritualized state of individual existence in a life after this one. The hope for the Kingdom was a social and temporal one. Jesus was, in effect, a "society-builder."[38] The goodness which Jesus preached was a social goodness. The morality of the human being "consists in being a good member of his community."[39] The Kingdom of God, he insisted, was "the true human society."[40]

---

[36] Walter Rauschenbusch, *Christianity and the Social Crisis*, ed. Robert D. Cross (New York: Harper Torchbooks, 1964), xxiii. (The book was originally published in 1907.)
[37] Rauschenbusch, 8.
[38] Rauschenbusch, 65.
[39] Rauschenbusch, 67.
[40] Rauschenbusch, 71.

(We see in these words no real distinction between community and society. The power of the vision of the Kingdom was so great that it led most social gospelers to assume that, in the end, there will be only one united assembly of persons which can be called either community or society.)

Rauschenbusch, like most social gospelers, believed that love was the driving force moving society in the direction of the Kingdom. But love had an economic bite to it. A kingdom driven by love, he argued, "tends toward a social order which will best guarantee to all personalities their freest and highest development. This involves the redemption of social life from the cramping influence of religious bigotry, from the repression of self-assertion in the relation of upper and lower classes, and from all forms of slavery." The power that will drive this Kingdom is the power of love in a "progressive reign in human affairs." And this means, even more concretely, the end of "economic oligarchies . . . the abolition of constraint through hunger as part of the industrial system . . . [It will also] involve the redemption of society from private property in the natural resources of the earth, and from any condition in industry which makes monopoly profits possible."[41] In these lines, Rauschenbusch is trying to apply the general principles of the Social Gospel to the concrete economic problems of industrial America, thus giving specificity to an ethic of community that intended to speak to an entire society.

The Social Gospel contains a number of the ingredients that any responsible ethics of community must include if it is to address the negotiation between community and society effectively for our time. It understands that ethics must engage social structures and institutions, not simply individual moral traits and dispositions. That engagement must be practical and concrete, informed by facts "on the ground." It must penetrate the arcane areas of economic philosophy and practice. It needs to analyze and utilize the processes and procedures of politics, even walk comfortably (though with critical insight) down the corridors of political power and be at home with the concepts of political philosophy. And above all, though this is the trickiest and most subtle part, it must keep alive a vision of a social reality that is neither the captive of present forces nor so abstractly removed from them that it drifts off into utopian fantasy. The Social Gospel did not in fact always keep the dreamy romantic dimension of its message from undermining its concrete engagement with society. But at least it reminded those who adopted its message that they needed some idea of where they

[41] Rauschenbusch, *A Theology for the Social Gospel* (New York: Macmillan, 1918), 142–3.

wanted to take society, and how a vision of community could light the way forward.

Reinhold Niebuhr and the Niebuhr Caution

The sobering voice of Reinhold Niebuhr must always be heard in any discussion of the ethics of community. Niebuhr, with whom the words "Christian realism" will always be associated, was virtually obsessed with the issue of community (the term he used most frequently). But for him the "community" of greatest interest was society or the nation-state. His trenchant analysis of the nature of society, provoked in part by what he sees as the dangerous naiveté of the Social Gospel, must be taken into account by any assessment of the negotiating possibilities between intimate communities and impersonal societies.

Against the backdrop of his belief in the pervasiveness of sin and his idealistic notion of love as completely non-self-regarding, Niebuhr argues that love is not truly applicable to societal relations.[42] "The new life in Christ represents the perfection of complete and heedless self-giving which obscures the contrary impulse of self-regard. It is a moral ideal scarcely possible for the individual and certainly not relevant to the morality of self-regarding nations."[43]

The very best one can hope for from groups is the practice of justice which presumes the reality of self-interest and the exercise of social coercion. Nations or societies represent the collective interests of individuals, each of whom is driven to join them in order to advance his or her self-interests, in the selfish sense Niebuhr associates with sin. "In every human group there is less reason to guide and to check impulse, less capacity for self-transcendence, less ability to comprehend the needs of others and therefore more unrestrained egoism than the individuals, who compose the group, reveal in their personal relationships."[44]

Failure to understand the nature of group morality and the "stubborn resistance of group egoism to all moral and inclusive social objectives"

[42] Niebuhr, *The Nature and Destiny of Man*, vol. 1, *Human Nature* (New York: Charles Scribner's Sons, 1941), 287.
[43] Reinhold Niebuhr, *Man's Nature and His Communities* (New York: Charles Scribner's Sons, 1965), 42.
[44] Niebuhr, *Moral Man and Immoral Society* (New York: Charles Scribner's Sons, 1932), xi–xii.

leads to a profound lack of realism about what to expect of group behavior.[45] Social conflict is an inevitable part of human history. Relations between groups will be determined by the exercise of political, economic, and military power wielded in defense of the group's interests. Justice is the moderating influence that seeks to adjust these power relations in a fair and equitable way without transcending them.

Justice presumes the absence of perfect love in human relations. It presumes an inequality in power and the existence of conflicting interests. Justice is primarily about rectifying the imbalance between those without power and those with disproportionate amounts of it. As John C. Bennett describes Niebuhr's position, "the strength of the egoism of all social groups is such that the power of every group needs to be checked by the power of those of whom it is tempted to take some advantage. The struggle for justice consists largely in the effort to increase the power of the victims of injustice."[46] Love may be the "final norm of justice" but equal justice is the "approximation of brotherhood under the conditions of sin."[47]

Politics will be the arena in which the struggle for a just balance of interests will take place. Niebuhr believes that democracy is provisionally the best form of political order because it recognizes the virtues of balancing competing centers of power. But it is not a perfect politics. Man's capacity, he once quipped, for justice makes democracy possible but his inclination to injustice makes it necessary.[48]

Niebuhr knows that no person can live without community of some kind. It is only in community that one gains the resources by which to express the fullness of human life (albeit always incompletely and ambiguously). Community is necessary for the self to be able to give itself to others. If the community protects and nurtures it, the self is then freed to be self-giving which, Niebuhr insists, is a necessary ingredient in self-realization. These communities include the family, civic associations, churches, tribes, and nation-states. Thus community can be seen as complementing and fulfilling the basic needs of the self, even though under the conditions of finite existence it is also often hostile to some of the interests of the self especially when they would threaten group unity.

---

[45]   Niebuhr, *Moral Man*, xx.

[46]   John C. Bennett, "Reinhold Niebuhr's Social Ethics," in Charles W. Kegley and Robert W. Bretall, eds., *Reinhold Niebuhr: His Religious, Social, and Political Thought*, vol. 2 (New York: The Macmillan Company, 1961), 60.

[47]   Reinhold Niebuhr, *The Nature and Destiny of Man*, vol. 2, *Human Destiny* (New York: Charles Scribner's Sons, 1943), 254.

[48]   Niebuhr, *The Children of Light*, xiii.

Of course all communities, the church included, resonate with ambiguity. No community is capable of maintaining or sustaining a perfect moral life for its members or for its relation to other communities. Christian communities in particular, therefore, need to be disabused of their naive attitude toward the exercise of power and self-interest even in groups such as their own churches that are dedicated in principle to advancing the common good and the welfare of the least well-off. Asking either the church or the society to adopt the morality of self-sacrifice and love, without calculating the inevitable presence of power politics is a profound illusion. Politics is an essential and necessary ingredient in group relations and will, perforce, require an interpenetration of the ethics of persuasion and the tactics of coercion. While individuals might mitigate to some degree the threat to their own self-interest that they see in others by an infusion of moral teaching and the moral spirit, "as racial, economic and national groups they take for themselves, whatever their power can command"[49] because only such taking is believed appropriate for overcoming the insecurity that led to sin (the arrogant belief that we can't trust God to look after us) in the first place. The most we can expect from dedicated persons who appreciate the virtues of community is a society "in which there will be enough justice, and in which coercion will be sufficiently non-violent to prevent the common enterprise from issuing into complete disaster."[50]

This suggests, contrary to some more pessimistic readings of his thought that for Niebuhr, that while religion and the ethics of love can never overcome the brutalities of power completely, they can modify and qualify them. Religion can provide an ethical grounding for the pursuit of justice so that it does not become a merely mechanical and cynical distribution of power based on nothing more than collective self-interest. While religion's vision of an ideal community is, in an historical and empirical sense, an illusion, it is an important illusion. "Without the ultrarational hopes and passions of religion no society will ever have the courage to conquer despair and attempt the impossible; for the vision of a just society is an impossible one, which can be approximated only by those who do not regard it as impossible . . . For what religion believes to be true . . . may become true if its truth is not doubted."[51]

The relation between the religious community and the larger society will remain forever ambiguous and paradoxical. If religious people can learn to overcome the fear of using force in order to establish justice (a fear

[49]   Niebuhr, *Moral Man*, 9.
[50]   Niebuhr, *Moral Man*, 22.
[51]   Niebuhr, *Moral Man*, 81.

legitimately based on the truth that the exercise of coercive power can easily corrupt the morally sensitive conscience), then "religious ideals may yet achieve social and political significance." But this significance is always qualified, incomplete, and ambiguous itself. In the end the role of morality in social life is for Niebuhr, at best, one of tempering a steel forged in the heat of self-interest. But the "illusion" that morality can make a difference in social life by energizing the drive for justice ought never to be expunged. "Justice cannot be approximated if the hope of its perfect realization [a clear illusion] does not generate a sublime madness in the soul. Nothing but such madness will do battle with malignant power and 'spiritual wickedness in high places.' The illusion is dangerous because it encourages terrible fanaticisms. It must therefore be brought under the control of reason. One can only hope that reason will not destroy it before its work is done."[52]

I don't think the "Niebuhr caution" regarding the dangers of utopian expectations for society needs the kind of ontological despair reflected in these final words from *Moral Man and Immoral Society*. Niebuhr's dualism has so distanced God from the historical process that he has only human beings, in their sinful ambiguous condition, to count on for building societies of justice. The track record is not, to be sure, one that would justify undue optimism about developing "perfect" systems of justice. But Niebuhr continually underestimates the power that God can bring to the historical process, both in terms of God's own unique actions in history as well in terms of God's renewal and transformation of human lives. If God is truly at work in the world building the kingdom of God, with the cooperation of human agents, then belief that such a kingdom is capable of instantiation in history is not an illusion, or a madness of the soul. It is a belief grounded ontologically in the will and power of God and presupposes a God who can act in history.

The "Niebuhr caution" reminds us not to baptize or bless human achievements prematurely, or to blind ourselves to the presence in all of them of some degree of self-interest and the moral ambiguities of the exercise of power. Nor must we too easily seek to close the distance between love and justice in practice. They are not the same and expecting to be able to create either a community or a society based solely on love is unrealistic and dangerous. It can lead people, in the name of love, to legitimate communities in which individual freedom and dissent are too easily suppressed in the name of a greater good. Justice must always adjust relations that love alone cannot complete, just as love must instruct justice as to its place in the full relationship of persons. But Niebuhr himself may

---

[52]   Niebuhr, *Moral Man*, 277.

in the end be the one who undercuts true realism: if God is real, then God's actions are real, and underestimating their power to bring about communities of greater love and justice than Niebuhr seems to allow is the ultimate form of nonrealism.

The Struggle between Individualism and Community in America Today

Despite Niebuhr's realism about the possibilities of community there has been a rise of interest in recent years in small communal groups that reflects a larger yearning for community in America and Great Britain. Although both societies are grounded in liberal philosophies of social contract that privilege the rights of the individual and the sacredness of private property against the claims of the society as a whole, they also have traditions of community that stand against the individualistic stream that has swept so much before it already.

That stream is still quite strong in rhetoric and in reality. It stands, in many ways, as the most important obstacle to developing an ethics of community that can address societal issues with realism and commitment. Most Americans speak a language of individualism that cuts hard against working for a larger societal common good. As Robert Bellah has observed, the first language for most Americans is that of individualism, private property, individual rights, self-reliance, and the sacredness of one's freedom to be left alone by others. But there is also a second, less overt language that they speak which reflects who they would like to be as persons. That second language is the language of community.

Individualism is deeply rooted in the American psyche, as Tocqueville observed over a century ago. At its core is a belief that only by exercising the greatest possible degree of personal freedom could the individual protect himself against the tyranny of an oppressive state or the unwarranted intrusions into his life by other people's imposition of their values and interests. The driving engine of individual action in this world was taken to be the pursuit of self-interest which fit perfectly into the ideology of a market economy.

One consequence of this individualism is the radical separation of one's private and public lives. The public world, the world of political, economic and other social interactions becomes either an oppressive obstacle to self-fulfillment or, at best, a remote, necessary evil with which one must engage only at the most minimal level in order to secure a social order in which the freedom of the individual to pursue its own private interests is protected.

But Americans were never entirely content with being a nation comprised only of atomistic persons always relating only out of economic and legal necessity and never committing themselves to each other in closer bonds of unity. There have always been echoes of the dynamics of belonging that resonate in the American experience. Individualism has never been unqualified. In their study of contemporary Americans, Robert Bellah and his colleagues "found all the classic polarities of American individualism still operating: the deep desire for autonomy and self-reliance combined with an equally deep conviction that life has no meaning unless shared with others in the context of community; . . . the inner tensions of American individualism add up to a classic case of ambivalence. We strongly assert the value of our self-reliance and autonomy. We deeply feel the emptiness of a life without sustaining social commitments . . . The tensions of our lives would be even greater if we did not, in fact, engage in practices that constantly limit the effects of an isolating individualism, even though we cannot articulate those practices nearly as well as we can the quest for autonomy."[53]

Bellah argues that Americans have a rich heritage, some of which we have already rehearsed, on which to draw in building up a sense of community. They have always belonged to communities that are constituted by a history and a memory of that history. They are held together from one generation to the next by a narrative of that history. They are communities of memory as well as communities of hope. "They carry a context of meaning that can allow us to connect our aspirations for ourselves and those closest to us with the aspirations of a larger whole and see our own efforts as being, in part, contributions to a common good."[54] This is precisely the kind of community one finds in the biblical tradition and in John Winthrop and the Puritans. It is also present in the work of those religious evangelicals and republican political philosophers at the time of the American revolution as well as in the reforming efforts of people inspired by the Second Great Awakening, and later by the Social Gospel. It is a community that takes seriously the notion of a common good that both transcends as well as preserves the worth and dignity of each individual.

A good ethics of community must be one that affirms both the individual (in all his or her uniqueness or "otherness") without succumbing to the false view that only by making our relationships with others tentative, provisional, and utilitarian can we protect the inner core of who we really are. Public and private are not dichotomous. Out of the biblical and

---

[53]   Bellah et al., 150–1.
[54]   Bellah et al., 153.

republican strands of our national "community of memory" might come
the resources for bridging public and private. We can move from intimate
community to public society without confusing them with each other or
demanding that we choose one over the other.

The Small Group Movement

One manifestation of the longing for community that Bellah has affirmed
has been the relatively recent rise of the small group movement in America.
Documented by Robert Wuthnow and celebrated by Scott Peck, the
small group movement includes the myriad of intentional communities
that have sprung up on almost every block in the country, catering to
some set of personal needs of those who eagerly seek to belong to them.

These groups seem to meet many Americans' need to move beyond the
isolating individualism that has characterized much of the American experience. There is a hunger for connecting with others and sharing with them
one's journey, anxieties, hopes, fears, and need for belonging. Small groups,
Robert Wuthnow argues, "temper our individualism and our culturally
induced desire to be totally independent of one another."[55] These groups
provide important emotional support to their members and help them
adapt to the demands of the larger society around them. The single greatest
satisfaction such groups provide is "having people in your life who give you
deep emotional support."[56] Groups work well, in the opinion of those who
join, when they enable individuals to discover how they are perceived by
others. "Interaction with others in a group . . . provides people with a mirror
in which to reflect upon their lives and reaffirm their self-definition."[57]

One energetic promoter and developer of these small groups is the
psychiatrist M. Scott Peck, perhaps best known for his book *The Road Less
Traveled*. Peck believes that at some basic level, in a culture saturated with
the "fallacy of rugged individualism," we are all lonely. It is this loneliness
that drives us into community. Peck says that if we are going to use the
word "community" "meaningfully we must restrict it to a group of individuals who have learned how to communicate honestly with each other,
whose relationships go deeper than their masks of composure, and who
have developed some significant commitment to 'rejoice together, mourn

---

[55] Robert Wuthnow, *Sharing the Journey: Support Groups and America's New Quest for
Community* (New York: The Free Press, 1994), 12.
[56] Wuthnow, 53.
[57] Wuthnow, 210.

together,' and to delight in each other, make others' conditions our own."[58] In community as Peck understands it the individual is accepted as he is. No one seeks to convert him and in the freedom this allows the individual may heal himself through the power of the group that he has chosen to belong to. The freedom to drop one's social mask frees one to become more himself in the presence of caring others.

Peck is quite vague about exactly what the communal consciousness will mean for the political and economic arrangements of societies. He is also, perhaps, overly optimistic about the ease with which one can overcome one's empirical "situatedness" in one historically contingent, particular community of the kind the communitarians extol. He hopes for a transcendence of particular cultures and their replacement by a planetary culture, but does not fill in the details of what kind of political and economic order it will have. Despite this frustrating lack of concrete analysis and prescription for the kind of global society/community he envisions, Peck is right to remind us that the capacity for transformation is "the most essential characteristic of human nature."[59] When this claim is linked to a moral ontology that has room for divine action in history, it opens up possibilities for community that cannot be dreamed of in philosophies that cannot think beyond the categories of individualism, self-interest, and the principles of private property and the free market. Peck is trying to point to potentials that are not limited by what we have been told by economists and political realists about what human nature really is and is capable of.

Wuthnow's own analysis and evaluation of these groups, however, is not as celebratory as Peck's. While appreciating many elements in the movement, Wuthnow makes the point that these groups are not always offering an alternative to the philosophy of individualism but are, in effect, carrying it out by other means. For each small group is often a reflection and a repository of personal, private needs that the individual members bring to it, and when those needs are not met, the individual moves on to other groups. The core value of the group is what it gives to the individual: it has no value of its own and belonging to a community for the sake of others or for the sake of the sheer joy of communion itself is not generally intelligible to most who belong to these groups. These groups have no "common good" to which the members are expected to subordinate their own individual interests.

---

[58] M. Scott Peck, *The Different Drum: Community-Making and Peace* (New York: Touchstone Book, Simon & Schuster, 1987), 59.
[59] Peck, 178.

Because their focus is so much on the emotional and psychological needs of the members, small groups often fail to think beyond themselves to the moral issues facing public, social institutions in the political and economic spheres (from which, in fact, members in the small group are often trying to escape, at least psychologically if not materially). By providing a haven of comfort and security away from the pressures of public life, the small group actually often winds up helping its members accommodate themselves to the society. The group becomes a kind of valve that helps the individual suffering under social demands let off steam. But this does not lead, in many cases, to a critical questioning of the policies, principles, and practices that have created the pressures in the first place. Their reluctance to question the values and beliefs of others spills over into their hesitation to hold up to critical scrutiny the values and beliefs that constitute the larger society. By providing an alternative community to those impersonal associations that constitute the political and social order, small groups actually weaken both our attachment to these broader communities and our zeal to challenge their defects and inadequacies.

Small groups can give practice in learning to hear and appreciate the variety and diversity of human beings; to sympathize with their needs; to discover the commonalities that even diverse people share; to learn the skills of reconciliation and commitment to others. Small groups can help people experience the joy of mutuality and an openness to others. The question is whether they can take these skills and practices into the larger society.

Some small groups have begun to take on controversial moral issues in the public realm, but the issues tend to be "personal" and conservative. They often attack the State for its intrusions into private life, especially the life of the family. But the principle of considering the effects of public policies on human life is one that could be applied equally well to issues of social and economic justice. But small groups will need to be much more intentional about confronting the public dimensions of community and society if they are to make a contribution to responsible transactions between them. They will need to take up issues of social justice and not just private charity. "An ethic of caring that extends beyond the group must be cultivated, issues of peace and justice must be kept on the agenda, and a spirituality of sacrifice will need to be brought into juxtaposition with conceptions of personal gratification . . . Only by focusing explicit attention on the character of community and on the needs of the wider society are small groups likely to realize their potential for creating a genuine sense of community."[60]

[60] Wuthnow, 340.

Chapter 4

Building a Philosophy of Community

John Macmurray and the Philosophy of Community

As we move from a historical narrative of experiments in community to a dialogue between philosophies of community and society, it is time to lay out a philosophy of community that is grounded both in a construal of a Christian vision and in a philosophical analysis of the nature of human persons. The work of the late Scottish philosopher John Macmurray provides, I believe, a solid, comprehensive, and metaphysically adequate foundation for a philosophy of community. Macmurray's work is, I believe, basic to the moral ontology developed earlier in this volume. If Christian ethics is committed to the belief that God has created the essential conditions of reality, that human nature participates in those conditions, and that human history is moving, under God's guidance, to a telos of a social Kingdom, it is thereby committed to a philosophy of the person and that which presumably completes the person, the telos of community. If the person and the community through which he/she is fulfilled is central to a Christian ethic, then some understanding (traditionally called metaphysical) of both is necessary if ethics is not simply to be done ad hoc with no coherent overarching sense of its fundamental grounding and direction.

Macmurray's principal expression of what he called the philosophy of the personal is found in his Gifford Lectures of 1953–4, which he titled the "Form of the Personal" and which were published as *The Self as Agent* and *Persons in Relation*. Macmurray sets out to "exhibit [in philosophical form] the unity of human experience as a whole."[1] The thesis guiding this

---

[1] John Macmurray, *The Self as Agent* (London: Faber and Faber Limited, 1957), 13. This book has recently been reprinted by Humanities Press (New Jersey and London) with an Introduction by Stanley Harrison in 1991.

exhibition is that "all meaningful knowledge is for the sake of action, and all meaningful action for the sake of friendship."[2] (Friendship is synonymous for him with community.)

Epistemological Revision

To clear the ground for his full development of the form of the personal, Macmurray begins by recasting traditional Western philosophical epistemology. He rejects the Cartesian understanding of the self as primarily a thinker because it leads, in his opinion, to an unbridgeable gap between our understanding of the relation between thinking and acting. Modern philosophy, since Descartes, begins the search for the foundations of knowledge with the self in isolation from its practical relations with others. In its isolation the self is conceived primarily as thinker searching for the foundation of true thought. But if the self is essentially thinker, how can it account for the fact that thinking is only one of its many actions? A dualism between thought and action emerges and the unity of the self (as both thinker and agent) is shattered.

We can restore the unity of the self, according to Macmurray, by starting our epistemological journey by thinking not from the standpoint of thought but from the standpoint of action. That is, Macmurray argues, we can begin by postulating that the self is essentially an agent, one of whose actions is the act of thinking. Conceived in this way, thinking becomes subordinate to the more inclusive category of action: it becomes an instrument for helping the self to guide its practical actions more successfully in the real world in which it is already fully engaged. The self already exists as a self in relation to the not-self. We are embedded in a reality that is other than ourselves. We can partially withdraw from this larger-than-ourselves reality in thought in order to get a conceptual grasp on it, but our thoughts presume, arise from, and must be directed back to that larger whole from which the self has temporarily withdrawn itself. (The tennis player may withdraw mentally from the acts of hitting the ball in order to figure out why his shots keep going into the net. He becomes a thinker in order to help his more physical actions become more "successful" in realizing his intentions.)

At a more abstract level, thinking is a necessary device by which the self can conceive the relevant differences between different not-selves. Some are conceptualized as having only material characteristics (e.g., a table),

---

[2] Macmurray, *The Self as Agent*, 15.

some as having material and organic dimensions (e.g., a dog), and some as being fully personal (containing material, organic and personal aspects simultaneously). The chief exemplification of these latter characteristics are other persons. To properly characterize them requires conceiving them as having the same ability to reason and to intend as oneself.

If the self is defined by thought, its noncognitive actions become a mystery or must be conceived as radically different from its thinking. Action is not a thought. On the other hand, thinking is clearly an action. It is one of many things that agents *do*. Therefore, action is the more inclusive and more basic category through which to conceptualize the human person.

The significance of this recasting of traditional epistemology is hard to overestimate. It means, for example, that the truth of a belief is ultimately "proven" by its reference to action in the world. "Proof" in this sense is usually determined over the long run, and for a theist always in reference to the long-range intentions of God and the fundamental structures of reality.

This means that the truth of the person can only be validated by his/her actions in relation to others. And those actions are validated only in and through the development of a community of persons living in bonds of mutual love and friendship. This means, of course, that truth is historical. It cannot be established conclusively solely by acts of cognition or by meeting the criteria of coherence and consistency (though the latter are important provisional and intermediate tests of truth). In this sense Macmurray's epistemology is distinctly relevant to a Christian ethics of community because both are grounded in the conviction that God is at work in history cooperating with other agents in bringing about the conditions for the establishment of a fulfilling community of persons (Kingdom of God).

Given the multitude of agents and the contingencies and complexities of history, this would lead us to expect that there would be many different historical experiments in community and many different attempts to work out the appropriate relationship between communities and the societies of which they are a part. And this expectation has, of course, informed the structure of the development of this particular version of an ethics of community. Ultimately the final proof of an ethics of community is whether it works in practice for the long run. And that can't be known until the possibilities of history have been exhausted. (Though it doesn't rule out intimations, hints, glimpses, or foretastes in the midst of history of what can and will ultimately be achieved.)

Toward the end of *The Self as Agent* Macmurray argues that if we are seeking to represent philosophically the unity of the person, then we must take into account the unity of history, because history is the joint work of human and divine agency. If action is constituted by intention, then the unity of history must be a unity of intention. "Historical understanding is . . . a comprehension of the continuity of human intention, and so far as it succeeds, it exhibits a multitude of individual acts as constituting a single action, in virtue of a community of intention."[3] This rather cryptic and condensed assertion simply means that the philosopher *thinks* the unity of historical action *as if* it is the work of a community of persons intending the same outcome. Ultimately Macmurray will represent that unity as God's overarching intention for the world. But in the short run it led him to the challenge he takes up in *Persons in Relation*, namely articulating the relationship of persons in action for community.

As the self acts it encounters resistance from the Other, the not-self, or, more accurately, many not-selves. If the self's intentions are to be success-fully realized, it has the practical task of figuring out just what kind of object the not-self is that is resisting it. An adequate "reading" of the not-self is essential for the resumption of successful action in relation to it. At this point we find, Macmurray argues, that we can characterize the Other as either material, organic, or personal. (Each of these three forms of repres-entation in order contains the one(s) preceding it but goes beyond them. The person is material, organic, and constituted by that which is uniquely personal; the organic contains the material but has no personal dimension; and the material has neither organic nor personal characteristics.)

Personal Relations

The thesis of *Persons in Relation* is simply stated: "the Self is constituted by its relation to the Other; that it has its being in its relationship; and that this relationship is necessarily personal."[4] Macmurray insists that there are distinctions to be drawn between types of personal relationships. And these distinctions, as we shall see, have a crucial bearing on the distinction between community and society, a distinction I have been insisting is central to any adequate ethics of community. Macmurray says that personal relationships can be either direct or indirect. Direct relations are "those which involve a personal acquaintance with one another on the part of the persons involved. Indirect relations exclude this condition: they are rela-tions between persons who are not personally known to one another. All

---

[3] Macmurray, *The Self as Agent*, 213.
[4] John Macmurray, *Persons in Relation* (New York: Harper and Brothers, 1961), 17. This book was reprinted by Humanities Press with an Introduction by Frank G. Kirkpatrick in 1991.

indirect relations are therefore necessarily impersonal. Direct relations are those which may or may not be personal, at the will of the persons related."[5]

I have an indirect impersonal relationship with the individual who responds to my mail inquiries at my health care insurance company. I have a direct relationship with my next-door neighbor. But my neighbor and I don't like each other very much and so we don't, by mutual choice, have a personal relationship. I do have a direct and personal relationship with my wife. Communities will be those groups constituted by direct personal relationships and societies those associations characterized chiefly by impersonal direct and indirect relationships among the members. Societies meet Macmurray's condition that persons are constituted by their relations with others, but only communities can meet his condition that persons are fulfilled and have their being in direct personal relationships with others.

Mother and Child

One of the most direct relations possible is between mother and child.[6] Macmurray insists that this relation is not to be understood solely in biological terms since the survival of the human infant requires the free, intentional actions of its parent(s). If the infant relied solely on its own motives and behaviors it would die since it is helpless without the aid of capable intending agents, chief among whom is the mother.

The mother–child relation is the "basic form of human existence," a "personal mutuality," a "'You and I' with a common life."[7] The personal, therefore, is a relationship, not an individual. This relation is constituted by the infant's impulse to communicate with the world which, originally, *is* wholly the mother before it can begin to discriminate the various forms and modes of "otherness" around it. Eventually out of this mother–child relationship are developed positive and negative poles of the infant's

---

[5] Macmurray, *Persons in Relation*, 43.

[6] In light of the feminist critique of traditional views of the family, Macmurray explicitly argues that his use of the term "mother" is not a biological one. It simply means the adult who cares for the infant. "The mother may be an aunt, or an elder sister or a hired nurse. She need not even be a female. A man can do all the mothering that is necessary, if he is provided with a feeding-bottle, and learns how to do it in precisely the same fashion that a woman must learn." (Macmurray, *Persons in Relation*, 50.) This assertion both opens up the boundaries of what a family can be and might be argued to have overlooked the importance of breast-feeding, which is now regarded by many as essential to the physical as well as emotional health of the developing child.

[7] Macmurray, *Persons in Relation*, 60.

motivations. They are respectively love and fear. Fear is of isolation from the Mother: love is the delight in being cared for and in intimate communion with her. Macmurray argues that the negative pole (fear) falls within and is subordinated to the positive (love). When the positive is fully functioning the child and mother enjoy their relationship as an end in itself, for its own sake. There is a mutual delight in the relation "which unites them in a common life" expressed through various symbolic gestures.[8] This is the genesis of community.

Resistance and Discrimination of the Other

The infant must be brought through the developmental process to the point where it can exercise free agency so as to intend a positive relation with others. And one crucial part of this process is the *resistance* that the parent provides to the infant's motives. The resistance of an object to my action is the essential basis of my knowledge of the Other as Other. The resistance from the Other is essentially a frustration of my will. In practical experience "Self and Other are correlatives discriminated together by their opposition; and this opposition constitutes the unity of the experience."[9] The first "other" the infant experiences in this way is the mother. Before the process of gradual differentiation completes itself, the mother is to the infant "the whole community of persons of which [it is] an individual member."[10]

The practical process of differentiation begins with a characterization of the whole world in which it is enmeshed as personal and gradually distinguishes on a purely practical basis between those parts of the whole that respond personally (and hence are taken as persons) and those that do not (and are taken as nonpersons, whether solely material or a combination of material and organic). This process is essential to the full development of the individual self. "Personal individuality is not an original given fact. It is achieved through the progressive differentiation of the original unity of the 'You and I.'"[11] What is particularly significant about this is that "the child discovers himself as an individual by *contrasting himself, and indeed by wilfully* [sic] *opposing himself to the family* **to which he belongs**; and this *discovery* of his individuality is at the same time the *realization* of his individuality" (bold mine).[12] This means that individuality requires resistance from the Other and therefore the actualization, within a particular context,

---

[8]   Macmurray, *Persons in Relation*, 62–3.
[9]   Macmurray, *The Self as Agent*, 108.
[10] Macmurray, *Persons in Relation*, 80.
[11] Macmurray, *Persons in Relation*, 91.

of the negative pole of relationality. The personal Other, originally the mother, must *withdraw* from a fully positive relation with the child in order to help the child differentiate positive from negative and thus differentiate itself from the Other(s). If the Other simply melted away at our touch, or absorbed us into itself with no resistance, there would be no possibility of distinguishing ourselves as individual persons. We need the resistance of the Other to become ourselves since central to our self-identity as persons is our individual agency. "Without the support of a resistance there can be no action; and the resistance must . . . be the resistance of a personal Other."[13] Eventually, of course, the infant must learn that there are nonpersonal Others in the world who will also offer resistance. Without this knowledge, the developed self will be a helpless and ineffective agent in the world.

One part of this process is the necessity of the child's learning to distinguish between negative and positive. Macmurray believes that his distinction undergirds the later distinctions the adult will have to make between real and unreal, good and evil, beautiful and ugly, true and false.

The essential task for the emerging self is to develop a reliable understanding of what is truly negative (i.e., not personal) without remaining stuck in negativity (i.e., becoming so fearful of the nonpersonal, withdrawn, and resisting Other that one adopts an egocentrism out of fear of that Other). The ideal is to use the knowledge of the reality of the nonpersonal in the service of developing healthier personal relationships. The child will ideally develop a healthy will of his own: but he will have to choose whether he wants to exercise that will to wall himself off from Others who, he believes, intend him harm, or to guide him toward personal others who, he hopes, will welcome him into community and mutuality. The loving resistance and opposition that the mother, and more expansively, the family, provide the infant must be delicately and carefully handled.[14]

This leads directly to what Macmurray takes to be the basic problem of life itself: the problem of personal reconciliation. If the child responds out of fear to the mother's strategic and lovingly intended withdrawal and

---

[12] Macmurray, *Persons in Relation*, 91.

[13] Macmurray, *Persons in Relation*, 92.

[14] This is why, perhaps, Freud and other psychologists have rightly focused on the importance of the early years in child-raising and why those years are so fraught with danger and expectation. It also suggests some interesting connections between Macmurray's work and that of object-relations theorists who stress the importance of relationality, and in particular of the "good enough mother" in the development of a healthy self. It may be no accident that Macmurray's work and the development of object-relations theory both occur at the same time and in the same place: W.D. Fairbairn was a contemporary Scot and Harry Guntrip was Macmurray's student.

resistance, the negative motive will dominate his later egocentric actions. He will become either submissive to or aggressive toward the other as a way of dealing with his fear that the Other intends him harm. But these behaviors toward the Other are self-defeating because the only thing that will truly fulfill the self is "the full mutuality of fellowship in a common life, in which alone the individual can realize himself as a person."[15] Only if one intends this state of mutuality can one be understood as positively motivated. But this requires the opposite of fear, which is love: love for the other as other. That is why Macmurray calls it "hetero-centric" since its object is the other (hetero), not the self (ego). But this heterocentricity is possible only in community, in which the unity of persons is based on mutual positive personal motivation.

Community provides the fullest possible conditions for individual flourishing and individual flourishing provides the means for the flourishing of all the others who are the objects of the individual's love. Such flourishing presupposes direct personal relations between those who are bound together by mutual love. But it also presupposes that those direct relations have a material foundation that includes indirect relations between persons as well.

Society

Those cooperative indirect relations relative to the material foundation of community are what constitute, in Macmurray's view, a society. He believes that the basis of any human society "is the universal and necessary intention to maintain the personal relation which makes the individual a person, and his life a common life."[16] But many societies are based on what Macmurray calls a negative motivation, namely fear for the self and therefore fear of the other, fear that the other is a threat to the material possessions and social status by which the self has come, falsely, to define itself. The unity of this kind of society is intended, for example, to advance the interests of "aggressively egocentric individuals" (as in Hobbes' conception). For Hobbes society is the necessary evil that permits these "inherently isolated or unrelated" atomic units to live together. "They are united in a whole by an external force [the power of the State maintained through the sanctions of the Law] which counteracts the tendency of their individual energies to repel one another."[17] In such a society, because the self fears the other, its

---

[15]   Macmurray, *Persons in Pelation*, 105.
[16]   Macmurray, *Persons in Relation*, 128.
[17]   Macmurray, *Persons in Relation*, 137.

freedom to express itself fully is inhibited. It is afraid to open itself to others, to share its goods, to sacrifice some of its narrow interests for the sake of others because it fears that everything it gives away will diminish it and will entail a loss of self-identity and meaning. It can only assume that the others are just as negatively motivated toward it as it is toward them. In this kind of society, basic trust has been eroded, and with it the necessary conditions for other-regarding behavior. The result can only be the further disintegration and alienation of the society and its members in relation to each other.[18] "Society is maintained by a common constraint, that is to say by acting in obedience to law. This secures the appearance of freedom, for it secures me from the expression of the other's animosity. But it does so by suppression of the motive which constitutes the relation."[19]

A community is distinguished from a society by the positive apperception of its members toward each other. If a society is held together by a negative bond of unity, the unity of a community is a personal and positive one. A community in its fullest possible sense has overcome the fear for the self and its correlative fear of the other. And in so doing it has opened up the possibilities of freedom for the other.

In community persons will care for one another in love. A community, he asserts, "is for the sake of friendship and presupposes love."[20] To establish and maintain such a community is the function of religion which is, for Macmurray, concerned with "the original and basic formal problem of human existence, and this is the relation of persons . . . religion is aboutthe community of persons."[21] Religion exists because the communal relation of persons has been broken and needs restoration. Once restored these relations are direct, personal, and mutual. There is no "purpose" behind a community to which it is an means: the relations that constitute it are ends in themselves, characterized by joy and delight in the mutuality of the relationships as such.

---

[18]   This is the thrust of recent work being done by the African–American philosopher Laurence Thomas. See especially his *Living Morally* (Philadelphia: Temple University Press, 1989).

[19]   Macmurray, *Persons in Relation*, 151.

[20]   Macmurray, *Persons in Relation*, 151.

[21]   Macmurray, *Persons in Relation*, 157. Macmurray makes rather sweeping statements about "religion" in general and often fails to note the different functions different religions play in different cultures. It is clear that his understanding of religion is derived from a western European theistic tradition. Since that is the tradition on which this ethics of community is built, however, it seems fair to draw upon Macmurray's treatment of it in this regard.

"The structure of a community is the nexus or network of the active relations of friendship between all possible pairs of its members."[22] One self's fulfillment is dependent on that self being the object of other selves' love, just as it loves other selves. The relation between the selves in community is truly "heterocentric; the centre [sic] of interest and attention is in the other, not in himself . . . But this is mutual; the other cares for him disinterestedly in return. Each, that is to say, acts, and therefore thinks and feels for the other, and not for himself. But because the positive motive [love] contains and subordinates its negative [fear], their unity is no fusion of selves, neither is it a functional unity of differences – neither an organic nor a mechanical unity – it is a unity of persons. Each remains a distinct individual; the other remains really other. Each realizes himself in and through the other."[23] Clearly, in Macmurray's view of community the individual is not suppressed or subordinated to a greater whole in which he is only a functional part. The flourishing of the individual with his own unique gifts and talents is integral to the very meaning of community itself. Individual and community are not polar opposites.

Sometimes Macmurray uses language about community that is truly excessive and asserts more than is justified. A universal community, he suggests, is one "in which each cares for all the others and no one for himself."[24] Taken in context, however, this only means that if the relationship is truly mutual then one can let go of a preoccupation with self because others will be caring for him, just as he is caring for them. This is not an absence of self-concern but a communal resolution of the problematic found in individualistically based associations of how persons can relate at more than a utilitarian level.

Macmurray also argues that any genuine community of persons must, by intent, be inclusive of all persons. This means simply that no one can be deliberately excluded since such exclusion would have to be grounded in fear (the negative motivation). And to live in fear of the other is to live with less freedom than to live in love. Fear inhibits the actions of the self: it becomes self-defensive and is not free to reach out to or receive the gifts that others bring to it. Only love can transcend the inhibitions created by fear and therefore only love can truly free the self to be itself. But in practice no communities as we know them can be inclusive of all persons. Practical community is necessarily limited in size. Macmurray does say that a universal community is an "ideal of the personal" and thus seems to

22 Macmurray, *Persons in Relation*, 158.
23 Macmurray, *Persons in Relation*, 158.
24 Macmurray, *Persons in Relation*, 159.

recognize the practical limitations on community-building that will not be overcome without the active intervention of God. Until God's intention for community is fully realized, however, the role of religion is to "express the consciousness of community," to celebrate communion, and to express a consciousness of one's joy in it.[25] Religion's function is to challenge negative motivations and strengthen the positive ones (the task of reconciliation). Religion is to "create, maintain and deepen the community of persons and to extend it without limit, by the transformation of negative motives and by eliminating the dominance of fear in human relations. To achieve this would be to create a universal community of persons in which all personal relations were positively motived [sic], and all its members were free and equal in relation. Such a community would be the full self-realization of the personal."[26]

At this point Macmurray makes the intriguing suggestion that as societies have moved from the more "primitive" kinship groups to the larger nation-states, they have begun to approach something like universality. The notion seems to be that societies, even though limited in their motivation for truly personal relationships, can provide the material and political scaffolding upon which the movement toward a universal community can be built. This does not, of course, solve the problem of what a universal community of persons would look like. Macmurray fails to develop a coherent or adequate notion of how every single person could be directly and personally related to every other person in the world. But his failure should not obscure his basic point. Persons can approach universal community if they do not *deliberately and intentionally* exclude other persons from the potential for or possibility of direct personal relationship in a communal setting. As long as one is open to such personal relationships with any person in the world (regardless of race, gender, age, culture, etc.), one is expressing the fundamental motivation by which genuine community is built.

Until the Kingdom comes, however, it would be more realistic to expect that the communities in which people will actually live will be relatively small in size and limited in membership. But if they are positively motivated, they will be open to, even eager for, positive relations with other such communities as they become available. The hostilities and fear that presently mark international relations would be diminished, even though a single universal loving community, in the strict sense, would not replace them at least in the short run. By suggesting that the movement

25   Macmurray, *Persons in Relation*, 162.
26   Macmurray, *Persons in Relation*, 163.

of societies is toward becoming more inclusive in practice, Macmurray at least suggests a way by which the religious intent of expressing and celebrating communion could be linked with the devices of politics and nation-building that characterize the work of societies.

Macmurray does not believe that negatively motivated relations can, in societies of indirect personal relations, ever be entirely replaced by the positive (or "heterocentric") motive of love for all the others. It is utopian fantasy to believe that a society, especially one of the enormous size and complexity of the modern nation-state, can be turned into a community by the devices of politics. Societies cannot provide in and of themselves the substance of mutuality that constitutes the heart of authentic communities. Built as they are on indirect relations between persons, societies are only "potentially" communities. And because of this fact, the limitations of politics must be recognized as persons struggle to develop the conditions for full human flourishing, both for themselves and for others. But if we know what those conditions are, at least in a general kind of way (given a moral ontology in which the will of God plays a central role), then we have a fulcrum by which to critique, challenge, and reform the structures and institutions of society so as to best serve the purposes of community without replacing or becoming identified with them.

Material Foundations of a Just Society

The crucial function of a society is to provide the material foundations and the just parceling of power on which the flourishing of individuals within communities must be built. Macmurray is fully in accord with both liberals and communitarians in regarding what John Rawls (see pp. 81–4 below) calls the primary social goods as essential to a full, even spiritual life. These goods include rights and liberties, powers and opportunities, income and wealth, as well as self-respect.[27] The basic moral question for any society is whether these goods are fairly distributed in way that permits all persons to flourish in the most just way possible. And this is the question of justice,[28] as Rawls has also argued.

[27] Macmurray does not question whether these goods carry over into nondemocratic, nonliberal societies. Like Rawls, he seems to be working within the given framework of western liberal society and assuming that its basic goods are those that, for the most part, constitute the foundation, if not the full meaning, of human flourishing.
[28] John Rawls, *A Theory of Justice* (Cambridge, Mass.: Harvard University Press, 1971), 62.

Politics, for Macmurray, is the "maintaining, improving and adjusting [of] the indirect or economic relations of persons."[29] The institutional expression of politics is the State, "and its central function is the maintaining of justice." Justice, in this sense, is the minimum of reciprocity and interest in the other in the personal relation: it is a "kind of zero or lower limit of moral behavior." Justice is the negative aspect of morality but it is necessary to the constitution of the positive, though subordinate within it.

Nevertheless, justice must insist that the others remain differentiated from me and from each other. Justice keeps morality from becoming sentimental or lapsing into what Macmurray calls "a minor mutuality which is hostile to the interests of the larger" society. The other must remain other, both in society and in community, and justice ensures that this will be the case in both. Locating justice within community keeps the latter from degenerating into a purely sentimental or totalitarian whole in which the rights of the individual get swamped by the imperatives of group solidarity. Justice acts as a block on forms of social unity that privilege ethnic, gender, class, racial, or other types of identity to the exclusion of individual rights. In this sense justice will be necessary even when genuine fellowship has been attained. For even then "the negative aspect would still be present, though completely subordinated to the positive, and functioning as a differentiating force within it . . . There must be no self-identification of the one with the other, or the reciprocity will be lost and the heterocentricity of the relation will be only apparent."[30] If Macmurray is right about this, then an absolute dividing line between society and community is impossible. They mutually condition and inform each other, especially around the issue of justice.

The equality of persons, with respect to their functioning within society, is necessary and it is one of the ends of justice. "My care for you is only moral if it includes the intention to preserve your freedom as an agent, which is your independence of me,"[31] in the sense of remaining an autonomous being whose decisions are your own, even if those decisions are ultimately fulfilled only in communal interdependence with me. Whether in community or in society, therefore, "I can hope to secure justice in my dealings with [others] by limiting my activities for the sake of their interests, provided they will do the same in their dealings with me . . . We can consult together and come to an agreement about what is fair to each of us, so far as our separate courses of action affect one another

29 Macmurray, *Persons in Relation*, 188.
30 Macmurray, *Persons in Relation*, 189.
31 Macmurray, *Persons in Relation*, 190.

and impinge on one another. This can be achieved by a common consent to general principles by reference to which each of us can determine what would or would not be fair to the other person if we did it. Such agreement is a contract between us, which . . . determines reciprocal rights and obligations which we engage ourselves to respect. It is a pragmatic device to secure justice in cooperation and to eliminate injustice."[32]

There is much in this lengthy statement that anticipates Rawls' development of the principles of justice for a liberal society. It assumes society as a cooperative endeavor; that it is based on a contract; and that it protects the rights of individuals by limiting the activities of all for the sake of each. The parties to the contract must reach common consent (which is the purpose of Rawls' original position).

Given his commitment to the notion of the unity of the self, Macmurray insists that persons have all the requisite material resources necessary for living a fulfilling life in the world. The provision and control of these resources is the work of what he calls positive government. This government exercises a "positive control of the material life of its citizens, [and] determines what use shall be made of the material resources of the nation."[33] While acknowledging that socialist theory is better attuned to a doctrine of positive government, Macmurray's basic point (one that survives the failures of many socialist governments in practice) is that we cannot separate the spiritual life (the life of love and mutuality) from its material base. "Without material resources we cannot live. Without adequate material resources, the personal life must remain stunted and undeveloped . . . The means of life are also the means of a good life. Freedom is the life blood of all culture and the condition of the good life . . . [and] whoever controls wealth controls the means of cultural development and personal freedom."[34] Positive government sees its duty as providing for the common good by providing the "resources of the people for the welfare of the people."[35]

At the same time, however, Macmurray also holds that no political society should ever trespass into areas of personal life that depend upon

---

[32] Macmurray, *Persons in Relation*, 191.

[33] Macmurray, *Constructive Democracy* (London: Faber and Faber, 1943), 18.

[34] Macmurray, *Constructive Democracy*, 21–2.

[35] Macmurray, *Constructive Democracy*, 28. While Macmurray goes on to argue that the government "would plan and administer the economic life of the community" (29), I do not believe that he would necessarily subscribe to all the details of a communist or socialist command economy. In fact, his whole argument on behalf of positive government is couched in the context of a defense of political democracy and the prohibition on government from entering into the spiritual and personal lives of its subjects.

the free exercise of one's reason and spiritual conscience. This means that Macmurray would resist some of the more extreme communitarian emphases upon the complete or thoroughgoing embeddedness of persons in their tradition, culture, history, or community. It is vitally important, he would argue, that persons retain a degree of transcendence over even the most powerful of constraining and defining conditions in order to be able to critique and reform them. He locates this area of transcendence in the religious life and denies the government any right to interfere with it. "There is a department of social life in which the political authority has no competence. It lies beyond the limits of the State's authority."[36] Each individual and subgroup within the State ought to have the freedom to stand apart from their political, legal, and cultural traditions in order to reflect critically upon how they might be altered (or better defended) in the light of the overarching purposes of genuine community to which they ought to be the means. And for Macmurray this standing apart is possible, in part, because one can appeal to the will of God as that which transcends all particular and historically contingent cultural forms even while being enacted in and through them.

---

[36] Macmurray, *Constructive Democracy*, 11.

Chapter 5

Political Philosophies of Society

From Private to Public

As we move from the intimate communities of direct personal relations to the public societies of indirect and often impersonal relations, we enter the world of public space. This is a movement that has become highly contested in recent years in the United States. The world of public institutions (especially those associated with government particularly at the federal level) has come to be regarded as a world hostile, or at least alien, to the interests of the self and its local affiliations and attachments.

This means that political philosophies as such are having less and less relevance for many people. An ethics of community has to insist, however, against the primacy of individualism, that commitment to a larger public society is part of a commitment to God's intention for humankind, given the moral ontology on which this ethics is based in which God's concern encompasses all of human life in its manifold social forms. The Kingdom of God toward which an ethics of community is oriented must encompass both the small fellowships and the larger societies in which they will necessarily have a place. Political philosophy is an entry into that larger world.

Political philosophy has given us a variety of alternative understandings of what life in society is and (when it is bold enough to be prescriptive) ought to be. While eschewing for the most part underlying ontological or metaphysical principles, these philosophies do raise fundamental (and often fundamentally different) understandings of the human person, both in relation to him/herself and in relation to others. If theology rests on a basis of what is ultimately true about human beings it must, at some point, cohere with or complement what is true in a philosophical understanding of persons in societal relation.

Two of the most important forms of political philosophy today come at the questions of justice and the meaning of societal life from different angles and presuppose, at least on the surface, different understandings of human beings and their social relations. One, liberalism, presumes the primacy of individual interests within a cooperative social contract framework. The chief contemporary rival of liberalism, communitarianism, tries to reverse the priority by placing the "community" (which in most cases is really a "society") ahead of the individual. It argues that communities shape and define us, and provide us with our sense of who we are and what we value.

Both political philosophies attempt to find a place for smaller communities within larger overarching societal frameworks. If an adequate ethics of community is also to speak both to community and society, it must take account of the salient features in these prevailing political philosophies.

The Political Philosophy of Liberal Democracy:
John Rawls

There is no political or social philosopher of the contemporary period who has elicited more interest and commentary than John Rawls. His work, *A Theory of Justice*, and his subsequent development of its thesis in numerous articles, have become the benchmark by which most contemporary political philosophy is done. He lays out the case for liberalism as a political philosophy with impressive care and detail, and with a remarkable ability to tie his analysis to previous political philosophical systems and principles. I will argue that his case for liberalism is ultimately unconvincing in certain crucial respects, but there is much in his argument that is true and must be taken seriously. He fails in the end to take community as seriously as an ethics of community would desire (though he does have a significant place for communities, which he calls social unions, within the liberal society). He also overemphasizes the differences between individuals at the expense of the unity of the social group, but his notion of justice is one that, I believe, can be successfully accommodated to a viable notion of community consistent with the moral ontology underlying this book and with Macmurray's philosophy of community previously developed.

Rawls begins with the assumption that society is "a system of cooperation designed to advance the good of those taking part in it. [It] is a cooperative venture for mutual advantage."[1] To generate the principles

---

[1]   John Rawls, *A Theory of Justice* (Cambridge, Mass.: Harvard University Press, 1971), 4.

of social justice that will assign rights and duties to all the members and institutions of society, as well as to articulate the just distribution of the benefits and responsibilities of social cooperation, Rawls engages in a thought-experiment. He calls this the "original position" in which the participants are to determine what is fair and just in the arrangements of society to which they will give their rational consent. We are to imagine that the parties in this (nonhistorical but theoretical) position are behind a veil of ignorance as to their actual life situations. All they know is that they will (when the veil is lifted) belong to a society of some kind and that they are rational enough to determine by what principles of justice they would wish to be governed once they "discover" their actual life situations. They are assumed to be motivated primarily by self-interest, that they have conflicting claims to the division of social advantages and goods, that they may have no extensive ties of natural sentiment to each other, and that they take no interest in one another's interests.[2] None of these assumptions may turn out to be true for any given individual, but the original position has to assume them in order for the parties to reach rational consensus on the most basic procedural principles for determining what everyone will ultimately agree is just once they "reenter" society and "discover" what their actual interests and situations are in fact.

Rawls assumes, contrary to some communitarian readings of him, that individuals will hold some minimal (or in some cases even extensive) "metaphysical" visions of the good, even though he denies that these will play much of a role in the constitution of the just society. But, given the reality of self-interest, no one, Rawls claims, has a moral reason to accept any loss to himself in order that someone else might have greater satisfaction.[3] Society cannot be essentially altruistic or, in Macmurray's terms, heterocentric.

From the "original position" rational people would emerge having agreed to two fundamental principles of justice: the first, or equality, principle is that "each person is to have an equal right to the most extensive basic liberty compatible with a similar liberty for others."[4] The second, or difference, principle holds that: "social and economic inequalities are to be arranged so that they are both (a) to the greatest benefit of the least advantaged . . . and (b) attached to positions and offices open to all under conditions of fair equality and opportunity."[5]

[2] Rawls, 127–9.
[3] Rawls, 14. In this respect Rawls qualifies traditional utilitarian theory.
[4] Rawls, 60–1.
[5] Rawls, 302.

There is no presumption that there will be any agreement as to any substantive good to be pursued by all, nor that there will be any harmony between individual life-plans. In fact, Rawls' individualism leads him to believe that there will inevitably be "conflicting and incommensurable conceptions of the good."[6] This pluralist assumption is one of the hallmarks of liberal political philosophy. Individuals are assumed to have many different comprehensive religious, philosophical, and moral commitments. These differences require that agreement on *procedural* principles in a cooperative society must be made solely on the basis of how best to protect individual rights since one cannot presume unanimous agreement on a common good for all (except the good of individual freedom). This is particularly true of the right to choose freely one's own life-plan according to one's own lights, not on the basis of an overarching common notion of the good (i.e., a common life-plan everyone should follow in order to attain personal fulfillment). This leads to Rawls' insistence that "justice as fairness [is] the concept of right prior to that of the good."[7] It is based on the idea that persons must first agree to the principles for a *process* for organizing their life together before they can begin to contemplate what is *actually* good for each of them individually. We must first define the social principles that will "govern the background conditions under which" our individually chosen aims "are to be formed and the manner in which they are to be pursued. For the self is prior to the ends which are affirmed by it."[8]

This latter "ontological" assertion about the self is the claim that attracts the greatest criticism from the communitarians. It is a highly abstract claim, but its point seems to be that there must, in some sense, *be* a self before it can determine for itself what its good is and how it will attain that good. Rawls is not offering a full-blown ontology of the self. By exaggerating the nakedness of this Rawlsian self, his communitarian critics tend to paint him unfairly as indifferent or insufficiently sensitive to the social conditions in which selves are born, nurtured, and participate.

Rawls goes on to argue that the most we can hope for in a liberal, morally diverse society, is an "overlapping consensus" in the political realm as to what the rules of engagement are as individuals pursue their personal life-plans as they see fit. The political conception of justice does not require acceptance of any particular religious or metaphysical

---

[6] John Rawls, "Justice as Fairness: Political not Metaphysical," *Philosophy and Public Affairs*, 14 (Summer 1985), 245.
[7] Rawls, *A Theory of Justice*, 31.
[8] Rawls, *A Theory of Justice*, 560.

doctrine about the nature of the good or of human beings, or of the goal of history.[9]

What Rawls has described is the form of a just *society*. It is the form of impersonal cooperative association among persons each seeking his or her own good under the conditions of the greatest possible degree of freedom and in accord with an overlapping consensus of general social principles. Given Macmurray's philosophy, this form of life together is clearly a society not a community since the latter presupposes a greater degree of mutual love and a sense of being bound together by a common sense of the good for all. Communities, being more intense, intentional, and intimate, are not the same as but cannot exist in the absence of more formal, impersonal, and just forms of human association, i.e., societies.

For the liberal, carrying forward the individualistic premise on which liberal political philosophy rests, the purpose of the State (the governmental dimension of society) is simply to ensure that all citizens have equal opportunity to advance whatever conception of the good they might individually happen to hold provided only that they do so without violating the initial two principles of justice.

The Political Philosophy of Libertarianism: Robert Nozick

Another version of liberalism is provided by Robert Nozick who carries the primacy of the individual in political terms as far as it can go in an essentially anticommunitarian, anti-Statist direction (with one important qualification). Nozick has argued that "there is no *social entity* with a good that undergoes some sacrifice for its own good. There are only individual people, different individual people, with their own individual lives."[10] There is no social good which can justify using one individual for the sake of others. No individual without his consent ought to be forced to give anything up for the sake of others. "*He* does not get some overbalancing good from his sacrifice, and no one is entitled to force this upon him – least of all a state or government that claims his allegiance (as other individuals do not) and that therefore scrupulously must be *neutral* between its citizens."[11] We have "separate" existences and "no moral balancing act

[9] John Rawls, "The Priority of Rights and Ideas of the Good," *Philosophy and Public Affairs*, 17 (1988), 252.
[10] Robert Nozick, *Anarchy, State, and Utopia* (New York: Basic Books, 1974), 32–3.
[11] Nozick, 33.

can take place among us; there is no moral outweighing of one of our lives by others so as to lead to a greater overall *social* good. There is no justified sacrifice of some of us for others."[12] Given these radical individualistic assumptions, Nozick tries to develop a justification for the most minimal possible "state," or society organized to protect its individual citizens against such things as violence, theft, and fraud.[13]

One implication of Nozick's position is that at the social or political level, none of the qualities appropriate for family or intimate community models of personal relationships ought to apply.[14] Nevertheless, Nozick does recognize the importance of such qualities as love in the actual lives of human beings. The point is that these qualities are not the subject or concern of the minimal state. Love is actually a bit of a puzzle to Nozick who confesses that he cannot fully understand why one would love another person and not simply the qualities of character that person embodies.[15] Individuals seem a bit too messy and complicated to elicit Nozick's rational interest.

The Communitarian Critique

The major alternative to the political philosophy of liberalism is communitarianism. It began essentially as a critique of liberalism and only developed into a philosophy of its own subsequently. While it forcefully deploys the term "community" in its criticism of liberalism, it turns out that in practice what the communitarian really has in mind is often only a particular kind of *society* and should not be confused with what an ethics of community as developed in this study has understood by the term "community."

The communitarian criticism of liberalism objects that it leaves the human self in a naked, isolated, and radically untenable individualistic posture, cut off from the very others whose relationships with it enable it to flourish and become a self. Such a view of the self, the communitarian critics argue, is not true to the fact of the self's actual historical embeddedness in a particular culture's or community's traditions, language, and views of the good.

I am, in liberalism's view, essentially a solitary chooser, an "unencumbered self" who is not "constituted" by his choices. There are for liberalism no

[12] Nozick, 33.
[13] Nozick, 26.
[14] Nozick, 167.
[15] Nozick, 168.

"constitutive ends" that define the self prior to its choosing of its particular personal ends.

Michael Sandel agrees that this unencumbered self is capable of joining a "community" by an exercise of choice, but what is denied to such a self "is the possibility of membership in any community bound by moral ties antecedent to choice; he cannot belong to any community where the self *itself* could be at stake. Such a community – call it constitutive as against merely cooperative – would engage the identity as well as the interests of the participants, and so implicate its members in a citizenship more thorough-going than the unencumbered self can know."[16] While acknowledging that the liberal view of the self has a liberating quality to it, Sandel denies that it is true.

Sandel's target is clearly liberal theory, not liberal practice.[17] We cannot, he argues, view ourselves as so independent that our identity is separated from those "loyalties and convictions whose moral force consists partly in the fact that living by them is inseparable from understanding ourselves as the particular persons we are – as members of this family or community or nation or people, as bearers of that history, as citizens of this republic."[18]

The liberal self that exists prior to her choice of attachments is a self without character or moral depth. To have character is to "move in a history I neither summon nor command, which carries consequences none the less for my choices and conduct." The liberal self is "beyond the reach of its experience, beyond deliberation and reflection. Denied the expansive self-understandings that could shape a common life, the liberal self is left to lurch between detachment on the one hand, and entanglement on the other."[19]

---

[16]   Sandel, "The Procedural Republic and the Unencumbered Self," in Shlomo Avineri and Avner De-Shalit, eds., *Communitarianism and Individualism* (New York: Oxford University Press, 1992), 19.

[17]   See Bernard Yack, "Liberalism and its Communitarian Critics: Does Liberal Practice 'Live Down' to Liberal Theory," in Charles H. Reynolds and Ralph V. Norman, eds., *Community in America: The Challenge of Habits of the Heart* (Berkeley: University of California Press, 1988), 155–7.

[18]   Sandel, 23. (Richard Rorty seems to split the difference between this communitarian attack and the liberalism against which it is directed. He, too, accepts the ethnocentric preconditions of the self's "community," but as a liberal democratic wants to emphasize the right of the individual within that community to question its values and self-understanding. Whether this gives Rorty a completely coherent and consistent political philosophy is an open question.)

[19]   Sandel, 24.

Communitarians such as Alasdair MacIntyre insist that the liberal self has a "certain abstract and ghostly character" because it is so separated, in theory, from its social embodiments.[20] MacIntyre prefers to rest his argument for human society (which along with the other communitarians he persists in calling a "community") in a particular philosophical understanding or ontology of human being. There really is, he argues, a human life that is ultimately "good" for persons, lived in accordance with the appropriate virtues. The virtues exist only in the context of particular structures and conditions of human life, embodied in particular historically constituted communities (societies). And they exist only relative to a conception of the goal or "telos" of human life, which is not radically different for individual persons.

At the heart of MacIntyre's argument is the notion of a "practice" which he defines as "any coherent and complex form of socially established cooperative human activity through which goods internal to that form of activity are realized in the course of trying to achieve those standards of excellence which are appropriate to, and partially definitive of, that form of activity, with the result that human powers to achieve excellence, and human conceptions of the ends and goods involved, are systematically extended."[21] The problem with the liberal political philosophy is that it completely underestimates or neglects this communal dimension necessary to the cultivation of the structures, narratives, and traditions by which we learn to value certain practices and the virtues which sustain them in the first place. Like Aristotle, MacIntyre argues that the whole notion of practices and virtues requires some "overriding conception of the *telos* of a whole human life, conceived as a unity." This telos, given that the person is a social being, must mean some historical "community" with its own set of defining and shaping narratives and traditions in which its practices are embedded. And as a self that is itself defined by its practices and virtues, I am also the "product" (up to a point) of the community into which I am born and through which I am educated.

While criticizing the liberal for starting with a self that has no history, no concrete attachments or engagement in practices that are constituted by a narrative and a tradition, MacIntyre admits that while the self may be fully embedded to begin with it is not confined to its original community. He only denies the possibility of escaping from that community absolutely. And the liberal, in turn, never denies the social embeddedness of the self, but insists only that he/she must have some freedom to stand back from

---

[20] MacIntyre, *After Virtue* (South Bend: University of Notre Dame Press, 1981), 31.
[21] MacIntyre, 187.

that social construction in order to critique and move forward from it (or embrace it after reflection). The communitarians insist more on the historical context of self-reflection; the liberals more on the freedom to subject that context to critical analysis. But each philosophy ultimately recognizes (albeit grudgingly) the truth in the other.

A Critique of the Communitarian Critique

Liberalism is not without its own criticism of its communitarian critics. Derek Phillips has put a number of communitarian claims under the historical and conceptual microscope and found them wanting. But in the process Phillips reveals some of the most important confusions that still characterize the liberal–communitarian debate.

In his book *Looking Backward: A Critical Appraisal of Communitarian Thought*, Phillips argues that many pivotal communitarian thinkers make a number of fundamental mistakes. First, they naively idealize, contrary to the historical evidence, a number of historical societies that, according to Phillips did not meet the criteria of community that the communitarians themselves have advocated. Second, they overlook the ways in which their ideal communities have often been bastions of privilege for the powerful and agents for the oppression of the marginalized. Third, they swamp the importance of individual rights and the freedom to dissent from prevailing oppressive structures under the claim that individuals are who they are only through their roles in a community.

Phillips also believes that the communitarians have had great difficulty in coming up with a suitable definition of community. But he believes he can tease one out from their writings. He describes their notion of community as: "a group of people who live in a common territory, have a common history and shared values, participate together in various activities, and have a high degree of solidarity."[22]

According to Phillips, and this is crucial for an appraisal of his own view, community for the communitarian is essentially a whole culture or society, not an intimate personal fellowship. He claims that while some communitarians emphasize the necessity of "direct, intimate, face-to-face relations as a defining characteristic of community [and our preferred definition of community would fall under this description] . . . the communitarians

---

[22] Derek L. Phillips, *Looking Backward: A Critical Appraisal of Communitarian Thought* (Princeton: Princeton University Press, 1993), 14.

being considered here do not include regular face-to-face relations as an element in their conception of community."[23]

Now if this is the communitarians' conception of community (and it does not seem unfair to a reading of Sandel and MacIntyre) then their use of the term "community" is not the same as the one we have adopted in our ethics of community. For us community is more closely aligned with the face-to-face fellowships of direct personal relations such as the early *koinonia*, some of the monasteries, the Puritan villages, the communal experiments of the nineteenth century, and some of the "small groups" now dotting the landscape. None of these communities of intimate friendship are broad enough to encompass the fullness of what communitarians think of as a community. In fact, the examples they often use of good communities are, in our terms, a whole set of large, complex societies: ancient Athens, the Middle Ages, early and revolutionary America.

This has the implication that Phillips' critique of communitarianism's "communities" is not inconsistent with our development of an ethics of community. The two entities are simply not the same and to deconstruct the medieval world as failing to meet the criteria of community is to mix apples and oranges, for the medieval world was never and could never be a community in our sense. It would be more helpful, therefore, to think of community in the communitarian sense as what we have called society. Phillips scrutinizes the historical instances of community cited by the communitarians and shows, convincingly I think, that they failed in almost every respect to live up to the ideal image they have in the minds of communitarians. At the heart of the gap between ideal and reality is that these so-called communities often attained their solidarity and unity at the expense of smothering diversity and difference and restricting individual freedom, especially among those persons who did not belong to the communities' white male ruling elites.

Communitarian appeal to these "communities" also leaves out the individual thinker who wrote or thought against the grain of the prevailing ideology of the community. As long as these individuals are omitted it becomes much easier to claim a unity and cohesion of thought and practice for the group under consideration, but such a claim is not supported by the historical evidence.

I do not deny the force and truth of many of Phillips' claims. But our ethics of community does not assume that those "communities" cited by the communitarians were, *in practice*, what their ideology hoped them to be. Ironically, it is within a theistic theological framework that one can

---

[23] Phillips, 15.

most easily understand why social ideals are never fully exemplified in practice. The Niebuhr caution is a theological reminder of what can and will go wrong with any attempt at community, both intimate and societal. I think Phillips' surprise at the failure of the communitarian ideal arises, at least in part, because he has no discernible notion of sin or of the gap between ideal and reality that any theologically based ethics of community would immediately recognize.

Surely Phillips would not suggest that communities (or societies) have no ideals, no long-range expectations and aspirations, hopes and dreams for themselves that, while not reachable in the short run, are nevertheless necessary for grounding the work of community in something greater than what has been achieved up to the present. If we don't have a sense of the possibilities of community (which in theology must be grounded in God's intentions and actions, as well as ours), then we will settle for something less than what might otherwise be accomplished in history. The status quo, conformity to what is, imprisonment in the past will prevail. For example, while the Puritan village never attained the high ideals Winthrop set for it, his vision of community at least gave the village a sense of what to strive for and some criteria by which to gauge its failure to achieve the vision. The republican revolutionaries' vision of America at the end of the eighteenth century was never fully implemented but, as Gordon Wood himself has observed, it does suggest that there are intellectual and historical resources available to us even now for thinking that present day American life is not frozen in time and could be transformed, to some extent, by ideals that once had been firmly lodged in the minds of some of its earliest thinkers and dreamers.

Only with a clear ontology of community can one have a firm foundation for the criteria by which abuse of the community ideal can be recognized for what it is. We cannot name something as abuse unless we have a prior understanding of what is proper and right. Only a moral ontology can provide that understanding. It may well be, for example, that a good community, one that truly fosters human flourishing, requires a degree of pluralism, democracy, and an encouragement of diversity (given the complexity of human nature as it manifests itself in various social groups) in order to foster the very conditions that make a community vital, exciting, and capable of growth.

What Phillips lacks, in short, is a sense of the transcendent source and goal of community. He seems to assume that the communitarians cannot look beyond the community itself: that in its present historical form it becomes the final judge of what is proper, right, and good. And that is true if communitarianism is itself without a transcendent reference point. An adequate philosophy of community grounded in a philosophy of the person and in a theology of God's intentions will have a built-in critique of any self-limiting and parochial "communal" practices. Such a theology looks beyond each community taken in isolation from others and turned in upon itself.

It is interesting to note that Phillips takes communities to task precisely because they tend to exclude "foreigners, women, racial and ethnic minorities, and the poor."[24] But it was precisely these groups that, with more or less success in practice, many of the intentional experiments in community that we have examined intended to include. Ancient Israel (under the prodding of the prophets), the early *koinonia*, many of the antebellum communal groups, and the Social Gospel reached out beyond the racial, economic, and sexual stereotypes of their time to people who had been marginalized by society and fell outside the prevailing categories of "acceptable" and fully equal members. Without a transcendent reference it is not clear whether this inclusive, universalist dimension would have been possible.

Feminist Criticism

Women have often been the victims of stereotypical thinking about their roles in community. While suspicious of some of the more extreme individualist dimensions in liberal philosophy, many feminist thinkers are also wary of the communitarians' resistance to critical analysis of the way in which women have been treated in so-called historical communities.

Iris Marion Young has been particularly clear about the danger of abusing the notion of community to nullify the distinctiveness of individual persons in relation and to privilege the prevailing subordination of one group of persons within a "community" to another.[25]

Like the communitarians, Young appreciates that living in community requires paying particular attention to the "particularity" of others' needs and interests.[26] But she argues that the "ideal" of community (she fails to

---

[24] Phillips, 164.
[25] Iris Marion Young, "City Life and Difference," in *Justice and the Politics of Difference* (Princeton: Princeton University Press, 1990). ("Community" is still a term that is used by the critics of communitarianism to refer both to the same thing the communitarians do – a society with a common set of traditions, values, history, and narrative – and, at the cost of ongoing confusion, on occasion also to more intimate face-to-face associations. Young's criticism is directed primarily at the latter even though communitarianism in general focuses almost exclusively on the former.)
[26] Young, 228.

distinguish different conceptions of community from each other) desires a *"fusion of subjects* [emphasis mine] with one another which in practice operates to exclude those with whom the group does not identify. The ideal of community denies and represses social difference . . . in its privileging of face-to-face relations."[27] Its ideal is the *"copresence of subjects,* that is, the transparency of subjects to one another."[28] But this ideal of copresence, she argues, is a metaphysical illusion.[29]

The uniqueness that characterizes each individual can never be completely comprehended.[30] In addition, privileging face-to-face relations winds up avoiding the political question of justice between the various units of relationship.[31] The liberals, she points out, deny difference by understanding the self as completely autonomous and self-sufficient, separated and undefined by others. Communitarians deny difference by fusing the self with others in a single totality.[32]

Avoiding politics means, in effect, avoiding having to deal with the maldistribution of power among individuals and groups in the social body. In so doing, the crucial political question of how to nourish justice while minimizing oppression among these units remains unasked and unresolved.[33]

Young's arguments are quite telling against visions of community that reduce the individual to an organ in an organism, or that fail to appreciate individual difference and otherness. She is also correct in calling for a political engagement with society beyond the internal relationships of a face-to-face community. But she completely fails to grasp the vision of community in the Christian moral ontology undergirding my ethics of community precisely because she assumes it requires "fusion" between the partners. Such fusion flies in the face of the centrality in a Christian ethic of respecting the "otherness" and distinctive particularities of the other persons whom one wishes to flourish. It fails to account for what Macmurray's philosophy of community called "heterocentricity" in which the unique otherness of the "other" is always the focus of attention and concern. Like Macmurray, she wants to avoid minor mutualities that obscure the need for major structures of social justice. (See the section

---

[27] Young, 227.

[28] Young, 231.

[29] Young, 233. (Obviously Young has not taken in Rorty's and Rawls' contention that no metaphysical judgments about the human self and its relation to others can be made.)

[30] Young, 232.

[31] Young, 233.

[32] Young, 229.

[33] Young, 234.

on the "The Family as Community" in chapter 7 below.) As long as lovers live in a larger social world in which indirect relations will be necessary, justice will be essential.

Communicative Ethics

The ethics of community arising from the moral ontology we've adopted would agree with much of what has been called the communicative ethics position, in particular its criticism that Rawls' original position runs the risk of obscuring the uniqueness of the concrete other, the individual person who cannot be reduced to a general, purely rational self. Seyla Benhabib, a feminist moral philosopher drawing on the discourse ethics of Jürgen Habermas, calls this position "interactive universalism."[34] Like Macmurray, she holds out for some form of ontologically based universal moral principles. Her stance is pragmatic, based on the actual discourse of persons in interactive communication with each other in any particular form of human association. She agrees with the communitarians that the self is "embodied and embedded." She also agrees with liberalism that the moral point of view is a contingent achievement, not a "timeless standpoint of a legislative reason [the Kantian factor]."[35] An interactive discourse ethic asks what principles of action the participants engaged in practical discourse can agree upon.[36] This clearly tracks with both Rawls' and Macmurray's notion of persons consulting together to reach common consent about the principles of justice in a social (if not fully communal) order.

Consistent with her search for the universalization of moral principles, Benhabib rejects the extreme claims of the cultural relativists like Richard Rorty. She denies, for example, their conviction that there is nothing beyond the incommensurability of moral frameworks through which they can be brought into conversation with each other. There is no reason, she argues, why we cannot engage other frameworks in dialogue, provided one is truly prepared to hear a different voice from one's own and to reformulate one's views as a result if the arguments are persuasive. There has been much more interaction (and not always of the imperialist kind) between cultures than the "armchair philosophers of cultural relativism"

---

[34] Seyla Benhabib, *Situating the Self* (New York: Routledge, 1992), *passim*. Benhabib's notion of universalism has strong parallels with Susan Frank Parsons' work, discussed below.

[35] Benhabib, 6. The bracketed words are my addition to her quotation.

[36] Benhabib, 28.

have been willing to acknowledge. In the process they ignore the real, though incredibly complex, ways in which a common humanity can move from being an abstract ideal to becoming a concrete reality.[37]

Unlike the strict liberal proceduralists who insist that procedures determining the right are more basic and universal than any particular conceptions of the good chosen by individuals (e.g., Rawls and Nozick), Benhabib insists that communicative ethics entails strong normative assumptions about the moral status of persons within the communicative community. Among these are the "principle of universal moral respect" and the "principle of egalitarian reciprocity."[38] Both of these principles accord with Macmurray's notion of equality and the differentiation of the other as truly other in any genuine personal relationship. "We ought to *respect* each other as beings whose standpoint is worthy of equal consideration," and "we ought to treat each other as concrete human beings whose capacity to express this standpoint we ought to enhance by creating, whenever possible, social practices embodying the discursive ideal (the principle of egalitarian reciprocity)."[39]

The second principle requires us to engage in what Benhabib calls the reversal of perspectives. We should be able to think from the other person's point of view and see how he or she judges others. Benhabib also insists that discourse requires the participants to make sure that they have genuinely heard the voices of those others who have traditionally been excluded from the conversation, namely women and minorities. Benhabib criticizes Rawls on just this point. She argues that Rawls' argument, by ignoring the standpoint of the *concrete* other[40] tends to assume the point of view of "the disembedded and disembodied *generalized* other."[41] Behind the veil of ignorance "the *other as different from the self* disappears." The particular self is abstracted from her concrete and specific identity within the complex of human social relationships and treated simply as one of many indistinguishable selves whose common attribute is the ability to reason abstractly. As a result her "voice" as this different and unique other is effectively silenced. What remains is the Kantian self that is everyone in general and no one in particular. To create the conditions for real community in which real persons are real contributors, the concrete, embedded lives of different concrete others must be included (what Macmurray calls the heterocentric dimension of relationship).

---

[37]   Benhabib, 62–3 n. 48.
[38]   Benhabib, 29.
[39]   Benhabib, 31.
[40]   Benhabib, 161.
[41]   Benhabib, 160.

The inclusion of traditionally excluded particular others also under-cuts the privileging of certain individualistic moral ideals, such as the abstract "economic" or "political man," both of which seem to predicate the superiority of the male autonomous morality free from the constitutive bonds of family, and personal and communal interdependence. Benhabib, echoing themes found in feminist thought, argues that there is no reason, once the voices of women are brought into the conversation, why moral-ity should continue to be understood primarily as the rational actions of impersonal agents in a field of indirect relations, such as economics and politics. Employing the term that has come to characterize the Christian vision of community (but apparently without any intent to link it to that vision), communicative ethics "projects a utopian way of life in which *mutuality* [emphasis added], respect and reciprocity become the norm among humans as concrete selves and not just as juridical agents."[42]

Susan Parsons' work on feminism and Christian ethics picks up the theme of recognizing the other as unique and particular, not to be brought under categories that deny difference and diversity in human life. This is especially true of those male constructed categories that have been imposed on women to their political and personal detriment. As a Christian ethicist, however, Parsons is looking for what she calls an "appropriate universalism" which doesn't simply fall into the atomistic separations of a complete decon-struction of all categories, or "individualism run riot."[43]

Parsons wants to hold out for criteria of normativity in personal rela-tionships[44] without retreating into oppressive constructed categories that have been used to demean women in the past, including in societies that have often been lauded by communitarians. Drawing on the work of ethicist Sharon Welch, Parsons argues for "an appropriate universalism, sustained by the compassionate presence of God, and continually offering opportunities for . . . love to be interwoven into relationships with our fellow human beings and the natural world . . . [Parsons wants to encour-age] women to engage in the kinds of interactions with the world and other persons that may both embody the tenderness of God towards the creation, and also transform human life in the context of that creation into the beloved community."[45] Not only does Parsons' language here remind us of the transforming (and also political) vision of the Social Gospel (as

[42]   Benhabib, 60 n. 34.
[43]   Susan Parsons, *Feminism and Christian Ethics* (Cambridge: Cambridge University Press, 1996), 193.
[44]   Parsons, 196.
[45]   Parsons, 198.

exemplified in the work of Martin Luther King, Jr. who continually used the phrase "beloved community") but it squares nicely with the moral ontology behind this ethics of community because it embraces the role of God in history.

Parsons agrees that theological affirmations are important when they touch on "the sustaining matrix in which human welfare and flourishing is nourished and inspired."[46] That matrix, we have argued, must include both community and society, each with its own proper role to play in the fulfillment of the relational self, though at different levels and with different foci. Parsons notes that feminist thought "traces a path alongside" some of the communitarian emphases, emphasizing as it does the embeddedness of the moral agent. But she joins the liberals in cautioning that some "necessary space for some personal separation" must be provided, otherwise women are likely to be exploited for their tendency to be cast into and to accept as their primary role that of care-givers.[47] In a truly redemptive community, Parsons suggests, three things will be held together in mutual tension: the self, its relations with other selves, and their connectedness with nature. "For each element brings a measure of transcendence to the others, in which the divine presence can be discovered at work. It is with reference to this theme that Christian feminism claims a source of critical distance, of power, and of envisioning a new future, which may lead towards a redemptive community."[48]

Contemporary forms of liberalism abandon the dream of such a community because of their pessimism of ever constructing a society around a common vision of the good. Contemporary forms of communitarianism imprison the dream too uncritically in present or past societies that have, in practice, betrayed the content of the vision of the good that is grounded in God's intention, not in our own constructions erected to serve our self-interest.

Empowering Positive Liberty

One important implication of the communicative ethics view, as well as Macmurray's Christian social ethic, is that a society has a special obligation to empower all persons with the necessary material means to engage in the reasoned conversation from which a mutual consensus will be reached

---

[46]   Parsons, 199.
[47]   Parsons, 209.
[48]   Parsons, 217.

about the principles by which all those participating in the conversation agree to be governed. These conditions of empowerment, or positive liberty, go far beyond the negative liberty that conservatives and libertarians are so interested in, a liberty simply to be left alone by others in order to pursue one's private life-plan with as little interference from others as possible.

Carol Gould has argued (echoing Isaiah Berlin and paralleling Macmurray's notion of positive government) that positive liberty is the right to be provided with the means, economic, social, and personal, necessary for the full exercise of one's personhood; the right, in short, to have "access to enabling conditions." Positive freedom presumes the importance of social relations in providing the "fundamental context" for the self-development that each person intends for himself and for others. This context requires that a wide range of actual life options be made available to people. And they require, in turn, "the availability of the objective conditions – both material and social – without which the purposes [of the self] could not be achieved." [49] Among these conditions are the means for daily subsistence, the means for labor and for leisure activity, and access to training and education. I would add simply that any Christian social ethic that is incarnational and nondualistic (i.e., does not believe that full flourishing can exist solely at a spiritual level) must also embrace this kind of positive social freedom and justice as indispensable conditions for both community and society.

The Limits of Communitarianism

Within a theistically grounded ethics of community, the critical distance between the self and her social conditions is made possible because she can appeal to the will of God as that which transcends all particular and historically contingent forms of society even while she is historically embedded and "constituted" in large part by belonging to one of them. Being able to retain one's individuality, even against the community in which one is embedded, is essential to the full flourishing of the human self.

As political philosopher Will Kymlicka argues in defense of liberalism and against some its more extreme communitarian critics, "we *can* be mistaken about even our most fundamental interests, and because some goals *are* more worthy than others. Liberty is needed precisely to find out

---

[49] See Carol Gould, *Rethinking Democracy: Freedom and Social Cooperation in Politics, Economy, and Society* (Cambridge: Cambridge University Press, 1988), 39–41.

what is valuable in life – to question, re-examine, and revise our beliefs about value."[50] It is significant, however, that while Kymlicka provides a solid foundation for the right to stand in judgment on one's community, he does not insist that the liberal must *always* do so. "The capacity to revise one's way of life is a liberal value, but the ceaseless exercise of that capacity is not."[51]

Sandel himself acknowledges the importance of the central values of liberalism, i.e., egalitarianism and freedom of choice. In doing so, he effectively closes the gap between his abstract understanding of communitarianism and his practical commitment to values that track closely with those that the liberals have insisted upon. Even MacIntyre has admitted that one of the practices that ought to be engaged in by a member of a community is critical analysis of it. He says "I can always put in question what are taken to be merely contingent social features of my existence."[52] Given this concession to liberalism, one critic has asked of Sandel's views: what then is left of communitarianism?[53]

On the other hand, a liberal society is itself a community of sorts. It is one *kind* of community (one that cherishes liberal values) but it *is* a community (as that term is used by most political philosophers). As such it has a history which instills its values in its members. As Amy Gutmann has conceded of liberalism's chief value "the unencumbered self is . . . the encumbrance of our modern social condition."[54] Rawls himself has admitted that his principles of justice are historically conditioned and applicable primarily in a constitutional democracy and not in each and every historical society throughout the world.[55] Ronald Beiner has put it this way: "Liberalism itself instantiates one particular vision of the good: namely, that choice in itself is the highest good."[56] But to instantiate a vision of the good is to do exactly what communitarianism says communities do: they have a notion of the good into which all the members are enculturated.

[50]   Will Kymlicka, "Liberalism and Communitarianism," *Canadian Journal of Philosophy*, 18, 2 (June 1988), 185.
[51]   Will Kymlicka, "Communitarianism, Liberalism, and Superliberalism," *Critical Review*, Spring 1994, 272.
[52]   MacIntyre, 220.
[53]   Jeffrey Friedman, "The Politics of Communitarianism," *Critical Review*, Spring 1994, 308.
[54]   Amy Gutmann, "Communitarian Critics of Liberalism," in Avineri and De-Shalit, eds., 129.
[55]   John Rawls, "Justice as Fairness: Political Not Metaphysical," 226.
[56]   Ronald Beiner, "What's the Matter With Liberalism?," in Allan C. Hutchinson and Leslie J. M. Green, eds., *Law and the Community* (Toronto: Carswell, 1989), 45.

The communitarians are right to insist that there is an intrinsic virtue in contributing to the political community which, through its political acts, makes possible individual rights as well as ongoing conversation about the nature of the good among people with divergent views. The question is whether this debate and contribution, organized around a common commitment to the principles of justice, is enough to sustain the kind of bonds that ultimately constitute the fuller meaning of community life as envisioned in a deeper ontology of the person.

Can one truly share with others the political value not to have to share with others anything else of fundamental importance?[57] David Gauthier argues that a mutually beneficial enterprise (Rawls' definition of a just society) enables its members to interact in ways that foster such things as civic friendship. The result will be, he argues, that an "essentially just society thus fosters interpersonal bonds while being less dependent on them for its continuance. And so an essentially just society can afford to let interpersonal bonds be freely chosen by its members."[58] This suggests that a liberal society need not be hostile to interpersonal bonds provided that such bonds are to some significant degree freely chosen (or at least subject to periodic critical review), not imposed coercively once and for all from above.

The debate between liberals and communitarians therefore is not over whether one's membership in a society is part of one's identity, part of what it is necessary to have if one is to develop certain ideals and values. Of course it is, and both communitarians and liberals will concede this. The important debate is over *what kind of society and/or community* provides *in fact* the conditions and values most fulfilling to the self. The liberal needs to make the case that at least some of those values must include individual freedom to choose one's life plans, diversity in the make-up of the society, a strong degree of personal moral autonomy, and the right to have one's God-given (if they are theists) dignity and autonomy respected by others. This includes the right to subject all social values (though not all at once) to critical scrutiny. But liberalism must acknowledge that there is one kind of society it cannot sanction and that is one in which the dominant conception of the good rules out the right to choose one's own version of the good even if that choice ultimately is for the dominant conception of the good.

The communitarian needs to make the case that the right of free choice is an empty right unless it intends a way of life in and through political

---

[57]   See Robert Bellah, "The Idea of Practices in *Habits*: A Response," in Reynolds and Norman, eds., 273.
[58]   David Gauthier, "The Liberal Individual," in Avineri and De-Shalit, eds., 155–6.

relations in which part of the meaning of one's life is a common participation in the work of the polis, and part is through deeper nonpolitical personal relations of intimacy, trust, and love of others. It must argue for the importance of substantive ends by which a community defines and orders itself. Without such ends (no matter how much they are subject to ongoing conversation and revision) the community/society is merely a container within which nonattached atoms rattle around with no common sense of what makes their movement meaningful and with no common direction by which they are united in a common historical venture. But if common substance of vision and direction constitute a society, it must make the case for a sacrifice of some self-interest on behalf of a common good without suppressing the right to individual freedom and appropriate critical distance from the society. It must acknowledge its tendency, at least among its contemporary defenders, to occasionally valorize totalitarian societies, ancient traditions that privileged the inherited power of men, and to be drawn primarily to nation-states rather than to mutual communities as such.[59]

It is impossible to view ourselves as totally without social embeddedness, but we can envisage ourselves without our *present form* of embeddedness. As long as we have the possibility of interactive conversation among and between equal partners in relation, and the social bonds that make it possible, we can enter the process of ethical reflection and compare one "encumbered" potential self with another. We can continually expose ourselves to other views of the good and in the process keep open our right to reexamine "even our most deeply held convictions about the nature of the good life."[60]

For Macmurray, a society is ultimately to be judged by how far it succeeds in "achieving and maintaining justice in the indirect or economic relations of men . . . The appeal must be to a sense of justice of all those affected, and the pragmatic evidence of this is a common consent."[61] And a common consent is best reached in a democratic society by an inclusive conversation among all the members, including those who have been historically disenfranchised by the unjust exercise of disproportionate power on behalf of economic, gender, and political elites. Thus Macmurray's commitment to justice is congruent both with Rawls' principles of justice and Benhabib's discourse ethics of communicative interaction.

---

[59] See Friedman, 298.
[60] Kymlicka, "Liberalism and Communitarianism," 189.
[61] John Macmurray, *Persons in Relation* (New York: Harper, 1961), 203.

Communities within Liberalism

It is extremely significant that at the end of the day even Rawls, the arch-liberal, has room for tight-knit communities within his liberal society. Critics and defenders have so focused on the priority of the right in Rawls' liberal theory of society that they have often overlooked the importance he places on the possibility of the practice of life in what we would call community. As Roberto Alejandro has pointed out, Rawls has a strong sense of an encumbered self (quite at odds with what the communitarians criticize him for) who actually lives fully only in one form of community or another.[62] Rawls admits that "there should be for each person at least one community of shared interests to which he belongs and where he finds his endeavors confirmed by his associates."[63] This suggests that, even for Rawls (who eschews a metaphysical view of the self) selves, ontologically and empirically, do not fully flourish until and unless they are affirmed and appreciated by others. This has parallels to Macmurray's claim that because it is "natural for human beings to share their experience, to understand one another, to find joy and satisfaction in living together; in expressing and revealing themselves to one another,"[64] it is necessary to enter what Rawls calls a social union. Thus for both Macmurray's Christian moral ontology and Rawls' liberal social philosophy, a goal of radical self-sufficiency is neither possible nor desirable. One ultimately depends upon others "to confirm his sense of his own worth."[65]

Rawls concedes that "only in social union is the individual complete."[66] He seems to understand that persons require a closer, more direct and

---

[62] See Roberto Alejandro, "Rawls's Communitarianism," in *Canadian Journal of Philosophy*, 23, 1 (March 1993), 75–100.

[63] John Rawls, *A Theory of Justice*, 442.

[64] John Macmurray, *Reason and Emotion* (New York: Barnes and Noble, 1962) 98.

[65] John Rawls, *A Theory of Justice*, 445. This also echos Marx's notion that in a truly human society, through your enjoyment of the product of my labor, "I would have had the direct enjoyment of realizing that I had both satisfied a human need by my work . . . and would have been for you the mediator between you and the species and thus been acknowledged and felt by you as a completion of your own essence and a necessary part of yourself and have thus realized that I am confirmed both in your thought and in your love [and] in my expression of my life I would have fashioned your expression of your life, and thus in my own activity have realized my own essence, my human, my communal essence." Karl Marx, "On James Mill," in *Karl Marx: Selected Writings*, edited by David McLellan (Oxford: Oxford University Press, 1977), 122.

[66] Rawls, 525.

personal form of community than society in general and this fact opens Rawls up to a consideration of communal relationships that go beyond, without replacing, societal principles of justice.

If this is true, Alejandro is right in claiming that "for a Rawlsian community is far from being a mere attribute . . . it is *constitutive* [emphasis added] of the individual's identity," just as the communitarians claim.[67]

But Macmurray and the biblical theist would want to make the metaphysical determinations that liberalism and communitarianism shy away from, drawing on their construal of God's intention for the fulfillment of human persons in and through mutual love. In this respect, Macmurray keeps alive the importance of a moral ontology grounded in the will of God as the basis for a full understanding of the relationship between society and its devices of politics, and community with its mutuality of love.

---

[67]   Alejandro, 94.

Chapter 6

Community and Society: Difference and Engagement

A Theology of Difference

The engagement or disengagement of the church (more or less understood along *koinonia* lines) and the secular society is an issue that presently divides many Christian ethicists and theologians. This is not simply a question of what the proper relation between church and state ought to be.

Underneath the legalities of church/state relations, there is the deeper, more fundamental question for any ethics of community of what attitudes and engagements between the ecclesia and society (sometimes limited to what is called the State) are theologically and morally justified. This is a more basic question in some ways than deciding which form of society (e.g., liberal or communitarian) is the most desirable from a Christian ethical point of view. Sometimes the question is posed as one of the relation simply between the church and the "world."

It is important to note that the term "the world" is often used in more than one way in theological conversations over this question. On the one hand, as the object of theological focus the world is what God created, loved, and, in Jesus, died for. On the other hand the world, as the object of ethical polemic, is the complex of institutions, forces, principalities, and powers that either stand against the will of God, or try to live apart from it (consciously or unconsciously). The way in which the issue is framed today by many theologians is by putting one community, the church, against another (more amorphous) community, the world (or society). The church is often seen as the custodian and representative of God's will, the world as the unregenerate complex of forces that are indifferent to or ignorant of God's will. This complex is taken to be "secular," meaning that it is world*ly*, with no transcendent reference point or ultimate grounding, a passing and transitory "age" that will eventually be superceded by God's world or Kingdom.

The problem that faces any religious group is how to relate its orientation to and grounding in a transcendent reality to its place in a society that is not so oriented and grounded. An explicit lack of such grounding is characteristic of most contemporary political philosophies of society. Any church, on the other hand, will have its ultimate authority in the transcendent power and will of God. No human institution can, short of the final realization of the Kingdom of God, fully embody God's unvarnished and pure intention for humankind. This means that all human institutions fall short of perfection and cannot arrogate to themselves the powers and loyalty owed only to God. Inasmuch as the Church claims to represent, even in broken form, the revelation of God for the world, it will also stand (and be seen by its members to stand) in critical tension with the principalities and powers around it.

The crucial question is whether this critical tension amounts to a kind of *cordon sanitaire* around the church, limiting its engagement with the "world," or whether the church is commanded by God to penetrate the world in myriad places precisely because its mission is to serve the world in God's name. The tension is inevitable in a theology which affirms both that God loved the world and came to serve it, and that God's work in the world is not yet done in part because it meets resistance from the world. God's love for the world undergirds the imperative to engage the world; the not-yet-completed aspect of God's engagement with the world (through the church) undergirds the caution not to get too cozy with the world.

Using H. R. Niebuhr's categories, one might say that the danger of too close an affiliation between church and world makes religion into a captive "of" worldly culture, while too great a distance between church and world creates a state of antagonism in which the church stands "against" the culture.

There is a tendency among a number of contemporary Christian ethicists to draw increasingly hard lines between the church as community and the secular political order as something less or other than genuine community. They are driven by a fear that if the church gets too comfortable with the prevailing norms and practices of a secular society it will betray its mandate to preach and practice only the politics of the Kingdom, not the politics of a fallen and idolatrous world.

Often linked to the philosophy of communitarianism, what one might call the theology of difference argues that the ethics of the church and that of the state (the governmental form of society) are radically different.

This theology holds that we learn our ethics only from within the culture, tradition, narrative, and practice of a particular community. By insisting that the Christian community is qualitatively distinct from the secular and civil societies that constitute the world (meaning that the latter derive their authority from humanly devised forms and norms of social life), the advocates of this position stress the uniqueness of the church and its incommensurability with the values of the world. The truth of God's revelation for human life is found, appreciated, and applied only within the church, not outside.

At one extreme we even find the argument that morality cannot be Christian because morality is the rational product of human insight, articulated and applied according to "universal" human principles and norms and thereby not grounded in the divine will. John Milbank declares forthrightly "no, morality cannot be Christian."[1] He goes on to develop a clear divide between Christian morality and the morality of the world. "Christian morality is a thing *so* strange, that it must be declared immoral or amoral according to all other human norms and codes of morality."[2] The fear of and resistance to evil that underwrites the world's morality is incompatible with the faith of the Church. This faith holds that "evil . . . can be altogether rooted out within the fellowship of those who follow the way of Christ, who has recovered for us the true pattern of perfection, the original *logos* of human existence, which is a power working prior to any taint of evil."[3]

From this point of view (reminiscent of Anabaptism) the church is a community unto itself, living an "alien citizenship" in the world, with which it ought to have as little to do as possible. Christians may not enter into active disobedience of the world's laws, nor seek to undermine its secular functions, but they will practice a virtue and a way of life that is radically differentiated from that of the world. The church will be sectarian, not established: it will renounce any pretensions to "Christendom"; it will even be, in Milbank's words, antinomian. According to George Lindbeck, the church is to live solely in light of the narrative of God's work in Jesus Christ, a narrative that is not identical or reducible to or commensurable with any other narrative of life in the world.[4]

---

[1] John Milbank, "Can Morality Be Christian?", in *The Word Made Strange* (Oxford: Blackwell Publishers, 1997), 219.

[2] Milbank, 219.

[3] Milbank, 251.

[4] See David Fergusson, *Community, Liberalism and Christian Ethics* (Cambridge: Cambridge University Press, 1998), 34–7 for an analysis of Lindbeck's work.

Hauerwas and Community

In the contemporary discussion of an ethics of Christian community that is claimed to be discontinuous with the ethics of the world, it is imperative that we confront the challenge of Stanley Hauerwas. Hauerwas has taken a concept of community and deployed it in defense of what he sees as an embattled and unique form of life together, the Christian church, which he calls a "community of character." He sees this church virtually in a state of war with the culture around it, staking out its own understanding of what constitutes community as grounded solely in the grace and power of God, not in the resources of a secular and fallen (especially liberal) human society. The church, he argues is "a distinct society with an integrity peculiar to itself," grounded and sustained by convictions that are peculiar to Christians, convictions derived from the particular and unique story of how Christians came to be, thanks to the actions of God in history.[5] The community called the church has an overriding obligation to form its people by reference to virtues that are peculiar to Christians. It should be known by "the kind of people it develops."[6] And those people will be, in some clear and distinct way, set apart from people formed by other traditions and political philosophies.

Hauerwas insists that this is not an ethic of withdrawal or rejection of the world by the church "but a reminder that Christians must serve the world on their own terms." What that means, in turn, is that Christians must not seek to do public policy or the work of nations in the terms defined by the nations of the world, in particular terms defined by modernist, liberal political philosophy and practice. This leads Hauerwas to his basic oppositional stand (at least as he rhetorically deploys it in multiple polemics): "the church does not exist to provide an ethos for democracy or any other form of social organization, but stands as a political alternative to every nation, witnessing to the kind of social life possible for those that have been formed by the story of Christ."[7]

His position has been described (with Hauerwas's approval) as one in which the church is an "alternative *polis* or *civitas*, which is constituted 'by the new reality of the Kingdom of God as seen in the life and destiny of Jesus.'"[8] This new reality is to be sharply distinguished from other political

---

[5] Stanley Hauerwas, *A Community of Character: Toward a Constructive Christian Social Ethic* (Notre Dame: University of Notre Dame Press, 1981), 1–2.

[6] Hauerwas, 2.

[7] Hauerwas, 9–12.

[8] Arne Rasmusson, *The Church as Polis* (quoted in Stanley Hauerwas, *In Good Company: The Church as Polis* (Notre Dame: University of Notre Dame Press, 1995), 6).

and social organizations, especially the modern nation-state. Since many communitarians tend to use the notion of community to describe their ideal for the nation, Hauerwas backs off from even using the term "community" to describe the church. "I seek," he says, "not for the church to be a community, but rather to be a body constituted by disciplines that create the capacity to resist the disciplines of the body associated with the modern nation-state and, in particular, the economic habits that support that state."[9]

While shunning the label "communitarian," Hauerwas nevertheless echoes one of communitarianism's persistent themes when he insists, against modernism and liberalism, that the unrestricted freedom of the individual from all community constraints is fundamentally wrong-headed and ultimately idolatrous. He understands liberalism to be represented by "those societies that take as their primary aim the freeing of the individual from arbitrary "accidents" of birth and community."[10]

For those in the church, their identity is, in a sense, a divine "accident," a gift from God, not from the world given to them without their having "earned" it. Their beliefs about who they are and what God has done for them cannot be understood outside the church. They constitute a kind of epistemological and theological ghetto, but one which issues in convictions they are bold enough to claim are true, against the beliefs of the world "outside." Hauerwas insists that the church is unlike any other human society or community. In this respect Hauerwas is driven, I think, by a fundamental fear of the non-Christian "other," a fear that the other will contaminate, dilute, distort, and idolize things that the Christian will, hopefully, always keep in the proper perspective as utterly dependent on the grace of God. (By contrast, however, within the body of the church, the "other," as individual person, is welcomed because the uniqueness of the community formed by Christ "enables its members to trust the otherness of the other as the very sign of the forgiving character of God's kingdom . . . The otherness of the other can be welcomed as a gift rather than a threat."[11]) But outside the church the other is the person, or more often the structure, institution, or ideology, that represents the nation-state, the quest for individual freedom and moral autonomy, and the pursuit of a kind of common denominator justice. The "other" is whatever stands in opposition to the unique activity and wisdom of God in

[9]   Hauerwas, *In Good Company*, 26.
[10] Stanley Hauerwas, *Against the Nations* (Minneapolis: Winston Press, 1985), 81 n. 14.
[11] Hauerwas, *A Community of Character*, 50–1.

graciously selecting those who will be formed within the narrative and tradition of God's acts in the world. Any "other" in this sense is to be shunned because all such others are dilutions and distortions of the Christian life, which can be lived fully only within the church.

Hauerwas is deeply suspicious of any ethical appeals that transcend the particularities of individual communities and traditions. In this sense he and Milbank are in agreement: morality cannot be Christian.[12] Morality is humanly generated, and what a Christian practices is divinely generated. "There simply is no generally accepted Christian theory of justice."[13] Justice as such (for example, as developed by Rawls) is a meaningless abstraction for the Christian in his own community. (This is not to say that justice is absent from the *koinonia*, but its character and quality are radically different from the kind of justice that a non-Christian secular world must endorse in order to undergird a secular society.) The world might try to live by a general, nonparticular, perhaps Aristotelian or Rawlsian sense of justice, but the world, Hauerwas insists, "can never be the church . . . for the world, while still God's good creation, is a realm that knows not God and is thus characterized by the fears that constantly fuel the fires of violence."[14]

The question that Hauerwas poses to an ethics of community is how the church, as the community that is peculiar unto itself, is to serve the world with which it is so clearly contrasted. Hauerwas knows that God has not stopped loving the world which, after all, God created and for whose sake he sent his son to become human, die, and be resurrected so that all persons within it might be forgiven and live again, renewed and transformed.

So what then is the role of the church? At one level Hauerwas answers this question (repeatedly in his numerous and often repetitive books) by insisting that the church serves the world just by being itself, by practicing the Christian virtues within its own life. These virtues include accepting and loving the stranger, showing compassion to the weak, refusing to resort to violence, speaking the truth in love, testifying to the reality, power and grace of God, living out of God's resources and not their own,

---

[12]   In this sense both Hauerwas and Milbank reflect, to a degree, Dietrich Bonhoeffer's claim that "ethics" is a sign of the fall of human beings from grace. Bonhoeffer claims that Christian ethics intends to "invalidate" the knowledge of good and evil which is the aim of all ethical reflection. Instead, Christian ethics wants to know only God (ethical knowledge is already a separation from God). See his *Ethics*, edited by Eberhard Bethge (New York: Macmillan, 1965) 17–18.

[13]   Stanley Hauerwas, *After Christendom?* (Nashville: Abingdon Press, 1991), 56.

[14]   Hauerwas, *A Community of Character*, 109.

and so on. At another level the church serves the world by embodying, or incarnating the "truth" about the "essential" nature of human persons. Ultimately, Hauerwas concedes, Christians cannot "give up claims of universality," even though "the basis of our universalism comes by first being initiated into a particular story and community."[15]

An ethics of community can be instructed by Hauerwas about the importance of locating the dynamics and constituents of community in particular sites. He is right in insisting that there is no such thing as community in general. He is right to insist upon the historicity, particularity, and uniqueness of each community in the world, of which the Christian ecclesia is one. But his commitment to particularity has the tendency to come back and bite him. He has not given us a set of criteria transcending each of the particular historical communities that openly call themselves Christian by which we can decide which ones are, in fact, more authentically Christian than others. Surely he does not intend to say that any body of people that calls itself Christian does, in contingent historical fact, fulfill all that he means by a Christian community. (If he does believe this then his insistence on the localized nature of authentic communities is fundamentally misleading.)

On the other hand, not all communities that call themselves Christian mean the same thing or practice the same form of Christian virtue. Hauerwas does not intend, presumably, to say that the German Christians who conformed their behavior to Hitler's policies are practicing the same Christian virtues and living the same Christian story as the French Christians of LeChambon who hid Jews from the Nazis. Does he wish to emulate the church that has practiced "an exclusively male, hierarchically authoritarian tradition, as a good example of Christian community?"[16] Hauerwas is somewhat evasive about which of the multiple Christian communities that have existed and exist today are closer to the story and virtues that he himself has identified as constituting the Christian way of life. He comes close to identifying the empirical, sociologically situated church as itself fully embodying what Bonhoeffer called the New Testament view of life in Christ: "the complete absence of this world of disunion, conflict and ethical problems . . . The life and activity of men is not at all problematic or tormented or dark: it is self-evident, joyful, sure and clear."[17] Would that the life of the church met this description! But anyone who has

[15]   Hauerwas, *A Community of Character*, 93.
[16]   Gloria Albrecht, quoted in Fergusson, *Community, Liberalism and Christian Ethics* (Cambridge: Cambridge University Press, 1998), 67.
[17]   Bonhoeffer, *Ethics*, 26.

belonged to a real church, as opposed to the ideal one that Hauerwas projects, knows that this description is often far off the mark.

As David Fergusson has pointed out, "the church advocated by Hauerwas nowhere exists. It is a fantasy community, the conception of which fails to reflect the ways in which the members of the church are also positioned within civil society."[18] But if there is nothing but contingent, particular, and idiosyncratic communities spread across history, then Hauerwas gives us little help in figuring out which ones truly reflect and embody what he takes to be the "core" Christian virtues. (This does not mean that he does not make such judgments – he does – but rather that in doing so he seems to be straying from his focus on particularity and rising to the level of abstraction that he thinks is so dangerous in the modernist or liberal point of view.)

The difficulty that I have with Hauerwas's sectarian understanding of church as community is that it fundamentally underestimates the scope of God's involvement with the world beyond the church. Hauerwas too narrowly limits the scope of God's actions in history to the church and only to the church (wherever and however he finds and defines it). He has a sense of the universality of God's intention for the world, he understands the world as that which God loves and that which the church serves, but he cannot bring himself to acknowledge that the world just may, in its own various ways, be doing more things to realize God's intentions than the church itself has done or has been able to appreciate. He rightly rejects the Constantinian appropriation of the church, just as he rejects medieval Christendom, but is there any reason to assume that the world has no possibilities, on its own, of glimpsing God's intention and enacting it in some authentic, albeit, partial and perhaps even unconscious ways? Is the world, even in its secular form, entirely devoid of wisdom and insight into how people grow, develop, and flourish as the human beings God has created them to be? Into how they can live more peacefully and justly with each other even under fallen and imperfect conditions?

I am not suggesting a kind of sanctification of the secular (à la Harvey Cox and the "secular city" theology of the 1960s), but the "secular" can be an arena for God's actions as much as can the church. It is not self-evident that when the world (or, more concretely, some of its nation-states), for "secular" reasons, chooses to use selective and limited violence in defense of helpless women and children who are being brutally raped and pillaged that it is idolatrously exploiting a power that God unequivocally condemns. The church might testify to the long-range futility of violence,

---

[18]   Fergusson, 66.

but in the short run many secular peoples and nations have often rushed to the defense of the victims of violence more readily and rapidly than the churches who ought to be, in Hauerwas's view, testifying "against the nations" and their idolatrous use of force.

Hauerwas is quite right to condemn the seductive allure of liberalism in its individualistic guise. But this kind of liberalism is not the only kind there is (and surely some defense of the rights of the individual in a multicultural society is well-justified, as we have argued in a previous chapter). Nor is liberalism the only cogent political philosophy around. By dismissing the "world" so contemptuously and absolutely (at least when he is being particularly polemical), Hauerwas runs the risk of shutting off both the resources of the church for the world and the selective but genuine wisdom of the world for the churches. There is a kind of arrogance, not warranted by scripture, in limiting God's decisive actions in the world to the formation of just one people, the Christians living in communities arrayed in their moral purity against the nations.

A fuller ontology that is more open to the diversity of God's acts is needed if the Christian community, with all its riches, is to be effectively engaged with the world beyond its communal borders. Christians need to be more than "resident aliens." Unlike the image Bonhoeffer evokes of the Church as "a sealed train travelling through foreign territory,"[19] the church has more right than Hauerwas, Bonhoeffer, and the theologians of difference suggest for making itself a bit more at home in the world, without becoming so comfortable that it allows itself to be seduced by the world.

Kierkegaard once said that the Church was like a fortress that, once it had built a bridge across the moat that separated it from the world, became a country seat, and naturally the enemy took it.[20] But Hauerwas, Bonhoeffer, and Kierkegaard are too pessimistic. The "world," when it is not just a rhetorical device used to ginn up a needed sense of the counter-identity of the church as something more than a pale reflection of secular interests, is still the place where work has to be done for the well-being of all people. Christians are being a bit disingenuous in declaiming against the world when they have for too long occupied positions of political and economic power in the world and benefited greatly from that privilege. It is a form of subtle hypocrisy to quietly retreat to the holy ghetto of the antinomian sect against the nations and wash their hands of what they have conspired

[19] Dietrich Bonhoeffer, *The Cost of Discipleship* (New York: Macmillan, 1959), 313.
[20] Søren Kierkegaard, *Kierkegaard's Attack Upon "Christendom,"* trans. with an intro. by Walter Lowrie (Boston: Beacon Press, 1956), 138.

to bring about when the world reveals that it is not always open to negotiation with the church solely on the church's terms.

Those who regard the church as "alien" to the world are right to warn it against too easy an accommodation with the world, but they often, as is the case with Hauerwas, draw the string connecting the world and church so taut that it breaks, sundering what God has intended to be kept together even in tension. Hauerwas jettisons the tension and the relationship itself, or at least threatens to do so with his overreaching polemic against the world. Just as two persons who marry do not lose their unique and particular identities in that vow of union (in fact they may now enjoy a condition which permits those identities to flourish in new and surprising ways), so church and world can retain their particular identities even when they join together, each performing its distinctive work, in furthering the advent of universal community, the Kingdom of God, in and for the world. One may do it by fostering interpersonal communion and the other by developing institutions of social justice, but both contribute to the work of God in bringing about God's Kingdom.

David Fergusson, drawing on the theology of Karl Barth, establishes a far more viable relation between church and world on a much sounder basis. He argues that God speaks one Word (or in my terms, reveals one overarching intention for humankind), but there can be a multitude of witnesses to that Word, both within and outside the Church. "The conviction that God is the creator and redeemer of the world gives grounds for the confidence that such witnesses will be encountered. . . . since God has not abandoned the world, we may expect signs of that same kingdom in strange and surprising places."[21]

Barth's Theology of Engagement

In a remarkable essay ("Christian Community and Civil Community") written late in his career, Karl Barth laid out a more adequate theology for engagement between church and world than that found in the theology of difference. Unlike Hauerwas and the theologians of difference, he acknowledges that there are "dead" churches that simply do not represent all that these theologians have claimed for the church. He goes on to argue that the Christian community has a vital and indispensable relation to the civic community. "Politics" is essential to both. (Even the concept

---

[21]   Fergusson, 74.

"kingdom" of God is replete with political connotations.[22]) The Church anticipates that the work of God in history will end not in an eternal church "but in the *polis* built by God and coming down from heaven to earth."[23] Until that time, all attempts to instantiate God's kingdom will be "external, relative, and provisional," and these include the civil community.

Drawing on Romans 13, for example, Barth sees one role of the civil community (the State) as providing the conditions for "humanizing" human life and providing a political order that will protect persons from chaos. The church remains the inner circle within this outer body (or community as Barth calls it). It benefits from the provisions and protections of the political order. Far from being hostile to the intentions of God, the civil community works with God (often unconsciously) in providing a bulwark against the destructive effects of sin. In this sense "the civil community shares both a common origin and a common centre with the Christian community," and like the latter is "an instrument of divine grace."[24] It renders a "definite service to the divine Providence and plan of salvation" precisely because it provides for "freedom, peace, and humanity" within its mandate.[25]

The work of the civil community, however, is not identical with or a substitute for the work of the church. While its circle is broader and more inclusive than the church, it must not identify itself with the church nor the church with it. The church, and not the State, proclaims the vision of the Kingdom to come. The State does not necessarily know its place in God's plan. But because the church is the inner circle within the State, it has an obligation to move out into society. "The members of the Church are also automatically members of the wider circle. They cannot halt at the boundary where the inner and outer circles meet, though the work of faith, love, and hope which they are under orders to perform will assume different forms on either side of the boundary."[26]

Barth here acknowledges the truth in Hauerwas's position: the church is not simply society writ small. It has a task of living more closely to the heart of the Kingdom of God (though still only provisionally and relatively). It can expect a higher degree of conformity among its members to

[22]   Karl Barth, "Christian Community and Civil Community," in *Community, State and Church: Three Essays*, intro. by Will Herberg (Garden City: Doubleday & Co., 1960), 152–3.

[23]   Barth, 154.

[24]   Barth, 156.

[25]   Barth, 156.

[26]   Barth, 158–9.

the virtues of love, self-sacrifice, forgiveness, tolerance, etc. than can the civil community among its citizens. But the members of the church do not forfeit their citizenship in the outer society. And since God is using that society as part of God's plan of salvation, Christians must exercise their rights of citizenship by wise and prudential engagement with and, when necessary, reform of the "secular" world of which they, too, are a part. Christians must, Barth insists, participate "in the human search for the best form, for the most fitting system of political organisation" even while they are deeply "aware of the limits of all the political forms and systems which man can discover."[27]

There is no such thing as "the" political philosophy of the state or society that Christianity has to offer. And there is no such thing as a "Christian" state or a Christian political party. Nevertheless, the church must take on the complex responsibility of engaging in practical, even pragmatic, determination of what policies and programs will work best in the "external, provisional, relative" world of the civil community. "The Christian community 'subordinates' itself to the civil community by . . . distinguishing between the just and the unjust State, that is, between the better and worse political form and reality; between order and caprice; between government and tyranny; between freedom and anarchy; between community and collectivism; [and] between personal rights and individualism."[28]

This is hard work, requiring an ability to live in the tension between the absolute and the relative, to live in uncertainty as to which political philosophy is actually (and not just theoretically) appropriate to this time and this place and these conditions. It requires a form of political realism (see the discussion of Reinhold Niebuhr) as well as a refusal to become cynical about the work of the polis (politics). It requires attentiveness to the realities of the world and at the same time an ability to think "outside the box" of those realities. The church will be critically selective in its support for or reform of political systems, without becoming apolitical. For Barth, and Fergusson, the church is called to share in the tasks and problems that are " 'natural,' secular, profane." The mandate to do so comes, of course, from God. In knowing the source of its imperative the church knows something the civil community, as such, does not know.

The church remembers that God's kingdom has not yet come but proclaims that it is coming. In this way it secures a place for the transcendent dimension in its politics without succumbing to the temptation to

[27]   Barth, 161.
[28]   Barth, 162.

abandon the world or to embrace it uncritically. The division or difference between church and world is not swallowed up but it does not justify the sect mentality so attractive to the theologians of difference. As Fergusson rightly notes, Barth's more complex understanding of the relation between civil society and church community helps us to understand that a path can be "marked out between withdrawal and assimilation by those whose citizenship was ultimately in the church but who were called to serve God in other places and communities."[29] A genuine ethics of community will take up this call and address itself directly to the relative, provisional, but necessary forms of political philosophy and political practice in the multicultural, pluralistic social world today.

Base Communities: Radical Engagement

The issue of the engagement of the church community with the world in ways that are consistent with Barth's views is exemplified, albeit in radical ways, by groups known popularly as "base communities" (CEBs) in Latin America. Their "praxis" is reflected in a theology of liberation that has explicit political, societal, and economic dimensions. Predominantly Roman Catholic, these base communities challenge the theology of difference's understanding of the way in which the Christian community should relate to its surrounding society. Because of their peculiarly intense dual focus both on community vitalization as well as on engagement with the larger political and economic order, they represent a significant example of how community can engage society without becoming its captive or blurring the essential distinction between community and society. While flawed in some respects, these CEBs point to possibilities for a creative negotiation between community and society that even non-oppressed religious communities in the developed world could, with appropriate qualifications, also develop.

The base community movement is squarely rooted in a moral ontology virtually identical with the one we have utilized throughout this study of an ethics of community. Liberation theology presumes (through its reading of Scripture and life experience) that God is an Agent working historically in the world with the cooperation of human agents to create a new future that will liberate all persons from all the forms of bondage that presently keep them from fullness of life. That future is one in which

---

[29]   Fergusson, 79.

persons will experience full communion with God and brotherhood with all other human beings. But it is a future which will be built through the historical acts of human beings who cooperate with the actions of God in realizing the divine intention for the Kingdom. And these historical acts will have an essentially political cast to them. The fulfillment of the human person includes his entire material as well as spiritual being. Nor can fulfillment be separated from the practical conditions that either retard or enhance the enjoyment of economic and social justice.

What is aimed at is a "total and complete fulfillment of the individual in solidarity with all mankind."[30] This aim is historical and as such requires the construction of "a just and fraternal society, where people can live with dignity and be the agents of their own destiny."[31] Gustavo Guttieriez, one of the seminal thinkers of the movement, links this aim directly with the biblical view of salvation which differs from it only insofar as it "gives the whole process of liberation its deepest meaning and its complete and unforeseeable fulfillment."[32] Anything in history which keeps this fulfillment from happening is to be overturned or transformed (this is reminiscent of the Social Gospel).

The political order is the primary place through which the historical work of liberation will take place. Only "in the political fabric," according to Guttierez, does the person emerge "as a free and responsible being, as a person in relationship with other people, as someone who takes on a historical task. Personal relationships themselves acquire an ever-increasing political dimension."[33]

In these comments Guttieriez is attempting to link the historical intention of salvation/liberation with the political means by which (though not exclusively by which) it is to be accomplished. But politics is essential to the liberation movement and this requires due attention to the institutions and structures of justice in society, not just in community.

Those societal structures will be, at least in the case of underdeveloped nations and especially among the poor, primarily economic. Thus liberation theology has focused upon transforming those economic practices (usually associated with capitalism in the countries of Latin and South America) that impede the full realization of the communal nature of persons and their ability to live together fraternally in solidarity with each other.

---

[30]   Gustavo Guttieriez, *A Theology of Liberation*, trans. and eds. Sister Caridad Inda and John Eagleson (Maryknoll, NY: Orbis Books, 1973), 33.

[31]   Guttieriez, x.

[32]   Guttieriez, x.

[33]   Guttieriez, 47.

The church exists within this overarching political/societal/economic framework as an essential community of persons who are oriented simultaneously to the deepest sources of fulfillment (God), to God's eschatological intention for history (the Kingdom), and to the political/historical tasks by which that divine intention can be realized under the conditions of time, space, matter, and history. Thus the church is both a community representing in its inner life a foretaste of the fullness of the Kingdom, and an agent of social change, working outward into the political and economic world to bring the Kingdom to completion. According to Guttieriez, "we have here a political hermeneutics of the Gospel."[34]

This reading of the meaning of the Gospel speaks directly to the distinction/correlation I have tried to draw between church as community and society as the institutionalization of structures of justice that enable people to make the world a better place in practice. The CEBs exemplify the ethics of community insofar as they retain a dual focus on building up the community from within and working from its resources to engage the world beyond in the cause of building up the Kingdom of God through political action.

Liberation theologian Leonardo Boff believes that the church today has a unique possibility of providing a much-needed alternative to the "wild atomization of existence and a general anonymity of persons lost in the cogs of the mechanisms of the macro-organizations and bureaucracies."[35]

Congregations can be built on intimate participation in a joint venture of living out Jesus' message of communion with all human beings and the building of the Kingdom of God.[36] Life in these communities, according to Boff, is characterized by "the absence of alienating structures, by direct relationships, by reciprocity, by a deep communion, by mutual assistance, by communality of gospel ideals, by equality among members." Absent are "rigid rules, hierarchies; prescribed relationships in a framework of a distinction of functions, qualities, and titles." There is present an "enthusiasm generated by a community life of interpersonal ties."[37] According to a 1972 seminar held in Brazil, the basic community is "a group, or complex of groups, of persons in which a primary, personal relationship of brotherly and sisterly communion obtains, and which lives

---

[34]   Guttieriez, 13.
[35]   Leonardo Boff, *Ecclesiogenesis: The Base Communities Reinvent the Church* (Maryknoll: Orbis Books, 1986), 1.
[36]   Boff, 4.
[37]   Boff, 4.

the totality of the life of the church, as expressed in service, celebration, and evangelization."[38]

Boff admits, in an echo of the Niebuhr caution, that no such communities have ever succeeded in "extinguishing all traces of conflict, selfishness, individualism, individual and group interest, the pressure to have order and rules, and the establishment of goals with a rigid process for their attainment."[39] Even within community there will be a power arrangement that will not be able to eradicate all inequalities or the tendency toward rigidifying social roles. In this sense, he suggests, communities will always have an element of society within themselves. As a result it would be unrealistic to expect a society that would be fully a community, absent all conflict. However, it would not be unrealistic for communities to "struggle for a type of sociability in which love will be less difficult, and where power and participation will have better distribution. Community must be understood as a spirit to be created, as an inspiration to bend one's constant efforts to overcome barriers between persons and to generate a relationship of solidarity and reciprocity."

If this goal can be approximated then, Boff argues the church can become an "approximate realization of this utopia."[40] "A large organization can be renewed by a community, but it cannot be transformed into a community."[41] The church is in the world, says Boff, but the world is not in the church.[42] This is a very apt way of putting the point. Societies cannot duplicate the work of communities. But communities can point societies toward possibilities otherwise perhaps never envisioned. In this sense "utopia" is not a futile project but a direction for historical action.

Only in the context of a moral ontology in which history is the arena of God's actions in bringing about the realization of God's historical Kingdom, does such directional action make sense. This makes the hope of the Kingdom both the greatest utopian vision imaginable and the one future reality guaranteed by the power of an acting God. Communities can indicate (in a fragmentary and broken way, to be sure) something of what God intends to accomplish in bringing the Kingdom fully into being.

---

[38]   Boff, 20.

[39]   Boff, 5.

[40]   Leonardo Boff, "Theological Characteristics of a Grassroots Church," in Sergio Torres and John Eagleson, eds., *The Challenge of Basic Christian Communities*, trans. John Drury (Maryknoll: Orbis Books, 1981), 134.

[41]   Boff, *Ecclesiogenesis*, 6.

[42]   Boff, "Theological Characteristics of a Grassroots Church," 127.

And only at that point, perhaps, will the distinctions and differences between community and society finally disappear.[43]

The CEBs are presently under challenge by Pentecostal communities in Latin America which stress a more individualistic understanding of the church's role. Despite the differences between these types of community, however, we must not lose sight of the point that both are to a large extent grounded in the political and economic condition of the poor at this particular historical time and place. In fact, the growing attractiveness of the Pentecostal community in Latin America simply testifies to the power of injustice to determine *what kind of politics* people who are its victims will practice. It is absolutely understandable that as the poor become more marginalized and powerless, they will find a politics of negotiating power distribution among the "haves" less and less relevant because they have no power base from which to negotiate in the first place. They will move to a politics of the community away from society rather than to a politics from the community toward society.

If some kind of politics must be practiced, whether inward or outward looking, then an opening is provided for a transition to ecclesial communities in those societies that are more developed. Congregations in the affluent, powerful and economically rich societies of Europe and the United States face a different kind of challenge from that of their fellow believers in underdeveloped countries. It would be disingenuous of them to take over lock, stock, and barrel the rhetoric and practices of the base communities in Latin America as if they were politically appropriate for wealthy churches in rich countries whose members exercise in their "secular" lives vast economic and political power. Nevertheless, such affluent communities

[43] Manuel A. Vasquez, *The Brazilian Popular Church and the Crisis of Modernity* (Cambridge: Cambridge University Press, 1998), 3, argues that alternative religions such as Pentecostalism "offer more flexible strategies to negotiate the demands of the economic and political crisis" in Brazil than do many of the CEBs. As the power of small groups to effectively confront the vast political power of entrenched elites wanes, many people become more attracted to communities that offer retreat from the conflicts and ambiguities of the political order. David Martin has shown how this fact contributes to the rise of interest in Pentecostalism which is, at one level, far less engaged with the political struggle. Pentecostalism focuses on renewing inner-group relations, even challenging traditional male–female roles, and giving its members havens of mutual support for those being oppressed by the injustices of the external world. They are strongly communitarian even while withdrawing from political engagement as the base communities defined it. David Martin, *Tongues of Fire: The Explosion of Protestantism in Latin America* (Oxford: Blackwell, 1990), 280, quoted in Vasquez, 80.

do face a political challenge. In meeting that challenge they can fulfill in their own ways the potential that communities possess for engaging societies creatively, with a vision of social and economic justice that can renew those societies.

Community for Society

A healthy relationship between community and society in continuity with the core principles of the base communities and of Barth's understanding suggests that there are some things communities can do for societies and other things societies can do for communities. We need to look briefly at some notional examples of how communities can inform a good society about its responsibilities and help prepare and morally ground its citizens for their work in the polis, and how such societies in turn can provide the empowering conditions for communities to flourish, as well as encourage them in the carrying out of their civil responsibilities, even on occasion moving in advance of communities in extending principles of justice to historically marginalized people.

In our history of experiments in community we have seen examples of communities struggling to find ways to engage the larger society around such social justice issues as economic, racial, and gender injustice. Except for those communities that chose withdrawal, most experiments in community took civic responsibility seriously to one degree or another. In doing so they were enacting (with varying degrees of self-consciousness) a transformative ethic aimed at altering the structures of social life in anticipation of and as contributing to the arrival of the Kingdom of God on earth.

While it may be true that a withdrawal from the struggle for social change can empower some communities to take on the tasks of *koinonia* for their members without distraction from the larger society, too great a degree of withdrawal is an abandonment of the historical thrust of the Christian ethic of community that seeks to influence society at large. That thrust, of course, must ultimately be on the moral terms determined by the community itself (and in this respect the theologians of difference are absolutely right), no matter how much it is receptive to news from the other side of the wall that separates community and society.

One of the most basic things communities can do is simply to be places that make possible the strategic withdrawal and critical distance people need in order to develop and sustain a critique of the society from a moral vantage point not completely complicit with the society's reigning values. This is the communal counterpart to the liberal insistence on the individual's right of temporary withdrawal from societal relations, norms and traditions in order to pursue his/her own life-plans on the basis of personal choice, not societal coercion. The difference is that in an ethics of community the individual does not retreat into critical reflection either permanently or in solitary seclusion but always in the context of a loving supportive community in service to God's whole creation. Given the primacy in community of direct, personal relationships in which each is caring for the other as much for himself, it provides an environment conducive for critical thinking without the fear of ostracism, rejection, or derision so common in noncommunal environments that encourage mindless conformity and superficial thinking. Communities can be "safe havens" where the "warming fires of home" provide a place of comfort and support. Within them people are free to explore new, even radical ideas in the company of supportive others whose criticisms will not be seen as personal attacks but as part of an ongoing mutually empowering conversation.

From within these communities new perspectives on society may emerge that might eventually feed back into the ongoing political debate that constitutes the heart of societal decision-making. Sometimes the new visions that arise from the smaller communities will be disturbing to the status quo, but unless a society is prepared to be challenged by unsettling ideas it will rigidify into a bastion of privileged elites with controlling power who will find ways to shut out dissenting voices, especially ones that question the present distribution of power and the foundations of an economic order which undermines the very bases of community and social interdependence. Such bastions remove themselves from the life-giving forces of transformation and renewal that new ideas and voices would bring to them.

Church communities in particular can become, to recall Gerhard Lohfink's notion, "contrast-societies," especially when they are modeled on the principles of the early *koinonia*, or Winthrop's ideal village, the communities of character Hauerwas extols, or the base communities. Such communities can live, as Larry Rasmussen puts it, "as if the barriers between rich, poor, and underclass were not the givens the present economy says they are; living as if the chief actor of the past two hundred years, the nation-state, were no longer the only chief power; . . . living as if the world were indeed a single public household or world house, or living as if [to recall one of Martin Luther King's images as well as John Macmurray's overarching philosophical principle] we constituted a single moral community wrapped in a common garment and shared destiny."[44]

---

[44] Larry L. Rasmussen, *Moral Fragments and Moral Community: A Proposal for Church in Society* (Minneapolis: Fortress Press, 1993), 149.

Although it would be highly unusual in most church congregations today, creating forums in which political philosophy is discussed could also be one vital role such communities could play. If communities have actually experienced a different way of being together in which power is shared equally, in which all voices are heard, in which irrelevant factors such as race or gender or age no longer determine the distribution and exercise of power, then they might be able to model for the society an openness to new ways of decision-making in both political and economic spheres.

An ethics of community insists that politics should be the arena in which all persons, including those of the church, express their fundamental values for life together in society with both friends and strangers, through both personal and impersonal relations. Among the central values of the church are those that speak to the social life of persons. And social life is, by definition, political life. We all act politically on the basis of some set of values. Democratic societies do not demand a filter through which only values that have been stripped of their religious grounding can pass. In this sense there are no values, whether religiously or secularly derived, which ought to be kept out of the societal political mix of discussion, debate, and decision-making. Bringing the voices of the religious community to bear on public issues that have a moral dimension (such as health care, the protection of children, and economic and racial justice, among others) is perfectly appropriate in a democratic polity. To do this effectively and intelligently, however, requires an informed citizenry. The churches could become arenas in which discussions about what constitutes a good society and an appropriate political philosophy and its application to the purposes and principles of public policy would become an exercise in joining the work of community with the work of society.

The concepts of political philosophy on the one hand and the practices of politics on the other will, of course, need to be demystified. There has been so much "trashing" of politics that many people now see it as not only alien to their lives, but as fundamentally hostile as well. But if politics is the work of the people in ordering their societal lives according to principles of justice, then politics is one of the noblest activities for Christians who want to carry their values out into the public arena where presumably God's work for the Kingdom is still going on. Discussion of political philosophy at the grass roots could become a reasoned conversation among people who trust each other enough to share their deepest values and have them opened for examination. This can and ought to happen in the context of a community in which the members would feel free to talk about what principles and purposes they believe society ought to have. As persons morally grounded in the ethics of their tradition they ought to have ways of seeing how that ethics applies to larger societal issues. It is not necessarily narrow partisan politics that they would debate or commit themselves to. They would engage in informed discussion about the more comprehensive politics and political philosophies of the society as a whole. By providing an environment of trust, openness, and honesty (the qualities peculiar to communities), churches could play a significant role in crossing the bridge from community to society.

Smaller communities could also enculturate among their members the ontological truth that we are all persons who live most fully in interdependence with others. If the ontological lesson *of* community (e.g., as articulated by John Macmurray's philosophy) is learned *in* community (where one is freer and more personally supported in the learning process), then it will be easier to teach the lesson to society which also depends, though in less intimate and directly personal ways, on the interdependence of its members. In the process communities may challenge the myths and fallacies of the ideologies of "rugged individualism" and complete self-reliance, which have crippled many contemporary capitalist nation-states. Persons can learn in community from an early age either to trust other people in the context of interdependent common activities, or to mistrust them in an environment of competitive rivalry for scarce goods. By practicing mutuality, cooperation, and even sacrifice for the welfare of others, healthy communities can be valuable places in which the social goods of trust, civility, mutuality, and cooperative actions can be learned and then transferred to societal life where their absence would lead to social impoverishment.

The task of building trust is a particularly appropriate task for the family. I will take this point up in more detail shortly. From the building of trust, families, and by extension communities, help to give the individual self not only a sense of his/her own inherent worth, but also a sense that as individuals with unique gifts and talents they are not cut off from the ministrations of others. A community can help create a healthy sense of self-regard without having it degenerate into selfishness, and a withdrawal in fear from others.

Communities are vital centers for the development of moral character and they must do this work consistent with their particular moral traditions. Hauerwas's point about the church as a community of character is clearly relevant here. Unless the individual is grounded and nurtured in the values of community from within the bonds of love, trust, mutuality, and intimacy, she will often find herself adrift in a society in which there are competing and often incommensurable values at play. Without communities at its base, society loses one of the most vital and enduring sources of moral formation. "If," as Rasmussen says, "we are able to live with thousands of total strangers at all, that is, live in modern society, it is only by way of what we have learned in the more circumscribed terrain of intimacy, among those who heard our borning cry, who heard our dying one, and who accompanied us on the wondrous and difficult adventure in between . . . No community, no moral life; no moral life, no society worth living in – it is as simple and basic as that."[45] Society itself benefits when its citizens enter the public square with moral foundations and character shaped by their intimate communities. Even Rawls recognized the importance of smaller communities or social unions despite his overriding liberal credo. Society itself is not usually the best initial teacher or nurturer of moral values, or at least they are not as well grounded and inculcated outside of smaller communities. But when a society characterized in its economic life essentially by values of self-interest and acquisitiveness is not open to the moral values lived by persons shaped by the values of mutual, loving communities, it will continue to fragment and dissolve even the less directly personal and relational bonds that hold it together. When the bonds of community are weakened the fatal attraction of false individualism gains strength. The community can help to counter this growth of self-defeating value by reminding its members that the "other" is not to be feared but to be welcomed (hospitality was always a trait of the early monastic communities). The other is not truly other but is together bound with all of us.

As Macmurray has argued, however, in embracing the other we must be careful not to erase her distinctive, individual characteristics, those which make her the unique individual she is. In true community otherness is celebrated, not feared. When this lesson is taken into the larger society, the other, whether she be someone of a different race or nationality, an immigrant, a stranger, someone poor and helpless, she is ultimately part of us and we of her. True life in community can be one of the most important living challenges to the anti-immigrant, anti-poor stereotyping the typifies much political rhetoric today.

One dimension of the refusal to accept the other as other is suspicion about providing political or economic help to those in trouble through governmental structures and institutions as opposed to doing so through individual charitable acts. In this context one often hears calls to greater personal responsibility and less reliance on government programs. But personal responsibility is learned as a matter of course within a community since each is trying to serve the other in developing his or her own talents and capabilities. Such service requires one to be personally diligent and responsible for the use of these gifts. Personal responsibility in this sense is for the sake of the other, not, as within an ideology of individualism, for

[45]   Rasmussen, *Moral Fragments and Moral Community*, 12.

protecting oneself from others. In fact, in community, others (being equally heterocentric) are trying to help each other become more self-integrated, more whole, and thus more fully capable of personal responsibility. It is only when society begins to lose its communal underpinnings that mindless cries for more personal responsibility without reference to the community begin to be uttered.

The exercise of individual responsibility in the context of community-building also requires the skills of organization, planning, cooperation, budget and time management, etc. These are all activities that also are appropriate to societies. In fact, congregations, especially the larger ones, necessarily must depend upon practices that are as much societal as communal (i.e., require more indirect and impersonal relations between people if the budget is to be managed, the property maintained, the weekly schedule organized, etc.). Church members therefore are already practicing skills in some spheres of church-work that are also necessary at the societal level. Thus, they should find the transition into public citizenry less difficult than it is for people who struggle under the myth of self-reliance and a fear of belonging to groups except on a provisional or contractual basis and only if they promise to serve their self-interest. And carrying those skills into public political activity is a direct contribution to the civic health of society. Rasmussen notes that the boundaries between community and society are or ought to be "porous." Nonetheless, he says, in a marvelous passage that captures the range of community work that is also preparation for society work:

It is largely by way of relatively intact, small-scale communities with some staying power that we learn trust, temper individualism as a moral style, agree to freely serve, hone leadership skills for work together, have and raise children, learn to give to charities, volunteer for dirty, difficult, and unpleasant jobs, clean up after ourselves, restrain appetites, take out the garbage, help friends, care for siblings, parents, children, relatives, and friends, learn to read, learn to return books to the library, observe meaning-giving traditions, receive all manner of moral direction, including basic moral rules and social etiquette, find out by increments what moral responsibility means from childhood up, develop qualities of character, practice decision-making, acquire a moral language, nurture moral sensibilities, take responsibility for a pet, plant, or sibling, recover from serious mistakes, find our first models of behavior, and, most importantly, learn to forgive and start anew. In a word, we discover in microcosm how the bewildering world works and how to find our way in it.[46]

---

[46]   Rasmussen, 71–2.

I would only add that in the practices that constitute the fullness of life in community it is important that the members not identify voluntary charitable work *within* and from the group with the need for justice work in the society as a whole. Charity is not justice, though a good society cannot do without either. In preparing their members for community, communities are also preparing them for more and more inclusivity of others. Communities that are entirely self-enclosed have lost the universal thrust toward inclusivity (actualized in the Kingdom of God) that ought to be present even when it cannot be fully realized.

Society is necessarily more universal than community in practice. And if John Dunn is correct, even society can be extended beyond the nation-state, at least in imagination if not in fact in the present socioeconomic conditions of the world. Civil life beyond community is necessary for the full maturation of the person: this is the counterpart to the claim that only a universal community completely fulfills God's intention for humankind.

In community the principle of full participation of all the members has theological and ontological grounding. This claim does not belie the fact that contemporary churches are often torn over how to reconcile institutional hierarchically grounded power with the full participation of all the believers (as we saw in the base communities' relation to the hierarchy of the Roman Catholic Church). Nevertheless, the rhetorical trend (if not always the practice) of the modern age is toward greater, not less, participation by all the people in all the spheres of life that constitute the community and the society.

Ironically, the move toward greater democracy in those religious bodies that have been historically resistant to it has been the result, in large part, of democratic trends in society. This is one example of how the work of "secular" society may actually be in advance of the work of the church in furthering God's purposes for the world. It could be argued, I think, that the drive for freedom in society preceded and eventually influenced the same drive within the church (though the battle has not yet been fully won in many of them). The argument that the church should be a bastion unto itself in order to protect its unique values and beliefs often overlooks the positive way in which the world can and has moved the church to embrace more fully some of its own incipient principles, including civility, tolerance, a deep respect for individual freedom, and human rights for every person and group.

Societies often precede the churches in actualizing some of the key principles of justice to which both are, in theory, committed. When eleven o'clock Sunday morning was the most segregated hour in America, and Congress was moving toward approval of the Civil Rights Bill, society exemplified a moral advance in racial justice far beyond where many of the predominantly white churches were on the issue at that time.

Even within the church, of course, true democratic participation in decision-making requires empowerment. When the poor, the uneducated, minorities, and women are systematically denied equal congregational power they are thereby excluded from equal participation in decision-making. Therefore, churches must find the means for empowering the historically disempowered within their own membership. Paradoxically, one way of empowering them is by recognizing and celebrating the power they already possess: the power to tell their stories, to let their experiences of oppression and liberation illuminate the Scripture, to understand how they have received the gospel in the midst of their poverty or helplessness.

Another form of empowerment is a re-visioning of hierarchical authority. Instead of seeing hierarchical power as grounded in some "essential" relationship between a hierarchical power structure and God, the community can regard hierarchy as primarily a functional device for more effectively carrying out the community's actions. There can be a hierarchy of talent, or of appropriate skills relative to particular tasks. The tellers of tales can be hierarchically empowered to lead the congregation in some respects, while those with the skills of analysis or administration would lead it in others. Many churches have begun to experiment with recognizing the non-ordained ministries of the members who work in society. Instead of focusing on the ministry of the ordained as the only ministry that truly "counts," churches can focus on the multiple and complex ministries of people whose primary work is in the political and economic structures of the world. Whatever power the ordained exercise is functional to their work of empowering the other ministers, not replacing them or putting themselves above them. In this way hierarchy can be functionalized, not sacralized.

Through the experience of empowerment in the community might come the courage and the power to move society to empower all its citizens, again especially the poor, to become full and active participants in its political and economic life. As people come to feel that the work they are doing in the world is important and can, in its own way, enlighten the members of the congregation, they will feel supported and encouraged to continue that work in the world. Using some of the values that the secular world first pushed the churches to take seriously, e.g., human rights and political equality, the churches will then find themselves in a position to question the failure of society to enact those very same values more fully in its own structures and institutions.

Communities can also remind their members that what they achieve is the result of cooperative community investment, not solely individual merit. In community individuals learn the limits of the quest for self-sufficiency. They learn that the work of the entire group is necessary for individual as well as group success. It does not depend solely on the clergy, on the wealthy, on teachers, or other functionaries. This experience of mutual support leading to communal achievement might then be carried out into society as a whole. The healthy community can remind the society that social goods are the result of cooperative social activity (thus undermining, for example, the legitimacy of huge income differentials between CEOs and workers). It can prepare the society for serious consideration of economic practices that recognize in a just manner the cooperative labor of all who produce economic wealth. The myth of self-sufficiency and self-reliance is exploded both in the theological understanding of the individual's dependence on God and in the experience of interpersonal interdependence in the communal activities of the group. And if that myth is shattered in the community it will be hard to sustain indefinitely in the society as long as the members of the church remain politically connected to and in the society with their feet firmly planted in communal values.

It almost goes without saying that religious communities can and ought to model for society the practice of full racial and gender inclusion. If the early *koinonia* practiced Paul's injunction not to recognize (at least as far as power and dignity are concerned) the difference between Jew and Greek, slave and free, male and female, then it established a principle that members of the community could have taken out into society (though as we saw they resisted for other reasons a move into full political participation at the time). While churches in our own time were often as complicit in supporting racial segregation as secular institutions, they could not escape the fundamental contradiction at the heart of the gospel when they did so. People who truly learn in community what it is like to practice nondiscrimination and racial and gender inclusion are far better prepared than others to advocate societal principles that would move in the same direction.

Communities also have the obligation to think, at least to a degree, metaphysically or theologically about the overarching purposes of human life. Part of the *raison d'être* of a Christian community is its place within the overarching intentions of God. It must therefore have some consciousness of that place and this means thinking about its underlying moral ontology. The practice of thinking theologically is not of course transferable as such to a secular society. But the practice of thinking universally, beyond the limits of the particular and the contingent is a virtue from which society can benefit. Societies need continually to ask themselves, usually in the form of some political philosophy or other, "what is our purpose? What ends do we serve, not just for our members but for the global 'community'"? While Rawls has warned us not to rely upon a common metaphysical understanding in order to develop and instantiate the principles of societal justice, I don't believe he has shown that thinking "outside the box" of particular societal interests is unimportant. And metaphysical thinking (of a certain kind) is a virtue for any community that must understand its location in God's intention for humankind.

In the developed world, many church communities have the privilege of exercising relatively significant economic and political power, both by virtue of the power of their members and of their institutional property and collective economic resources. This means that such churches might become players in the political life of their local societies. To avoid exercising that power would be an abdication of the opportunity given to them. Of course the Niebuhr cautions need to be kept in mind, especially those that warn against the arrogance of power on the part of institutions that think they have a moral superiority over the other contending players. Justifying institutional actions on the basis of moral self-righteousness is one of the most dangerous of all political acts.

There are many examples of churches trying to make a difference to the society in which they are embedded. In a study of urban churches responding to changes in their political environment, Nancy Ammerman observes that within the urban environment congregations provide "spaces of sociability."[47] "They are communal gatherings, collectivities, that afford their members an opportunity for connections with persons, groups, divine powers, and social structures beyond their own individuality." They also challenge the "calculating rationality" of the marketplace. In short they reconcile the Bellah contradiction by uniting American individualism (in which one chooses whom one will relate to) with commitment to community. The collective energy of a transformed and renewed community can then be transmitted into the fabric of the society beyond. "Precisely because of this concentration of social energy, voluntary congregations can carry at least as much weight as the established churches of yore. They may not be able to muster troops or tax the citizens for their support, but they can channel the energies of those same citizens in ways that equally affect the world."[48]

Individuals sometimes have great difficulty impacting the social order as a whole. It is perceived as being too monolithic, too huge and sprawling to find ways to make a difference. Communities, however, provide both a

[47]   Nancy Tatom Ammerman, *Congregation and Community* (New Brunswick: Rutgers University Press, 1997), 353.
[48]   Ammerman, 354–5.

space of sociability and a mobilizing opportunity for more effective, because united, public action. We belong to particular communities and through them rather than as individuals acting alone can make a difference to other collective entities such as the nation. Each community or even a confederation of communities can become public actors. And to the extent that we may belong to many communities simultaneously (church, neighborhood, affinity group, support group, etc.) we can through these groups impact society in different ways at different times over different (but often overlapping) issues.

Walter Brueggemann suggests a telling image of the relation between the church community and the body politic. He says each community must have a space for itself on one side of the wall that divides communities from the work of the polis. As Ammerman paraphrases him, "any community that wishes to sustain itself must have space (behind the wall) and language for telling its own primal narrative and imagining its own view of the future. Such views and practices . . . are essential for a society in which critical perspectives can be brought to bear on the issues that confront us. Sectarian communities enrich and critique the conversation on the wall."[49]

Communities create, in short, "social capital," i.e., energized people whose labor, intelligence, trust, and moral sense are major contributions to the maintenance of a good and just society. "Social capital in its most basic form, these relationships of trust [within community] facilitate communication and coordination of activities in society and provide well-being to their participants. Both individuals and society as a whole benefit from the act of belonging, in all its particularistic multiplicity. . . . [B]elonging to a religious community has a moral weight not always granted to other memberships."[50]

Congregations can bring their particular community's insights and moral claims into the public square or at the wall to join with the voices of other communities, both secular and religious. This is clearly not an isolation from society, but a linkage that takes seriously both the internal life of the community and its responsibility for shaping the external life of society. When communities are organized they make possible networks of cooperation with other communities and mini social unions.

In today's political climate there is an ongoing, flexible, creative relation between the resources of congregations, their programs, and the cooperative work of agencies in the society at large, from government to private philanthropic groups. Churches in the inner city that are working with

---

[49]   Ammerman, 359.
[50]   Ammerman, 363.

gangs or with kids hooked on drugs can often leverage resources from governmental as well as private agencies without transgressing the line between church and state. In this way churches can be agents of social responsibility without becoming captive to some of society's undesirable values and without cutting themselves off from society in general.

Society for Community

But what, then, does society do for the community which it cannot do for itself? Its primary work is create and maintain the structures of justice and foster a common commitment to a common social good. Such a broad societal climate can foster the development of smaller communities that know they and their members will have adequate, even abundant, social support in carrying out their more narrow communal goals.

The society can also provide to communities the material resources necessary for a flourishing life for all their members. These resources can be produced in many cases better by "economies of scale" than by having each community duplicate the economic work of all the other communities. Communities working cooperatively with a rational distribution of labor between them under the aegis of society are more likely to thrive than communities pitted against others each of which may be trying to take on the responsibilities best left to the governmental agencies of society as a whole. If they ignore or disparage the societal work that undergirds them all, they will fall into fratricidal warfare. This requires accepting the regulatory and mediating role of societal institutions over the external relations between communities. Without such regulation society will likely degenerate into competing smaller groups each seeking to suppress the demands of the others. A fair and just system undergirding a set of regulatory principles can do for the multiple communities what a fair set of rules in a family does for squabbling siblings. By means of these rules and regulations, a society can demonstrate in practice how to work out effective principles of justice since it will be less likely to be swayed by the mere power of interest groups or narrow constituencies. Societies at their best look to foster the good common for all their members.

In this respect, society can, as we have seen, often be far ahead of the churches in matters of social justice. Churches that focused only on their internal membership issues and "spiritual" concerns were often further behind society in coming to grips with racial and gender injustice. Ironically, by restricting itself to the external dimensions of justice (treating people in law without regard to skin color, gender, sexual orientation, age, etc.) society can often more quickly address public acts of discrimination that affect all its members than can a group with a purely voluntary membership. A community, for reasons of its own, may choose to deny women positions of leadership, but a society that has been transformed by principles of equality and justice does not have the luxury of segregating the treatment of women from the treatment of all persons equal under the law. A legal wrong is capable of rectification by law more directly and effectively than a practice that applies exclusively inside the community that can only be rectified by a change of heart or persuasion. That is why church membership has become integrated with respect to race and gender more slowly than the surrounding society.

Society can also utilize degrees of power that are often anathema to communities. Communities that will not use violence internally can accept (albeit with various shades of regret) the forceful protections provided by society against both external and internal threats to the life and safety of their members. Accepting protective force (by the military and the police) remains, of course, a divisive issue for some Christian communities, especially those committed to the principle of nonviolence. And all such communities have a duty to remind society that use of such force, even when given conditional approval by them, should not be the occasion for demonizing others as "the enemy." Nevertheless, societies can exercise power in ways that communities sometimes find morally troubling even though morally inescapable.

Societies can also remind communities of the voices and needs that they, given their limited size and necessarily exclusionary policies of membership, might otherwise not hear. By having the obligation to care for all its citizens, societies can instruct communities that there is a virtue to religious tolerance that left to their own devices many religious traditions have denied in practice. Principles of religious freedom, which have historically often been enacted politically by "secular" people more than religious, are a benefit to religiously pluralistic societies and can be seen as a gift to religious communities by the society.

Society, in short, can remind the religious communities of their finitude and limits. Those who claim the mantle of God's favor are often the first to fall victim to megalomania, self-righteousness, and, in principle, the totalitarian use of power. By exercising power that overrides the power of the individual groups within its boundaries, societies help communities remember the limits that some of their own theologies also affirm but their practices tend to forget.

If the church community is helping to prepare most of its members for service in the world, as the primary place of ministry, then society in turn provides concrete experience in doing the work of the polis and of multiple vocations in the "real" world. If these can be sites of ministry, then they can help instruct the congregations about how ministry is really and effectively carried out in the world beyond the church. This means that the society must have opportunities for meaningful ministry within (and sometimes in opposition to) the various institutions, structures, and vocations that constitute its political, social, and economic infrastructure. As persons morally formed by communities go out into those bodies they will be seeking to put the principles of justice into operation, appropriate to their particular vocational site. At the same time, they will be bringing back into the community news from the "other side of the wall." They will be able to report how things really are "out there" in the political and economic institutions of the world. More importantly they will be able to instruct the community on how to craft or understand public policy options appropriate for the political arena. Too often churches pass lofty sentiments without any real awareness of the political realities of the world to which they are addressed. A church member working in a major corporation, a banker, a grocery store clerk, etc. often has far more insights into the way public policies work in practice than do church members whose main focus is on the internal life of their community.

The work of the lay ministers in the world therefore involves an exposure to and training in the pragmatics of societal political and economic life. If the church is to be responsible for the society of which it is a part, then it must allow the society to inform it, ideally through its own members who are working in society, about what needs to be done to keep the principles of justice operative in the impersonal world of indirect relations.

In the end, therefore, there is a symbiotic relation between community and society. *Symbios* means literally "life together." The life of each is enriched by the life of the other: the one forms the fundamental moral character of each of its members, the other provides the broader social environment in which the moral life is completed. Neither loses its unique identity but neither, ideally, claims to be self-sufficient or to draw its full meaning solely from itself.

Chapter 7

Turning Inward to Community: The Family and the Dangers of Too Much Community

The Family as Community

No ethics of community can afford to neglect the importance of the family as community. As we have seen, one of the persistent dilemmas of contemporary social life has to do with the relation between the public and the private dimensions of human life. In many places the family has been elevated, at least rhetorically, to such a high moral status that the public and political dimension of life has been characterized as the enemy of what some have come to call "family values." Given that the family is often one of the most basic forms of community life, it is crucial to get straight what the relation between family, community, and society ought to be in an ethics of community.

I want to establish a framework, drawn from Macmurray's philosophy of the personal, for understanding the nature of the private and its proper relationship to the public spheres of life. Standing at the heart of this relation is the family as one of the most basic forms of community or locus of direct personal relationships.

In his defense of the family as community Macmurray is no apologist for the hierarchical, patriarchal patterns of family life that have historic-ally overridden women's rightful demand for justice and equal opportunity for flourishing, including those opportunities to help shape the public policies which impact family life. What I want to suggest is that there is a well-stitched unity (which preserves and does not annul vital distinctions) between the development of deeply personal relationships in the community of the family and the work of statecraft at the political and economic level in society.

What makes the relationship between family and society a unity, rather than an opposition, are the conditions necessary for the full development of mutual relationships and of the selves that participate in them. We are ultimately selves fulfilled only in and through the kinds of relationship that Macmurray calls "mutual" and which develop most fully in community. But he warns us against setting in opposition the "minor mutualities" of limited loves and the public structures of social justice.

Resistance from the Other is one of the most important factors in the healthy development of the self. It is most fruitfully and initially expressed in the context of the family. This means that the self is not absorbed into a minor mutuality that would eliminate its ability to stand back critically from its entanglements in that community. Nor is the self able to become the critical, reflective, and fully developed self that it can be apart from the nurturing relations that throughout its life, but most especially at its beginning, instill in it both the experience of love and the experience of resistance to and recognition of the "Other" as other.

Love must not override or swamp the imperatives of justice as long as persons stand in a relationship with each other that respects each partner's uniqueness and integrity. One important implication of this point is that the family cannot be exempt from the imperatives of justice, just as society cannot escape entirely from the imperatives, and the vision, first developed in the family, of care and compassion as moral guideposts for the fullest possible expression of human life. If the family is removed from public scrutiny it can become an enclave of unjust domination and oppression, especially for women. If the family is made little more than the servant of the State, it loses those capacities that make it a model of a community in which persons can relate to each other directly, personally, intimately, and mutually, in ways that are not possible between and among the totality of the members of a society. Relationships within communities are never to be summed-up or reduced solely to ones of justice. But love without justice is subject to the temptation of tyranny in which the self loses itself either out of fear of the other or out of an inappropriate desire to destroy itself for, or to allow itself to be swallowed up by, the other in the name of love. It must avoid what Iris Marion Young calls the fusion of selves. Macmurray's treatment of the family contains some important qualifications on excessive communitarianism. It also draws a strong link between the family and the public social order which permits a critique of false "traditions" and unjust tribal identities, as well as of liberalism's "naked" self.

For Macmurray, the family is in principle (though not always in fact) "the original human community and the basis as well as the origin of all subsequent communities. It is therefore the norm of all community."[1] In a community "each member of the group is in positive personal relation to each of the others taken severally."[2] A positive motive, however, always contains and is constituted by its own negative. What this means concretely is that even when I intend a personal relationship with another person, I carry with me a negative motivation insofar as I regard that other person as an object, a not-self. This view of the Other can never be entirely absent even from the most intimate of relationships. "Even in the most personal relationships the other person is in fact an object for us . . . The impersonal [or negative] aspect of the personal relation is always present and necessarily so."[3]

This means that I cannot subsume or absorb the other into my own self: she retains an obstinate, recalcitrant objectivity that I cannot (and ought not to try to) nullify by making our personal relationship so intimate and mutual that her own unique particularity and stubborn otherness disappear in me or in the relationship. Even in the family there is an objective, impersonal dimension always present. To the extent that principles of justice apply to our impersonal relationships, they should also apply to those dimensions of our most mutual relationships that contain the impersonal as a negative subordinated to a positive.[4] Thus, the family itself (and any other form of constituted social arrangement, such as those the communitarians appeal to) ought to be subject to the principles of justice

---

[1] John Macmurray, *Persons in Relation*, intro. by Frank G. Kirkpatrick (New York: Humanities Press, 1991), 155. David A. S. Fergusson, "Macmurray's Philosophy of the Family," *Appraisal*, 1, 2 (Oct. 1996), 68–74, has done an excellent job in bringing out the salient elements in Macmurray's treatment of the family and I'm indebted to his work on this issue. Note also that Macmurray may well be influenced here, as elsewhere in his philosophy, by Hegel, who called the family the "ethical root" of the state. (See G. W. F. Hegel, *Hegel's Philosophy of Right*, trans. with notes by T. M. Knox (London: Oxford University Press, 1967), 154.)

[2] Macmurray, 157–8.

[3] Macmurray, 33–4.

[4] We should note, as Macmurray does, that the distinction between personal and impersonal relations is not identical to that between direct and indirect relations with others. Direct relations involve a personal acquaintance with the other. Indirect relations are between persons who do not know each other personally. Thus all indirect relations are impersonal but not all direct relations are personal. I may know you (have a direct relationship with you) but not choose to have a positively motivated personal relationship with you. See *Persons in Relation*, p. 43.

even when there are essential elements in family life such as mutual love that go beyond the impersonal, objective dimensions of justice.

The positive and negative poles of the infant's motivations, which underlie this understanding of the private/public linkage, are developed out of the mother–child relationship. The infant must be brought through the developmental process to the point where he can exercise his free agency so as to intend a positive relation with others. And one crucial part of this process is the *resistance* that the parent provides to his motives.

We can recall that within the family, "the child discovers himself as an individual by *contrasting himself, and indeed by wilfully opposing himself to the family* **to which he belongs**; and this *discovery* of his individuality is at the same time the *realization* of his individuality" (bold mine).[5] The mother must *withdraw* in a strategic act from a fully positive relation with the child in order to help the child differentiate positive from negative. If the Other simply melted away at our touch, or absorbed us into itself with no resistance, there would be no possibility of distinguishing ourselves as individual persons. We need the resistance of the Other to become ourselves since central to our self-identity as persons is our free agency in relation to what is not ourselves. Ideally, within the family "the normal positive motivation is usually sufficient to dominate [not eliminate] the negative motives of self-interest and individualism."[6] Eventually, of course, the infant must learn that there are nonpersonal Others in the world who will also offer resistance without hope of reconciliation. Without this knowledge, the developed self will be a helpless and ineffective agent in the world, relying primarily on fear and hatred of the Other.

This leads directly to what Macmurray takes to be the basic problem of life itself: the problem of personal reconciliation. It can only be overcome within community in which the dominating and positive motive is love, or heterocentricity (making the other the center of one's concern).

Every positive contains its own negative, and the negative in relation to community is society. The social unions that constitute societies are primarily negatively motivated by fear for oneself and therefore fear of the Other. These fears do not annul our social relationship but they determine them on the basis of what serves the narrower interests of the self, or egocentrically. Macmurray has, in effect, articulated the basis of the liberal society: it exists to foster bonds of association that permit the individual the greatest possible latitude to pursue her own interests without violating the interests of others.

---

[5]   Macmurray, 91.
[6]   Macmurray, 156.

Society is necessary, however, because not all relationships all the time can be mutual, direct, and personal. There are simply too many persons with whom we are in social but not mutual relationship.[7] Because societies are configured at a less than fully mutual level, they will serve different purposes than direct personal fellowship, but the purposes they serve ought to support, complement, and enhance community. If the model community is the family, then it follows that societies are at least in part to serve the family. To this extent the conservative critique of liberalism is correct. But if society is the negative that is contained within the positive, it is also the case that the family (or any form of fellowship or mutuality) ought to adequately prepare its members to participate in and serve the society so that it, in turn, can serve the community. We have here, in effect, a dialectical dynamic, a form of what Macmurray calls the rhythm of withdrawal and return, or of resistance and response. The private sphere needs to prepare its members to play public roles so that society can best serve community without becoming confused with or reduced to it.

Just as the mother must withdraw temporarily from complete engrossment in the infant in order to allow it to grow and develop as an individual self, so the family must recognize the need of the individual to enter into relations that are not fully personal, mutual, and direct. All personal bonds need nurturing and support from persons who themselves often are not parties to those bonds. Lovers need among other things such social and material goods as food, clothing, shelter, education, healthcare, cooperation in the workplace, etc. When they live in social union with multiple others, they also need justice, law, order, and the complex political, economic, institutional and systemic structures that make living with others in nondirect, impersonal ways humanly and humanely possible. A society will be characterized to a large extent by the way in which it determines which social roles are necessary for maintaining a good and just society, what training must be provided to help people perform those roles effectively, and how those roles are efficiently integrated. At the same time it must not succumb to the false view that serving a societal role is an end in itself or that the full exercise of meaningful action is exhausted by performing our societal functions.

---

[7] Macmurray reminds us that no person ought to be intentionally or in principle excluded from the mutual relationships of community because such exclusion would be motivated by fear of that "other." But while open in principle to the possibility of entering into mutual relations with everyone and anyone, not everyone will be capable of entering into those relations nor will they in any given contingent social arrangement be able to act successfully on the principle of non-exclusion.

But if society is to serve community then individuals need to be given training in distinguishing the negative and impersonal dimensions of life from the positive and personal ones and subordinating the former to the latter. This is where the family can be crucial. The family might best be seen as the most effective forum for cultivating the essential traits and capacities of full personhood (love, trust, mutuality) without neglecting training in the negative elements necessary for societal relationship: i.e., resistance, impersonal relations, individual withdrawal into private space, justice, cooperation, and healthy self-interest. If the negative is never entirely absent from even our most personal relationships, the best families will be those that prepare their members to integrate or balance the personal and impersonal relations that constitute the relation between society and community. This means, among other things, preparing their members to take active and responsible roles in helping to shape the political and economic life of society. Unless justice, law, order, and the impersonal structures of society that provide for the most efficient distribution of necessary goods work well, the private life of individuals will suffer. The self will drown in the cloying quicksand of too much intimacy and too little critical distance from it. Or it will become the victim of larger impersonal forces the control of which it has ceded to other hands and structures.

Capacities for Personal and Social Life

What are the capacities for both personal and social life that the family ought to nurture?:

1) The capacity for informed free action. This means cultivating the habits of learning, rational thought, investigation, imagination, and critical analysis that maximizes the self's freedom of action. This would be one antidote to the myopic limitations of inherited traditions that pass themselves off as genuine communities in some communitarian philosophies. We need "ontic" space in which we can distinguish ourselves from others so that their individuality and uniqueness is respected while they respect ours. Clear thinking is one way to do this.[8]

[8] Objectivity in thinking is intimately related to the capacity for emotional objectivity: Macmurray insists that we need to develop appropriate emotional responses to others congruent with their "objective" natures. Emotional obsession with a toy to the exclusion of persons is not objectively appropriate, nor is emotional withdrawal from those with the capacity and willingness to love the child heterocentrically. But learning how and upon what appropriate objects to express one's emotions needs to be learned, at least initially, within the context of the family.

2) The ability to distinguish between those objects that have the capacity in themselves to bring flourishing and joy to the self, and those that instrumentally support and sustain the relationship without being intrinsically joy-bringing. Learning the appropriate difference between the primary material/social goods and the personal relationships they enrich is a capacity that is essential for understanding the transition from the family into the political/economic order; this suggests another capacity:

3) The capacity for understanding the importance and function of impersonal relations. Learning the utility of impersonal relations is an essential part of the full development of any person.[9] Since impersonal social relations are structured by principles of justice, it is crucial for these principles of justice as fairness to apply within the family itself under the appropriate conditions. Children need to know that there are many distinctly personal things they cannot appeal to for special treatment by their parents in matters of discipline (e.g., being more beautiful or athletically gifted than their siblings).

4) The capacity to both express and receive love: true love develops, of course, over time and presupposes a certain level of intentionality, emotionality, and free choice. Within the family the encouragement to express one's love toward others and the opportunities for doing so ought to be maximal. Not only should one be nurtured in giving love, but also in learning how to receive love from others. Only by learning how to be loved can one keep the negative motivation of fearing the other in check. Part of what it means to love, of course, includes learning how to love as many others as possible. Genuine love cannot arbitrarily foreclose the boundaries of the community that love is willing to embrace. (This is where the notion of a "universal community" and theology's reference to a Kingdom of God can play a role.)

5) A capacity for trust. Trust is an essential component of love. It is one crucial way of overcoming the negative motivation of fear of the other. Laurence Thomas has argued that "transparent" parental love which gives the child "basic psychological security" makes it possible for fear not to be a motivating factor in the life of the child.[10] And this requires what Thomas calls the establishment of "basic trust," trust that "others will treat

---

[9]   This fact explains why many psychiatrists do not have "personal" relationships with their patients. In order to serve their function as therapist or analyst they need to keep a distance between the skills they bring to their work and their personal needs and desires.

[10]   Lawrence Thomas, *Living Morally* (Philadelphia: Temple University Press, 1989), viii, 88.

one in accordance with the precepts of morality."[11] If this trust is established through good parenting, the child who becomes an adult will be much more able to will the flourishing of others without denying an interest in his own flourishing. In fact, it is primarily because others have loved us first that we can love ourselves (contrary to the popular wisdom that we have to love ourselves before we can love others). Out of trust and love, therefore, comes the capacity to love oneself in a healthy way. And the original venue for learning what it is like to be loved and to love others is the family.

One crucial implication of learning basic trust, Macmurray argues, is that we can then establish the basis of some kind of political order. "The possibility of the State depends upon an existing habit of cooperation which needs no enforcement; upon the existence of a society in which people do trust one another for the most part, though not under every condition or in all cases [but], provided we do in practice trust the majority of people to do in most circumstances what is expected of them, it is possible to devise mechanisms for dealing with the exceptions."[12]

It is this last point that suggests the transition from family to society. Most families exist in complex webs of interrelationship with other families and with a whole host of other forms of association and support structures, personal and impersonal, direct and indirect. Among these the two most important are the political and economic institutions of society. The latter provides the material goods which make human life possible, which empower people to use their liberty fulfillingly: the former provides the structural forms through which these goods can be most fairly provided for all the members of the society. Politics is the "maintaining, improving and adjusting [of] the indirect or economic relations of persons."[13] It expresses itself best in principles and institutions of justice which, in this sense, is the minimum of reciprocity and interest in the other; it is a kind of "zero or lower limit of moral behaviour."[14] And it can be summarized, I think, pretty much as John Rawls does, as "fairness." Justice is the negative aspect of morality necessary to the constitution of the positive. It does not require direct, personal, mutual relations, but it does require a set of mutually agreed upon principles of fairness that keep our impersonal relations from degenerating into "minor mutualities" that mask injustice and unfair treatment under the rhetoric of love.

---

[11] Thomas, 176–7.
[12] Macmurray, 191.
[13] Macmurray, 188.
[14] Ibid.

Dangers of Too Much Community

Perhaps the most important task facing a community internally, apart from empowering the family, is the need to balance commitment to a common or shared mission with enough individual freedom to permit dissent, difference, and diversity. And the resistance that is essential to the constitution of a good family can be the key to avoiding the dangers of overly oppressive communities.

Difference and diversity are in themselves good things because they reflect the rich panoply of human personalities. No one person can represent, express, or experience the manifold possibilities of human life and flourishing. Each of us flourishes in somewhat different ways from others (though we should not exaggerate the degree of difference). Each of us has different interests, talents, and abilities. And each of these, as gathered up into a whole host of different individuals, contributes to the richness, depth, and breadth of the whole community. Insofar as the community is what it is through the contributions of its members, their respective individual characteristics must be not only recognized but allowed to grow and develop as best they can so as to nourish not only themselves but also the growth and development of others. This is an obvious implication of what Macmurray calls the heterocentricity of community, the placing of the interests of the "other" ahead of one's own.

We cannot flourish without having the freedom to experiment with what works best for us under the changing conditions of history. But this is not unlimited freedom: if we are truly created for each other, then there will necessarily be some limits on our freedom to express ourselves. At one level, this limitation simply provides for the freedom of others. This kind of freedom is at the core of a liberal democracy. But at another level, our freedom needs to be limited so that we can enjoy and appreciate the contributions of others. It is one thing to hold back from expressing myself out of fear that the other will not respect my freedom unless I respect his. It is something else to refrain from exercising full liberty because I *want* the other to express himself without fear of me so that I can appreciate and take pleasure in what he contributes to me and to the community of which we are a part.

Limiting my freedom opens up space for the freedom of others. Absolute freedom is a contradiction in terms: I can only be truly free if there are others whose presence makes my freedom meaningful because it gives me something to engage with and in part to resist. The philosopher J. Melvin Woody has rightly argued that "to be free is . . . to be limited by an opposing realm with its own intrinsic determinacy and being. Freedom must have a milieu, or *world*, in order to exist and can only be consistently conceived as confronting that world and coping with it."[15] Pure freedom, with no boundaries or resistance, is sheer illusion. Without the strategic but lovingly intended resistance one finds in community (and the family), one is ill-prepared to confront the multiple and complex forms of more hostile resistance that necessarily characterize indirect and impersonal societal relations.

If communities are to be places where people can experience (even under the conditions of sin and finitude) some degree of the delights of mutual relationship, they will also need structures, institutions, and rules through which freedom is both limited and enhanced. To make these rules and structures appropriate, however, they must emerge from the freedom of the individuals who adopt them. Out of their freedom persons in community can choose how they want to be governed. (Government within a community is naturally going to be less complex, rigidified, or heavily structured than it will be within a society. But communities do need some form of government. Completely spontaneous unstructured relationships can constitute "peak" experiences in community but they cannot constitute the long-term basis of it. Sheer anarchy has never held a community together for any length of time.)

What makes government in a community distinctive is that it can, for the most part, arise out of common deliberations by all the persons, each of whom has been adequately empowered to speak in a voice which must be heard by all the others. In the early *koinonia* the voices of the marginalized and oppressed (women, slaves, the illiterate) had a place at the table, the table being the symbol and reality of a common feast in a common endeavor in communion with a common God. Naturally some persons may be unable to function fully in an informed participatory way in the work of the community. These will include infants or young children whose decision-making faculties still need development. Other persons who for reasons of mental impairment cannot contribute intelligently to group decision-making might also be unable to participate fully. But the communal decisions about who will and will not participate fully in its work need themselves to be discussed and determined with the greatest feasible amount of participation.

A complete cacophony of voices leading only to inarticulate rage or dissension will ultimately undermine community as well. At some point,

---

[15] J. Melvin Woody, *Freedom's Embrace* (University Park: The Pennsylvania State University Press, 1998), 116.

again through joint decision-making involving all the members of the community, rules will have to be established as to when and how dissension needs to give way, temporarily, to unity of action. Most successful communities have found ways to cycle through a process of discussion, dissension, agreement, revision, action, more discussion, and so forth. No decisions are cast in stone: they must, in an orderly way, be subject to review if they prove to be dysfunctional or harmful to the interests of the community or to particular individuals within it.

Communal Mechanisms of Commitment

Communities also need what Rosabeth Kanter has called commitment mechanisms. A community needs to build and sustain a conviction that, with God's help, its members can begin to live lives more in keeping with God's intention for a universal community of love. Most Christian communities will need to balance a sense of breaking some new ground for the Kingdom and a recognition that personal or communal perfection is not possible under the present conditions of the world and the state of human nature.

Communities will also need mechanisms for educating the emotions, not just the intellects of their members. There is much new literature coming out on emotional intelligence, just as there has been in the past on intellectual intelligence. Since friendship, love, and mutuality are strongly, even essentially, emotional, the community will survive only to the extent that it nurtures these emotional dimensions in its members.

Communities will need to provide systematic ways for the members to express their concerns, even criticisms of each other. Just as good families have learned how to do this effectively, so communities must adopt something along the lines of the "mutual criticism" practiced by the Oneida communalists. Insights from modern psychiatry and group psychology can be helpful in determining how this can be done compassionately and in support of community-building.

The ritualistic expressions of community commitment, belief, and unity are crucial. They reenact, or represent, the fundamental ideas and ideals of the community. They point to its underlying reason for being. Rituals, having a strong emotional component, are often more effective mechanisms for holding the community together than cognitive agreement on its basic principles and beliefs.

Unfortunately, no community has ever completely resolved the problem of how to handle the conflicts that emerge when some members find themselves at odds with the basic beliefs that once generated the meaning and foundation of the community. When the unity of the community is threatened over disagreements about ritual, belief, or practice, the question of tradition emerges and immediately becomes contestable. Some appeal to one part of the tradition (e.g., the apparent role of women as leaders in the early church) and others appeal to another part of the tradition (e.g., the denial of ordination to women at a later stage of the church's history). What parts of the tradition are considered binding on future generations and what parts are validly open for alteration is itself a deeply contested issue in many communities. Obviously splitting into different groups is one way of working out the problem, but each such fragmentation works against the long-range intention to create a universal community. Insisting upon maintaining the union, however, when it has already been broken in heart and mind also accomplishes nothing or at best camouflages real differences without resolving them. This is a tension and a problem all communities simply have to accept without papering it over with false, short-range solutions.

Kanter has argued that "commitment to group cohesion and solidarity requires the attachment of a person's entire fund of emotion and affectivity to the group."[16] It is true that no community can survive without an abiding and deep commitment to the relationships that constitute the group. But the attachment of the *entire* fund of emotion to the group would run the risk of leaving nothing left over for commitment to the larger society. This would mark, perhaps, one of the more important differences between the communes of the nineteenth century and communities in the present, provided that they have not abandoned their responsibilities in and for the larger society. Communities provide the emotional and moral foundation for the work that must be done by the members in the world beyond their group. This simply reaffirms the point that neither society nor community alone can do full justice to the person in the world who is seeking to do God's will.

In the past many communities were sustained, paradoxically, by their experience of being persecuted for their beliefs. The blood of the martyrs, it was once said, was the life-blood of the church. Persecution, however, is not the only form of conflict or tension between a community and its society. Communities can also find themselves in opposition to many of the prevailing values of the culture in which they exist. A community that

[16] Rosabeth Kanter, *Commitment and Community* (Cambridge, Mass.: Harvard University Press, 1972), 72.

has embraced a particular value on securing economic justice for the least well-off in society and carries that value out into the public sphere by working for the passage of certain public policies, might well face opposition by other groups with opposing viewpoints. (The clash of values over abortion has led some groups to claim persecution by their opponents, even though it clearly does not rise to the level of hostility experienced by the early Christians or the Anabaptists.) A group committed to the implementation of a particular social value must be willing to fight for that value in the political arena, as were many churches that had embraced the cause of civil rights. Losing the fight can itself sometimes inspire the community to fight harder. There were many peace groups struggling for years to call a halt to nuclear weapon proliferation. They were continually ignored both by the churches and the politicians, but eventually their message began to get through. In the early days of the struggle, however, many of these peace groups, and before them civil rights groups, felt like genuine communities, even support groups, and the refusal of the larger society to embrace them actually helped to develop group spirit and rededication to their mission.

These commitment mechanisms are useful ways of maintaining the unity of the community. But they have to be balanced or supplemented by an abiding commitment to principles of full democratic participation in community decision-making and to the maintenance of the material and political conditions that will empower all the members to engage in that participation. In these ways many of the dangers of too much or too oppressive community can be avoided or mitigated.

Chapter 8

Working Outward from Community: Economic Justice and International Order

A Good and Just Society

The question we have been dealing with throughout this treatment of the ethics of community is how principles developed in community can inform societal practices and values. This presupposes, in turn, a more basic understanding of what constitutes, from the perspective of an ethics of community, a good and just society.

Two of the basic issues facing a good and just society are how to define the good for the most vulnerable of its members and how to provide the appropriate legitimation of as well as the just conditions for economic practices within its borders insofar as they bear directly on servicing the needs of the most vulnerable. These questions are fundamentally political in the simple sense that their resolution ought to be reached through a democratic process of deliberation in which there is the greatest feasible degree of full participation by all the citizens of the society.

There has been no dearth of proposals in recent years for what general principles would constitute a good and just society. I want to touch on some of the more salient of these in order to suggest a foundation for building and sustaining a society that is most conducive to a healthy and vigorous relationship with an ethics of community.

Some of the basic principles of a good and just society are so well-established in western democratic political thought that they are virtually beyond dispute, even by those who are otherwise divided over the appropriate accents represented by the political philosophies of communitarianism and liberalism. A minimal definition acceptable to most persons is that good and just societies, in Rawls' language, constitute the organized life of people living together in cooperative ways for mutual advantage. The principles that constitute them include:

1) *Commitment to a common good: a good and just society will be one that orients its members toward the determination of a public or a common good.* This principle correlates with a moral ontology in which God has created persons to be for each other because they constitute a single fellowship under the justice and compassion of God. A good and just society, therefore, ought to be more than a contractual vehicle or protective association for the advancement of private interests. There are some goods (both material and spiritual) that we can acquire only together, by sharing our gifts and talents in and for a larger group to which we belong. Calvin's Geneva, the aspirations of Winthrop's Puritans, the revolutionary zeal of some of America's "founding fathers," the utopian dreams of the communalists, all testify to the possibilities of group work for the common good over and above individual efforts for self-advancement alone.

Commitment to a common good presumes, contrary to some versions of liberalism, a minimal moral claim that it is a constitutive good for persons to live together. If Macmurray's philosophy of the personal is correct, then even at the societal level (and not just in community) persons are more themselves, more capable of realizing the fullness of their personhood, when they do more than just cooperate with others but actually sacrifice some of their narrow self-interest in order to build a society that serves the needs of all in common. While our bonds with others in society are generally not as direct and personal as they are in community, society is a fundamental good for human beings. As such a society is committed to goods that serve the whole and not just the parts taken separately.

2) *A commitment to the common good includes the good of order: not anarchy or chaos.* This principle is clearly in line with the biblical awareness of the sin of self-seeking which requires some measure of restraint and coercion. Order follows from the need for a common good, not the other way around. If we are committed to a common good, we need to create and maintain the practical conditions for its realization. These conditions include the general reliability and fairness of the fundamental structures, laws, rules, processes, and procedures the society uses in carrying out its responsibility for fostering the common good according to the principles of justice. Order is, however, always secondary to the end it serves, namely the attainment of goods that are in the interests of the society's members taken both collectively and individually.

Once order has been established, the society can carry out its other tasks in a reasonably safe and reliable way. These tasks include:

3) *Due recognition of the freedom and the right of the individual to chart his/her own decisions and life-plans within the boundaries of the ordered commitment to the common good.* Any understanding of community requires a full recognition of the equality of each member in it and that, in turn, requires that each person be given the greatest possible latitude to express his/her freedom both to who they are and to the well-being of the group as a whole. Individual freedom is not an end in itself but it is essential to any meaningful relationships with others. There is no value in freedom in the abstract. Freedom must mean freedom *for* something. And in our ontology of community, the most meaningful kind of freedom is freedom for personal relationship. We know that we work best with others when we choose to work with them because it best suits our human nature. Only in community can we be most free to be ourselves in communion with others. Therefore, a good and just society must protect and enhance the opportunities for individual freedom as a precondition both for its own self-governance and for the delights of community.

In this sense the liberal insistence upon guarding the right of the individual to pursue her self-interest must be acknowledged. But if the moral ontology holds, then self-interest need not be construed primarily as the interests of the self in *opposition* to the interests of others. It can be better construed as living according to one's own nature, which in an ethics of community means living in community with others; liberty to do what one wants requires a moral ontology where what one ultimately wants is to be in communion with others. This is primarily positive liberty, with a place for negative liberty. Negative liberty is the right to be left alone by others (up to a point) and positive liberty, as Carol Gould has argued, is the ability to act effectively upon one's freedom. Society therefore has an obligation to provide the individual with all the necessary means to act effectively upon her freedom.

4) *The establishment of principles of justice is essential to any good and just society.* That there must be such principles goes without saying. These principles of justice, however, must be established, paradoxically, by just procedures. These include:

5) *Full participation by all the members in the determination of public rules and policies.* This requires ongoing conversation on the basis of equal power among diverse voices whose interests are at stake in the outcome of the deliberation. A genuine community, as Macmurray has argued, presumes the equality of all the members. This does not mean equal talent or equal functions: it means no member uses another member solely as a means to his own ends. No voices can be silenced or marginalized if the procedures of justice are to be followed in arriving at the substantive rules of justice.

Each must have a chance to articulate his interests and to hear the interests of others, as Benhabib has pointed out. This is one consequence of Rawls' first principle of justice that each person is to have an equal right to the most extensive total system of equal basic liberties compatible with a similar system of liberty for all.

It follows that an ethics of community when applied to society has an obligation to revive the integrity of politics. Politics is the work of the people in determining their own life together. It requires equal and full participation by all the members of the *polis*. The trashing of politics referred to earlier often comes from people who are deeply afraid of empowering those whose voices have historically been excluded from political decision-making. Politics, therefore, needs to be revitalized so that it becomes once again an honorable vehicle for those presently without power to exercise their voice and influence in crafting a good and just society.

One of the most important tasks of a transformed politics will be locating, debating, and addressing the social and economic inequalities that now disempower many persons and groups of persons in society. We will take up the issue of economic justice shortly.

Finally, however, we need to stress one remaining element in a good and just society and that is its provision of:

6) *Support for the creation and nurture of smaller communities in which persons can be most fully themselves.* Community life is both intrinsically delightful but, from the society's perspective, it is also a place in which the members can prepare themselves for their roles as informed, enlightened, and committed citizens of the society.

Economic Justice

One of the most pressing issues requiring the public responsibility of communities is that having to do with economic justice. Any ethics grounded in the intention of an acting God for a universal community of persons must necessarily be committed to an ethics of economic justice. In a material world created by God as good for human beings, the economic dimension of human life has a paramount place. Without its resources people are fundamentally disempowered as agents of their own destinies. We need food, clothing, housing, meaningful labor, and the beauty and integrity of nature not only for our well-being but also for our flourishing as the full persons God wants to be. All of these have a material foundation and all, except for nature itself before it is "worked" by human labor, are made available to us through economic activity of one kind or another. The economic "goods" labor produces are therefore also good for us in a moral sense as well. Because of the biblical doctrines of Creation, Incarnation, and the resurrection of the body, a Christian ethic is necessarily committed to a strong belief that "matter matters." It cannot, therefore, be indifferent to the ways in which matter in all its complexity is extracted, refined, transformed, marketed, distributed, and consumed. If matter matters then it matters how we get at it, how we transform it, what we use it for, and how fairly it is made available to all who need it.

An essential moral principle applied to the economic sphere is that: all economic activity (the production, distribution, consumption, and exchange of material goods) that takes place within a society ought to be morally and legislatively subordinate to the activity of *politics*. For some this is a controversial claim but it is predicated on the assumption that no human activity within the context of social life is outside the reach of public policies informed by the value of the common good.

Today in most advanced capitalist societies, when ethics is introduced into the economic field it often winds up being limited to the ethics of what goes on within and between corporations. What rarely gets examined is the larger social/political context in which businesses of any and all kinds are permitted to operate and regulated in how they do so. When Thomas Aquinas subjected economic behavior to moral scrutiny he reflected a common medieval view that carried over into the Reformation and Calvin's Geneva despite theological differences on other topics. Since the modern emancipation of economics from the moral oversight of a society steeped at least in part in religiously derived values, economic activity has come to be seen as a sphere of life independent of any external moral evaluation.

Nevertheless, even the most libertarian minimal states still set the rules and regulations for the behavior of their citizens, both in groups and, to a lesser degree, for individuals (depending on the degree of personal freedom a society recognizes). These rules and regulations are, minimally, intended to prevent harm to some by the actions of others. Any economic enterprise, individual or corporate, necessarily impinges on the lives of people within the society insofar as it requires employees, owners, stockholders, producers, consumers, and stakeholders (i.e., anyone whose life is affected even tangentially by the activities of the business). A single entrepreneurial hotdog vendor on the streets of any major city as well as a multinational pharmaceutical corporation have to meet certain codes of sanitation and safety in order to do business legally.

But all licensing decisions regarding standards and regulations for safety or sanitation in the workplace and for the goods produced there are ultimately political decisions. They ought therefore to be the result of reasoned and fully participatory deliberations determining public policy for the society in question. These fundamentally political decisions represent the most vital work of a representative democracy, through elected delegates and governmental administrators. They have the obligation of deciding even what will count as a business and under what conditions it should be given the freedom to operate in public space. Regulation of economic activity is one of the most vital political acts of social responsibility a society has to carry out. Even the decision not to regulate some aspects of economic activity is a political decision. As Robert Kuttner has pointed out "a decision to allow markets, flaws and all, free rein is just one political choice among many. *There is no escape from politics.*"[1]

Advocates of the free market in its pure form (hardly to be found in practice anywhere) abhor all deliberative, societal decision-making as an unwarranted intrusion into the voluntary commercial transactions of consenting adults. In its own way, therefore, a reliance solely upon the market to solve social problems in the absence of politics is, as Kuttner argues, "an insidious form of contempt for political democracy. Excluded by definition are the possibility of deliberation leading to social learning, institutional refinement, and an evolving conception of the common good. Indeed, the essence of the [Public Choice] theory [the political theory of the unimpeded free market] is to deny that such a thing as the common good exists, except as the sum of selfish individual goods."[2]

In the face of the rising dominance of Public Choice theory, Kuttner develops a forceful argument for the restoration of public democracy and the revitalization of politics, a task we have also argued belongs to a strong ethics of community. Political philosopher Hanna Pitkin says "What distinguishes politics [is] the possibility of a shared, collective, deliberate, active intervention in our fate, in what would otherwise be the byproduct of private decisions . . . [T]he distinctive promise of political freedom remains the possibility of genuine collective action, an entire community consciously and jointly shaping its policy, its way of life."[3] Only a strong democracy will be able to put markets in their place, under the oversight of the *polis* which they are ultimately to serve, not to master or be detached from.

Placing business and economic activity under the aegis of politics presupposes a prior public commitment to a common good by the society in

[1]   Robert Kuttner, *Everything for Sale: The Virtues and Limits of Markets* (New York: Alfred A. Knopf, 1997), 329.
[2]   Kuttner, 337.
[3]   Pitkin is quoted in Kuttner, 343.

which the business will operate. Such a commitment means that the fundamental needs of the people in the society for living lives of well-being and flourishing have been given a moral priority over the particular desires of any given individual or group within the society.

A good and just society usually agrees that it is in the best interests of everyone not to allow the sale and use of dangerous drugs without societal oversight because unregulated drugs can harm the individuals who take them. This is a harm that eventually ramifies into harm for others who comprise the neighborhoods and workplaces where the drug user lives and works. It also eventually hurts the society as a whole if it has chosen, through its health care system, to provide medical support for the drug addict and through its penal system incarceration for the dealer who has been convicted.

There is, of course, acrimonious debate over just what the appropriate limits of societal oversight of economic activity ought to be. But virtually no one, not even the extreme libertarian, would argue that society can afford to void all social regulation of economic behavior. Deceit in trade must be prohibited even if what is traded is subject only to market considerations. Less libertarian societies would also restrict the *kind* of product that can be offered for trade, e.g., certain lethal drugs or weaponry, and limit the persons eligible to purchase them – adults, not children.

If matter matters and is essential to a flourishing life, then one crucial political decision is how the society will see to it that all persons have access to the minimal quality, kind, and amount of material goods necessary for that life. And even if a society can decide what count as minimal standards for the availability of basic economic goods, it might, in the name of justice, also want to address the issue of the relative disparities of wealth among its citizens. A good and just society might see to it that all persons, including the poorest, have sufficient housing to sustain their bodily need for shelter, but if there are people who use their wealth to own and live in more luxurious homes than one can count, that degree of economic disparity clearly would have profound negative consequences on the spirit of the poor, as well as on their ability to contribute equally to the decision-making of the polity as a whole. Those who are economically disadvantaged are far less likely to have the political power to contribute equally to societal decisions and feel far less loyal to the social order itself and to the politics that sustains its basic institutions and shapes its policies. (This lack of loyalty might itself be a problem to the degree that it could lead to social unrest, a problem for both rich and poor alike.) Wealth, unfortunately, often gives those who possess it greater political influence and access to political power (through their ability to contribute disproportionately to political campaigns and politicians) than those without it.

Disparities in resources in and of themselves, of course, are not always a matter of economic justice: Michael Jordan's athletic gifts are clearly superior to those of most other peoples. But disparity in athletic talent would not affect those who are less well-endowed in that respect if their lack of athletic talent did not disadvantage them in securing the fundamental goods necessary for leading a full life. (They might not receive the public adulation or fame that he has acquired, but public celebrity, as such, is not a fundamental good to which all ought to have an equal claim.)

Nevertheless, when a school teacher in an inner city neighborhood earns only an infinitesimal portion of Mr. Jordan's income despite doing something that is arguably far more important for the common good, then one has to ask if economic justice is being served. The moral criterion on which this judgment is based is: what actions do the most to serve the common good? Serving the common good means doing what will help the most people, especially the most disadvantaged, lead lives of well-being and flourishing in the context of a cooperative mutual endeavor. If the schoolteacher is making a major contribution to the common good, her economic reward should not be wildly disproportionate to Mr. Jordan's even if strict equality of monetary reward is not feasible.

On the other hand, there are some persons whose essential needs are so great they are justified in receiving a disproportionate amount of the society's economic resources in order to meet their needs even if their contribution to the common good is minimal. An elderly person in need of nursing care will draw down more from the public pool of resources than a healthy teenager. Most people would find that disproportionate level of economic support fair and just even though it is based solely on need, not individual meritorious contribution to the overall social good. (Some might say that the elderly person's previous years of contributions to the society have "earned" him social support. But not all persons in need have made such contributions or could meet the standard of meritorious achievement.)

Disproportionate need, not merit, in a wealthy society is what justifies the focus in an ethic of economic justice on the needs of the poor rather than the desires of the rich. Generally within a philosophy of individualism the poor are treated as having less value than the rich (since they are often regarded as having failed to make good use of their presumably equally distributed individual freedom). They are disproportionately shut out of equal decision-making in the polity, they have less ability to take advantage of the resources available to the better endowed, and they are more likely to feel disempowered and their dignity disrespected. The effects of poverty on the poor are almost always negative and complex, ramifying deeply into their psyches, into the attitudes the rich have toward them, and into the social fabric as a whole.

Property, Poverty, and Politics

With these general principles of economic justice in mind, we can turn to the role small communities might play in dealing with their application at both the communal and the societal level. Treating issues of justice in the economic realm can be prepared for within Christian communities that operate by their own internal values. We can recall the early *koinonia* which practiced a primitive form of economic communism as did many of the communal groups in nineteenth-century America. Aquinas, Calvin, the Puritans, and the early Mormons all made clear that the economic resources of the members of the religious community were at the service of the poor and of the community as a whole. The principle in those religiously based associations was simply that those who had need would be given the resources necessary to meet that need from a common pool of goods.

Stewardship is the common term used to refer to the biblical notion that what we "possess" is, in effect, ours only as a loan from God. The prevailing contemporary notion that the individual is the unrestricted lord and master not only of his own person but of all that he can legitimately secure for himself through inheritance, contract, investment, financial dealmaking, or labor is clearly at odds with this notion of stewardship. And yet it is the strongest obstacle to dealing with the underlying issues of economic justice.

The individual's unlimited right to do with his private property what-ever he wishes has never been a controlling value in a Christian ethic of economic justice. Private property is always subject to the needs of the society as a whole, as they are defined especially by the needs of the poor. As Aquinas conceded, even a poor person has a right to take prop-erty from the wealthy if his fundamental needs, e.g., food, are not being provided by charity alone. "A starving man has a right to his neighbor's bread."[4]

---

[4] See John A. Ryan, "The Economic Philosophy of St. Thomas," in Robert E. Brennan, ed., *Essays in Thomism* (New York: Sheed and Ward, 1942), 246, for a fuller reading of Thomas's economic ethics.

This view of property as being at the disposal of the society for helping the most needy was fundamentally challenged by the rise of the
free-market economy and what C. B. Macpherson has called the philosophy of "possessive individualism." Connected with liberal political
philosophy, this term, according to Macpherson, refers to the belief that
the individual "is essentially the proprietor of his own person or capacities,
owing nothing to society for them. The individual was seen neither as
a moral whole, nor as part of a larger social whole, but as an owner
of himself . . . Political society becomes a calculated device for the protection of this property and for the maintenance of an orderly relation of
exchange."[5]

This view is profoundly at odds with an ethics of community which
simply cannot recognize the asocial nature of human persons, nor of their
unlimited right to private ownership of what ultimately belongs to God
and the commonweal. But western societies are so imbued with the notion of possessive individualism that it is hard to remember that property is
essentially to be valued primarily for its *utility* or capacity to serve the
fundamental interests of persons in society. Naturally, some forms of property, judged by their usefulness in serving human needs, have been determined in just societies to be best held privately. This would apply to such
personal items as one's clothing, house, books, etc., though the exact
boundary line between private and public proprietorship is hard to draw
and ought to be generally determined contextually and pragmatically. (If a
private pharmaceutical company develops the one and only drug effective
in combating AIDS does it have a moral right to a monopoly on its
production, pricing and distribution?) As Pemberton and Finn argue in
their excellent book on developing a Christian economic ethic, "every
individual has the right to own and consume what is needed for a basic
standard of living. On the other hand, when the ownership of material
things by someone stands in the way of the livelihood and flourishing of
others, the owner has the obligation to alter or terminate that ownership."[6] I would only add that it is not just the owner who has the right to
that decision: it is also up to the society to determine, by democratic
political decision-making, what inducements and/or penalties ought to be
developed to insure that that alteration or termination of ownership takes
place in the economic sphere.

[5]   C. B. Macpherson, *The Political Theory of Possessive Individualism* (Oxford: Oxford
University Press, 1972), 275.
[6]   Prentiss L. Pemberton and Daniel Rush Finn, *Toward a Christian Economic Ethic*
(Minneapolis: Winston Press, 1985), 170.

One of the fundamental reasons for insisting upon access to the goods necessary for well-being and flourishing is that our very dignity requires it. The US Roman Catholic bishops have recently addressed the economic order precisely on the basis of how that order can best respect and support human dignity. The bishops asked succinctly three moral questions of any economy: what does it do for people, what does it do to them, and how do people participate in it?[7] The principal themes of their pastoral letter include their convictions that all economic decisions must respect the dignity of the person, that that dignity can be realized only in community, that all have a right to participate in the life of their society, that the poor have a special need for protection from the ravages of economic deprivation, that economic rights are as important as other human rights, and that "society as a whole, acting through public and private institutions, has the moral responsibility to enhance human dignity and protect human rights."[8]

Some jobs that secure for individuals needed economic resources might be profitable to the individual in the short run but if they detract from the overall moral health of the society, they contribute to social injustice. Someone who works for a tobacco company or advertising agency which encourages people to take up smoking, or who works simply to satisfy his superficial needs by overindulgence in trivial pursuits is not contributing to the well-being of his society nor using his talents in the most morally worthy way. Communities can be especially effective in helping to educate their members on how to pursue their interests in ways that are both true to the individual's talents and contributory to the common good. If one decides to leave one job in order to train for another more in keeping with principles of social justice, the community can be a vital resource in providing transitional financial and emotional support for him and his family.

In many ways communities can also be essential to the feeling of personal worth and dignity for the poor. Within communities persons who are currently poor (poverty being often temporary and relative to the wealth of others) can receive the direct, personal attention that is sensitive to their individual situations. As the Pastoral Letter puts it, economic "decisions must be judged in light of what they do *for* the poor, what they do *to* the poor, and what they enable the poor to do *for themselves*. The

---

[7] National Conference of Catholic Bishops, *Economic Justice for All: Pastoral Letter on Catholic Social Teaching and the US Economy* (Washington: United States Catholic Conference, 1986), 1.

[8] Catholic Bishops, *Economic Justice for All*, ix–xi.

fundamental moral criterion for all economic decisions, policies, and institutions is this: They must be at the service of *all people, especially the poor.*"[9]

The poor must be treated as the full persons they are, not as statistics or
impersonal objects of a "case load" by a social worker. We also have to be
wary of labeling a class of persons as "the" poor, since poverty is both
relative to wealth and individuals who are poor at some times are not poor
at all times. Persons are not defined by their economic condition. An ethic
of economic justice must avoid depersonalizing and objectifying *persons*
simply because at one time or another they may suffer from poverty.
Communities can be a vital place in which the poor are given affirmation
of themselves as *persons*, not simply as members of a class.

Voluntary communities by themselves, however, or even in collabora-
tion with each other, are generally unable to alter the underlying economic and social conditions that produce and perpetuate poverty in the
first place. Nor are they able in any realistic or effective manner to respond
to the poverty beyond their own membership. The members can of
course do "charity" work, but this is primarily individual to individual, or
anonymous institutional transfer of money to charitable agencies or individuals, and does not reach all who are poor, nor does it address the
structural reasons for poverty in the first place.

To address poverty (with all its disabling, demeaning, and disempowering
consequences) requires a step into public policy analysis, reform, and political action. It is at this stage, contemplating what such action entails that
many people draw back into their community's direct personal responses
to poverty. They cannot face what looks like to them the intricate, complex, massively detailed and arcane aspects of economic and political analysis and policy formation through the political process. Besides, there are
an almost infinite number of policy experts and sophisticated analysts who
make entry into public policy formation daunting to those in the lay
public who are not indoctrinated in the jargon and mindset of the experts.

But we have to remember that in a democracy there is a distinction that
must be drawn between experts who have the analysis of data under their
control and the citizenry which has the formation of public policy as its
right and obligation. Citizens ultimately have the right and the responsibility to determine public policy by political means: they set the goals and
values for public action as it affects private and group behavior. They may
not know the details the way the experts do, but they can establish the
values they want policy to implement and then direct the experts to tell
them what would happen if they choose policy *A* rather than policy *B* in

---

[9]   Catholic Bishops, *Economic Justice for All*, 12.

pursuit of those values. The citizens through their representatives, can determine, for example, that a policy of taxing the rich proportionally more than the poor (through a version of progressive taxation) is more just than a regressive tax scheme in which the same percentage of taxes is taken from smaller incomes as from larger ones. The analysts can then tell the policy-makers that their preferred policy will in all likelihood yield x amount of revenues or y amount, as well as what effect this policy will likely have on the ability of the poor to afford basic goods. They can even make some reasonable predictions about the psychological effects of such a policy both on those who would benefit directly from it and those who would not. Then the policy-makers can take that data into account, determine what is a reasonable trade-off between one set of anticipated results and another, and still make a morally grounded decision as to which policy is relatively more just. The analysis does not determine the policy, but it does inform it with respect to its anticipated effectiveness. The policy determines which analyses are relevant to the issue at hand. Facts don't drive policy but a policy out of touch with facts is irrelevant and ineffective.

Within communities the discussion and debate about over-all social policy can be carried on without being side-tracked by esoteric references to arcane data. Utilizing the best talents of their members, of course, may permit them to hear from people in their midst who know, given their secular vocations, how to translate data into comprehensible concepts for lay persons. But the community is the best place to begin the discussion about the basic moral values at stake even though the decisions reached there will eventually have to carried over into the society through the societal political process. If the community is not the ultimate forum for moral conversation about basic social values, where else would it be found?

Economic Democracy

One crucial issue that ought to be the subject of such conversation is the application of democratic principles to the economic order as well as to the political one. If equal democratic participation is a virtue in the political arena, there is no reason why it should not also prevail in the economic arena. *Economic democracy* should be as important a value as political democracy. It is odd not that most businesses are not democratic but that few find this lack of democracy in the organization and running of the workplace problematic. The decisions within a business are usually made only by top management, with the ritual concurrence of the stockholders whose economic self-interest rarely extends to empowering the workers whose labor makes them rich. But if economic activity is secondary to enabling persons to live lives of well-being and flourishing in a just society, then why shouldn't the internal arrangement of businesses be subject to the same criteria of justice as prevail in the society as a whole? Charles W. Anderson has pointed out that because "we do not believe that voluntary associations have absolute license to define their own ends and assess their own performance," we ought to "believe that we are perfectly able, and entitled as a matter of political judgment, to decide what a corporation, or a union, or a school, *is* and what it is *expected to do*"[10] for us, the citizens of the larger society.

Inasmuch as economic institutions provide us with goods essential to our well-being and flourishing, and do so in ways that directly affect our public and social lives, we have, says political philosopher William M. Sullivan, a need "to extend the spirit of republican democratic life into the sphere of the major economic and administrative institutions"[11] of our society. If the social nature of human beings is to be given more than lip service when fundamental resources such as those provided by economic activity are at stake, then we need to think of the common good, as Philip Selznick has observed, "as more profoundly systemic, not *reducible* to individual interests or attributes, yet *testable* by its contribution to personal well-being. The common good is served . . . by institutions that provide collective goods . . . The strength or weakness of these institutions is a communal attribute, not an individual one."[12] Economic democracy is precisely the attempt to provide public institutional and communally-based values to the economic order.

This is not to deny that there can be, as there is in any good community, a place for some hierarchical economic power provided that it is justified by its effectiveness and by group consensus. A business (all those working for it) could decide that it will vest some decisions in those people whom it delegates to manage or administer its affairs. A church, for example, gives its administrative managers (who usually are, but need not

[10] Charles W. Anderson, "How to Make a Good Society," in Karol Edward Soltan and Stephen L. Elkin, eds., *The Constitution of Good Societies* (University Park, Penn.: The Pennsylvania State University Press, 1996), 110.

[11] William M. Sullivan, from *Reconstructing Public Philosophy* (Berkeley: University of California Press, 1982), in Robert Bellah et al., eds., *Individualism and Commitment in American Life: Readings on the Themes of Habits of the Heart* (New York: Harper and Row, 1988), 395.

[12] Philip Selznick, *The Moral Commonwealth: Social Theory and the Promise of Community* (Berkeley: University of California Press, 1992), 537.

be, clergy) the discretionary power to make many decisions for the running of the institutional dimensions of the community without constant interference or ratification by the membership as a whole. A business could adopt a similar strategy. As long as there are ample opportunities for the group to openly discuss and vote on policies of major importance, no harm would be done by delegating some discretionary authority to those whose "ministries" might be management and administration.

It would be extremely odd if the populace that is empowered to decide fundamental social policy *for* a business is regarded as too untrustworthy to decide fundamental economic policy *within* a corporation. If freedom is a high political virtue, why should a worker not be free to exercise his power in and through a more or less democratic decision-making structure within the business for which he works?

Regulation

It is the society itself, by democratic decision-making, that ought to determine what kinds of businesses are legitimate, under what conditions they can operate and what standards of safety and health their operations and products should meet. Regulation can, of course, be overly intrusive and bogged down in red tape and bureaucratic trivia. Governmental agencies can be overly intrusive and unresponsive to the practicalities of life on the ground. But the principle of societal oversight of business activity, from the safety of the workplace to the safety of the product itself, is essential in any good and just society.

Taxation

There is probably no more contentious public and economic issue today than that of taxation. Ironically, in most western democracies the only "obligation," other than obeying the laws, a citizen has to his or her country is to pay taxes. (In most societies one is free not to vote, and unless there is an emergency most do not have to serve in the military.) And yet, in spite of this minimal obligatory "contribution" to their society's welfare, most persons complain the hardest about being taxed. At the same time they are generally the most oblivious about what taxes are and what they do for themselves and others in the society.

One person in the United States was heard saying that she was tired of supporting people on welfare through her taxes. Stop taxing me, she said, for their support. Let the federal government take care of them. This attitude is part of the "trashing government" syndrome mentioned earlier. As long as people see government as remote, alien, and hostile to their interests they see no benefit in giving up what they think they have first claim on, their wealth, in order to help others.

Once again, it is necessary for communities to help their members understand what a societal taxation scheme really is and whom it is designed to serve. If the society has an obligation to provide for public goods, then it has to pay for the delivery of those goods. In accordance with principles of justice, it has been decided by most societies that if a good is truly public then the fairest way to raise the revenues for it is by a tax upon the public. This is true even when not every member of the public will benefit directly from the provision of that good. An elderly person with no school-aged children will be taxed as will a couple with school-aged children for the support of the public schools in that municipality. Likewise, all the citizens will be taxed for the construction of public roads, even though some will never drive on them. The elderly will, of course, ultimately benefit by living in a municipality that educates its children well because it will attract new families who will contribute to the life and well-being of that community. But to see this truth requires thinking politically and socially beyond private self-interest.

The question is not just who should be taxed for public goods but also by what means. And justice leads one to the conclusion that a progressive tax scheme is fairer than a regressive one. If every citizen pays 10 per cent tax on each item purchased, then for the wealthy that 10 per cent is far less damaging to their "discretionary" income than it is for a poor person who normally has little discretionary income after having paid out of his own pocket, in a free-market society, for the minimal amount of food, clothing, and shelter necessary for basic well-being.

But all the plans for fair taxation pale into insignificance if society has not convinced its citizens that their income is not solely theirs to do with as they want. When people talk about government "taking" their money they are indulging in the same myth that lies at the heart of possessive individualism, namely that what we "earn" is ours by right and can only be "taken" from us against our will and in violation of our rights. But in a just society, nothing is really being "taken" from individuals if there is a prior commitment to provide basic and essential goods to all persons empowering them to lead lives of well-being and flourishing both for individual fulfillment as well as for the society as a whole. In fact, in a just society taxes become the simplest and fairest way by which citizens can most effectively make their contribution to the common good. Only in a society imbued with the ideology of the primacy of self-interest, possessiveness and individualism do people feel aggrieved at any concept of taxation as a taking of what is primordially "theirs."

This is not to say that there cannot be serious and legitimate debate about the exact details of a fair tax system and how it is administered. Again, the smaller communities can both discuss with and instruct their members in the underlying rationale of taxation as such and, utilizing the talents of various members, even talk about the relative merits of various tax proposals. This is clearly not an illegitimate mixing of religion and economics, or religion and politics. It is a practical way by which communities (which are far less likely to be polarized than political organizations) can fulfill their obligation to be good stewards for the society of which they are a part.

An ethics of community must insist that discussion of political and economic issues within the group is not a violation of its primary focus on fellowship and communality. As long as there is a fundamental unity between body and soul, community and society, the personal and the political, the communal and the economic, then bridging the activities appropriate to each is an essential task for all those who comprise community.

International Order

To this point we have been concerned almost exclusively with the relation between communities and societies or nation-states. If an ethic of community is ultimately guided by a vision of a universal community, we need to touch briefly on the question of an international or global society. While there are many practical obstacles in the way of some kind of international political federation of nation-states, the idea is not as far-fetched as it might have seemed just a half century ago. The national boundaries that divide states along political, historical, and ethnic lines are being transcended daily by economic transactions and political alliances that are truly global in scope. Ideas, resources, technologies, finances, trading, communications, personnel: all cross national borders in the form of multinational corporations whose markets, investments, production, research, trading, and distribution extend into and certainly have effects upon virtually every country on earth.

Rosabeth Kanter has claimed that there is an emerging "world class," a social class "defined by its ability to command resources and operate beyond borders and across wide territories."[13] This "world class" is comprised

---

[13]   Rosabeth Moss Kanter, *World Class: Thriving Locally in the Global Economy* (New York: Touchstone, Simon and Schuster, 1997), 22.

of persons who have the ability to exploit concepts, competence, and connections throughout a vast interconnected global economy. She wants to believe that the rise of the world class can be harnessed to help local communities remain vital sources of identity and well-being.[14] But these communities must make their peace with what she takes to be the inevitability of economic globalization. The world is becoming a kind of gigantic shopping mall, which brings all the best material and informational goods together in ways that are accessible to people almost instantaneously no matter where they are located on the planet and "promises to give everyone access to the world's best."[15]

As producers and consumers move to develop international links, they are forced to upgrade local sites of production to world standards. Each local site therefore "has a stake in reinforcing the others' cosmopolitan thrust. Together they encourage governments to loosen local restraints, develop policies compatible with the rest of the world, and facilitate cross-border activity. And they develop cosmopolitan leaders who carry concepts from one place to another, pressuring local units to reduce their differences and join the world class."[16]

Any adequate ethics of community must acknowledge the rise of the internationalization of world commerce. How it accommodates it or responds to it is the crucial issue. If, as we have argued, economic activity ought to be subject to public political decision-making, regulation, and policy, then who constitutes the political decision-makers or the global polity capable of overseeing global business? The question that Kanter does not address adequately is what kind of global politics is a match for global business. She speaks approvingly of international companies working around or bypassing local governmental rules and regulations when the latter prove to be cumbersome or a hindrance to international commerce. While such bypass might be helpful in sustaining the global shopping mall, it also threatens to bypass the value question of whether it is an unqualified virtue to have such a panoply of goods available all the time to everyone on demand. She simply doesn't raise the question of whether all these goods are truly good *for* persons or ought to constitute the heart of a good society. She makes no value judgment as to the human worth of products, apparently content to let the market determine that. As we have seen, however, the market is a poor determiner of the value of essential public goods such as education, medical care, safety, or social security, etc. It also

[14] Kanter, 29.
[15] Kanter, 41.
[16] Kanter, 73.

shuts out those without the financial means to participate meaningfully. The unregulated free market is not a political democracy.

A second value question bypassed in her discussion is whether there is a virtue in having the people most directly affected by a global economy (those whose labor makes it possible, or those whose labor has been bypassed because they can't compete or contribute, or those who cannot labor meaningfully because of the material and psychological disadvantages they have suffered in poor debt-ridden countries) virtually shut out of the decisions made by the world-class elites. It might be true in the short run that handing over both the politics and the economics of a global economy to the entrepreneurs and CEOs of major multinational corporations would be economically "efficient" in getting goods into the marketplace where those wealthy enough to purchase them can be found. But market efficiency does not always correlate with political democracy, in which all the stakeholders (not just the stockholders) in an economic system ought to have a voice and an equality of political power to effect and affect crucial economic policies and activities according to principles of justice as fairness.

To date the only practical associations persons have found to exercise democratically based political power are societies (though people can, as we have argued, begin the first practice of democratic power in communities, when they function as communities of incipient citizenry). It would be naive to think that global networks constitute community, as we have defined the term, but a global society consisting of multiple units (i.e., smaller societies modeled on nation-states and even smaller units such as communities) all bound together by a kind of political confederation is not a completely unfeasible idea. Through the United Nations, nation-states have learned how to cooperate for mutual ventures that redound to the benefit of many nations in addition to their own. Europe is rapidly moving from a geography of states with mutual animosities, fears, and dense borders to a single self-styled commercially linked "community," with common economic and political features, including a common currency and porous borders.

The End of the Nation-state?

Nation-states themselves can now begin to be seen as no longer quasi-sacred entities whose boundaries have been defined once and for all time. Societies as we have known them are virtually coterminous with nation-states and as such are historically contingent forms of human association. As political philosopher John Dunn has observed, nation-states are not the

only or even ideal form of social grouping available to the moral imagination (quite apart from those we have called communities). Dunn argues
that the "fiercely demanding images of human fulfilment and human
liberty . . . indict the reality of *every* modern state and modern society."[17]
He argues that nationalism, the defense of the nation-state, is "the starkest
political shame of the twentieth century" and is simply a "habit of accommodation of which we feel the moral shabbiness readily enough ourselves."[18] The reason for this blunt assessment is Dunn's feeling that as a
body of persons that excludes noncitizens, the nation-state contradicts
some of the basic inclusionary moral tenets of natural law, Christianity,
and secular rationalism. It is nothing more than "one level in a conceptual
continuum which reaches from the single morally irresponsible individual
to the morally irresponsible species man the whole globe over [and as such
is] simply one version of the self-righteous politics of ethical relativism."[19]
Dunn does not, to be sure, see a practical alternative to the nation-state
given the present political and economic conditions of the world, nor does
he place any hope in an eschatological, transcendent goal for humankind.
But he does remind us that when we speak of society, we do so within the
context of an historically contingent period.

From the point of view of a Christian moral ontology, in which God's
purpose for the future is a central ontological factor, an ethics of community cannot give in to despair about ever reaching beyond the arbitrary lines of demarcation that presently define society as coterminous,
for political purposes, with the nation-state. But eschatological hope for
a universal "community" of humankind does not translate easily into
practical political programs for advancing toward a "global society." Therefore, we need to retain a certain degree of Niebuhrian pessimism regarding an advance beyond the nation-state at least in the short run.
Nevertheless, a Christian ontology must always retain an urge toward
a more inclusive society of persons and never absolutize or canonize the
nation-state as such. An ethics of community can embrace the move
toward a global society without fear provided that the principles of justice it has embraced are incorporated into the political policies of the
global society and that provision is made for the smaller, more intimate
communities that constitute the personal core of any society or group
of societies.

---

[17]   John Dunn, *Western Political Theory in the Face of the Future* (Cambridge: Cambridge
University Press, 1979), 18.
[18]   Dunn, 57, 59.
[19]   Dunn, 63.

One advantage that the emergence of a world class might have, if it is carefully managed, is in producing a growing awareness of human beings' fundamental interrelatedness and common humanity. As in any authentic community, of course, the uniqueness and particularity of each smaller unit must be celebrated and enhanced by virtue of the principle of heterocentricity. There is no reason to believe that a global society cannot encourage the appreciation and nurture of those distinct features of particular groups, nations, and ethnicities as they contribute to the multicolored, multitextured, multicultural tapestry that constitutes the global society.

While the global links between all the people of the earth are primarily defined by the world class at the present moment in economic terms, it is not difficult to see how economic commonalties might lead people to see deeper points of commonality between themselves and others. But if this advantage of world trade is to be a virtue rather than an end in itself, however, it must be linked directly to efforts to bring about a global sense of justice, stakeholding by all the world's people, and the empowerment of all to contribute to fundamental political decisions that affect the world "community."

In late 1999 the World Trade Organization held a meeting in Seattle, Washington. It was met by massive protest on the part of many different groups whose underlying message was that world trade had to be accountable to public values concerning exploitation of third-world workers and the environment. They were asking, in effect, that global trade be subject to the same moral principles as actions within a single nation-state. When the children of the Sudan are taken with the same degree of compassion and justice as the children of San Diego or Sussex, and when structures and policies are created and actions are taken to actualize that compassion and sense of justice, then the barriers to some kind of world federation of societies will have started to come down.

An ethics of community can embrace the goal of a global society as it is informed by the values of both community and a good and just society. The Niebuhr caution can be invoked to remind it that there is no easy walk to the Kingdom of God and that it is particularly dangerous to identify a way-station as the final destination. But if an ethics of community stops at the boundary of the nation-state it will have failed to carry forward the full power latent in the overriding element in its own moral ontology: the power of God's intention to realize itself fully and historically in the social and communal lives of all the world's people such that it would bring to mind, as a Puritan once said, a new heaven and a new earth wherein dwells righteousness and God himself will be with his people.

Chapter 9

Conclusion

This examination of an ethics of community has moved along a trajectory defined by the lure of intimate community and the demands of impersonal society. As the world becomes increasingly interdependent economically, the necessity for an ethics of political and societal responsibility becomes ever stronger. Christians simply cannot afford to ignore the imperatives of learning to live with others who do not necessarily share their religious faith. We live in a global megalopolis whose political and economic realities we can avoid only at our own practical peril. An ethics of community informed by Christian moral principles, however, has an additional reason to take these realities seriously: they constitute part of the world that God has created, loved, redeemed, and continues to care for.

If we have learned anything from our study of community we also know that we cannot find the resources for dealing with this world responsibly unless we also ground ourselves in the realities of smaller, more intense communities in and through which our full being as the creatures God intended us to be is called forth. From within a world intended by God for fulfillment through the values that community tries to embody (mutuality, heterocentricity, compassion, love), we are called both into community and into the institutions that comprise society. Community nourishes us at our deepest personal levels and society enables us to extend the principles of justice to those whom we may never know personally. It is highly unlikely that we could act justly in a world that operates primarily by impersonal rules and structures unless we were first empowered and enriched by a world that speaks to the very core of our being, a core that is by God's design essentially communal.

Community and society need each other. Without the resources of persons shaped by community societies would become nothing more than impersonal machines for the balancing of political and economic power.

Without the resources of society, communities could not survive nor could they act responsibly toward persons beyond their "boundaries."

One of the great tragedies of our time is the great divorce that has sometimes marked the relation between community and society. Christians often flee the dilemmas and perplexities, the moral ambiguities and power politics of society by retreating into communities increasingly withdrawn psychologically (though hardly ever economically) from the larger society in which they find themselves. People consumed with the pursuit of political and economic power often find communities cloying, irrelevant, or at best a harmless diversion from the realities that consume the better part of their lives.

In many western democracies today we are facing a crisis. More and more people have become distrustful of the government and believe that it has little to do with what they define as their "real" lives. Fewer people seem to vote each year and fewer still know the names of their representatives. While they often join small support groups to find the personal resources for avoiding alienation and isolation, they find little time or inclination to join political associations intended to advance the interests of the public good as a whole. The crisis of democracy can only be exacerbated by this centrifugal force that pulls communities and societies further apart. More and more people simply fail to see how their private and public lives are woven together in anything more than an incidental or superficial way. What they lack is an overarching philosophy of unity.

This is precisely why an ethics of community needs to be grounded in a moral ontology. The components of that ontology within the Christian tradition include:

1) grounding in an ontology in which God is the most decisive factor;
2) the belief that God's intentions and actions constitute the basis and direction for human behavior;
3) a construal drawn from the testimony of Scripture, reason, tradition, and experience, that the divine intention in history is the creation of an inclusive union of all persons;
4) at the core of this union will be the virtues and practices of mutual love, heterocentric actions, and delight in the fellowship of others;
5) until the final community or kingdom is achieved in all its fullness, human beings must learn to live with each other in societies characterized essentially by justice;
6) societal justice will apply primarily to the political and economic relations that constitute the society in question; and

7) these relations are to be taken with utmost seriousness because they constitute the material life of persons and, from God's point of view, matter matters as part of the well-being and flourishing of all persons.

The relation between community and society will remain one of creative tension, not radical separation or total identification. Communities will, ideally, always be fellowships of direct, personal, intimate relationships. In the Christian tradition they will be sustained in part but decisively by the power of God, not simply by the rules and forces of human sociality. The gracious actions of God (redemption, renewal, empowerment) will be experienced in these communities more fully than elsewhere.

They will not, however, constitute the whole of human life. Part of the unfulfilled nature of the human world that is still historically developing is the necessity to organize much of social life around principles of impersonal and indirect relations. Communities cannot responsibly claim that because they are the venue for the most direct and personal relationship with God and other persons in fellowship with them, they are therefore excused from responsibility for life in society. Communities can stand prophetically against the nations when the latter deviate from the standards of justice and decency, righteousness and civility. But they cannot be against the nations absolutely. The nations still remain the chief agents for the administration of social justice for all persons. Even while they ought to be working to transcend the boundaries of the nation-state (a mere creature of a particular historical epoch of human politics), communities must learn to deal with the political and economic structures of the nation-state because they are powerful shapers of concrete human life. Until those structures are brought under democratic control, they will remain instruments of oppression and alienation for many persons, especially under the conditions of the disproportionate allocation of power.

The religious communities that constitute the most powerful nation-states today need, therefore, to take their political responsibilities seriously. This means, as I have argued throughout, that churches ought to be centers for the discussion, debate, and reflection on overarching political philosophies as well as on concrete political and economic policies for the short run.

The potential power of the religious community is enormous, both for deepening the spiritual lives of its members but also for strengthening their attachments to the political and economic world around them. There is no place more conducive for teaching and experiencing the power of love than community. On the basis of that experience, there is no place more apt for preparing people to move out into a world in which justice (the approximation of love under the conditions of societal life) is to character-ize human relations. Love removes fear and unshackles the heart so that it can compassionately encompass a vast array of "others." Justice puts the heart to work in a world in which impersonal relations among the many others are the norm.

An ethic of community will have come a long way toward its final realization when communities provide their members with the resources for living most authentically and deeply in and through the power of God. Consequently, they will also fulfill their destiny when they live those lives for persons temporarily outside their boundaries. And that will mean living in the knowledge of politics and economics, debating the policies and principles that inform them, and taking their democratic responsibilities for the polity as a whole as seriously as they take the delight and joy of fellowship itself.

Bibliography

Alejandro, Roberto. 1993: Rawls's Communitarianism. In *Canadian Journal of Philosophy*, 23, 1, March, 1993, 75–100.

Ammerman, Nancy Tatom. 1997: *Congregation and Community*. New Brunswick: Rutgers University Press.

Anderson, Charles W. 1996: How to Make a Good Society. In *The Constitution of Good Societies*, eds. Karol Edward Soltan and Stephen L. Elkin. University Park: The Pennsylvania State University Press, 103–17.

Aquinas, Thomas. 1945: In Anton Pegis, ed., *Basic Writings of Saint Thomas Aquinas*. New York: Random House.

Aquinas, Thomas. 1972: In Mary T. Clark, ed., *An Aquinas Reader*. New York: Doubleday.

Arrington, Leonard, Feramorz Y. Fox and Dean L. May. 1992: *Building the City of God: Community and Cooperation Among the Mormons*, 2nd edn. Urbana and Chicago: University of Chicago Press.

Avineri, Shlomo and Avner De-Shalit, eds. 1992: *Communitarianism and Individualism*. New York: Oxford University Press.

Bainton, Roland. 1950: *Here I Stand: A Life of Martin Luther*. New York: New American Library.

Baldwin, Alice. 1936: *The Clergy of Connecticut in Revolutionary Days*. New Haven: Yale University Press.

Banks, Robert. 1980: *Paul's Idea of Community*. Grand Rapids, Mich.: Eerdman's.

Banner, Lois W. 1978: Religious Benevolence as Social Control: A Critique of an Interpretation. In John M. Mulder and John F. Wilson, eds., *Religion in American History: Interpretive Essays*. Englewood Cliffs, NJ: Prentice-Hall, 218–35.

Barth, Karl. 1960: Christian Community and Civil Community. In *Community, State and Church: Three Essays*. Introduction by Will Herberg. Garden City: Doubleday & Co.

Beiner, Ronald. 1989: What's the Matter With Liberalism? In Allan C. Hutchinson and Leslie J. M. Green, eds., *Law and the Community*. Toronto: Carswell.

Bellah, Robert, et al. 1985: *Habits of the Heart: Individualism and Commitment in American Life*. Berkeley: University of California Press.

Bellah, Robert. The Idea of Practices in *Habits*: A Response. In Charles H. Reynolds and Ralph V. Norman, eds., *Community in America: The Challenge of Habits of the Heart*. Berkeley: University of California Press, 269–88.

Benhabib, Seyla. 1992: *Situating the Self*. New York: Routledge.

Bennett, John C. 1961: Reinhold Niebuhr's Social Ethics. In Charles W. Kegley and Robert W. Bretall, eds., *Reinhold Niebuhr: His Religious, Social, and Political Thought*, vol. 2. New York: The Macmillan Company.

Boff, Leonardo. 1981: Theological Characteristics of a Grassroots Church. In Sergio Torres and John Eagleson, eds., *The Challenge of Basic Christian Communities*, trans. John Drury. Maryknoll: Orbis.

Boff, Leonardo. 1986: *Ecclesiogenesis: The Base Communities Reinvent the Church*. Maryknoll: Orbis.

Bonhoeffer, Dietrich. 1959: *The Cost of Discipleship*. New York: Macmillan.

Bonhoeffer, Dietrich. 1965: *Ethics*, ed. Eberhard Bethge. New York: Macmillan.

Brooks, Phillips. 1968: The Law of Growth. In William McLoughlin, ed., *The American Evangelicals 1800–1900*. New York: Harper Torchbooks, 158–70.

Bruce, Dixon. 1974: *And They All Sang Hallelujah: Plain-Folk Camp-Meeting Religion, 1800–1845*. Knoxville: University of Tennessee Press.

Brueggemann, Walter. 1997: *Theology of the Old Testament*. Minneapolis: Fortress Press.

Bushman, Richard L. 1967: *From Puritan to Yankee*. Cambridge, Mass.: Harvard University Press.

Bushnell, Horace. 1847: Prosperity Our Duty. Sermon preached in Hartford, Conn., Jan. 31, 1847.

Bushnell, Horace. 1968: Our Obligations to the Dead. In William McLoughlin, ed., *The American Evangelicals 1800–1900*. New York: Harper Torchbooks, 141–57.

Calvin, John. 1960: *Institutes of the Christian Religion*, ed. John T. McNeill, trans. Ford Lewis Battles. Philadelphia: The Westminster Press.

Calvin, John. 1964: Ecclesiastical Ordinances. In Hans J. Hillerbrand, ed., *The Reformation: A Narrative History Related by Contemporary Observers and Participants*. New York: Harper and Row.

Carnegie, Andrew. 1970: Wealth. In Joseph Frazier Wall, *Andrew Carnegie*. New York: Oxford University Press.

Conwell, Russell H. 1969: In Robert L. Ferm, ed., *Issues in American Protestantism*. Garden City: Doubleday, 236–239.

Cort, John C. 1988: *Christian Socialism*. Maryknoll: Orbis Books.

Crook, Roger. 1994: *An Introduction to Christian Ethics*. Englewood Cliffs, NJ: Prentice-Hall.

Curran, Charles. 1998: Absolute Moral Norms. In Paul T. Jersild et al., eds., *Moral Issues and Christian Response*. Forth Worth: Harcourt Brace College Publishers.

Deane, Herbert. 1963: *The Political and Social Ideas of St. Augustine*. New York: Columbia University Press.

Deidun, Tom. 1998: The Bible and Christian Ethics. In Bernard Hoose, ed., *Christian Ethics: An Introduction*. London: Cassell, 3–46.

Desroche, Henri. 1971: *The American Shakers: From Neo-Christianity to Pre-Socialism*, trans. and ed. John K. Savacool. Amherst: University of Massachusetts Press.

Dombrowski, James. 1966: *Christian Socialism in America*. New York: Octagon Books.

Duby, Georges. 1980: *The Three Orders: Feudal Society Imagined*. Chicago: University of Chicago Press.

Dunn, John. 1979: *Western Political Theory in the Face of the Future*. Cambridge: Cambridge University Press.

Dworkin, Ronald. 1992: Liberal Community. In Shlomo Avineri and Avner De-Shalit, eds., *Communitarianism and Individualism*. New York: Oxford University Press, 205–23.

Edwards, Jonathan. 1960: *The Nature of True Virtue*. Ann Arbor: University of Michigan Press.

Fergusson, David A. 1996: Macmurray's Philosophy of the Family. *Appraisal*, 1, 2 (Oct. 1996), 68–74.

Fergusson, David. 1998: *Community, Liberalism and Christian Ethics*. Cambridge: Cambridge University Press.

Finney, Charles G. 1878: *Finney's Lectures on Systematic Theology*. Grand Rapids, Mich.: Eerdmans.

Foster, Charles I. 1960: *An Errand of Mercy: The Evangelical United Front, 1790–1837*. Chapel Hill: University of North Carolina Press.

Friedman, Jeffrey. 1994: The Politics of Communitarianism. *Critical Review*, Spring 1994, 263–84.

Gauthier, David. 1988: The Liberal Individual. In Shlomo Avineri and Avner De-Shalit, eds., *Communitarianism and Individualism*. New York: Oxford University Press, 151–64.

Gewirth, Alan. 1993: Common Morality and the Community of Rights. In Gene Outka and John Reeder, Jr., eds., *Prospects for a Common Morality*. Princeton: Princeton University Press, 29–52.

Gladden, Washington. 1967: The Church, 1897. In Robert D. Cross, ed., *The Church and the City*. Indianapolis: Bobbs-Merrill, 40–51.

Gould, Carol. 1988: *Rethinking Democracy: Freedom and Social Cooperation in Politics, Economy, and Society*. Cambridge: Cambridge University Press.

Graham, Fred. 1972: *Jean Calvin: The Constructive Revolutionary*. Richmond: John Knox Press.

Greenberg, Jay R. and Stephen A. Mitchell. 1983: *Object Relations in Psychoanalytic Theory*. Cambridge, Mass.: Harvard University Press.

Greer, Rowan. 1986: *Broken Lights and Mended Lives: Theology and Common Life in the Early Church*. University Park, Penn.: Pennsylvania State University Press.

Gutman, Amy. 1992: Communitarian Critics of Liberalism. In Shlomo Avineri and Avner De-Shalit, eds., *Communitarianism and Individualism*. New York: Oxford University Press, 120–36.

Guttieriez, Gustavo. 1973: *A Theology of Liberation*, trans. and eds. Sister Caridad Inda and John Eagleson. Maryknoll: Orbis.

Handy, Robert F., ed. 1966: *The Social Gospel in America*. New York: Oxford University Press.

Hansen, Klaus J. 1981: *Mormonism and the American Experience*. Chicago: University of Chicago Press.

Hanson, Paul. 1986: *The People Called: The Growth of Community in the Bible*. San Francisco: Harper and Row.

Hardman, Keith. 1987: *Charles Grandison Finney*. Syracuse: Syracuse University Press.

Hauerwas, Stanely. 1985: *Against the Nations*. Minneapolis: Winston Press.

Hauerwas, Stanley. 1981: *A Community of Character: Toward A Constructive Christian Social Ethic*. Notre Dame: University of Notre Dame Press.

Hauerwas, Stanley. 1991: *After Christendom?* Nashville: Abingdon Press.

Hauerwas, Stanley. 1995: *In Good Company: The Church as Polis*. Notre Dame: University of Notre Dame Press.

Hayden, Dolores. 1976: *Seven American Utopias: The Architecture of Communitarian Socialism 1790–1975*. Cambridge, Mass.: MIT Press.

Hegel, G. W. F. 1967: *Hegel's Philosophy of Right*, trans. with notes by T.M. Knox. London: Oxford University Press.

Heimert, Alan. 1966: *Religion and the American Mind: From the Great Awakening to the Revolution*. Cambridge, Mass.: Harvard University Press.

Heyrman, Leigh. 1997: *Southern Cross: The Beginnings of the Bible Belt*. New York: Alfred A. Knopf.

Hostetler, John A. 1963: *Amish Society*. Baltimore: Johns Hopkins Press.

Johnson, James Turner. 1981: *Just War Tradition and the Restraint of War*. Princeton: Princeton University Press.

Jones, James. 1991: *Contemporary Psychoanalysis and Religion*. New Haven: Yale University Press.

Jones, James. 1996: *Religion and Psychology in Transition: Psychoanalysis, Feminism, and Theology*. New Haven: Yale University Press.

Kanter, Rosabeth Moss. 1972: *Commitment and Community: Communes and Utopias in Sociological Perspective*. Cambridge, Mass.: Harvard University Press.

Kanter, Rosabeth Moss. 1997: *World Class: Thriving Locally in the Global Economy*. New York: Touchstone, Simon and Schuster.

Kierkegaard, Søren. 1956: *Kierkegaard's Attack Upon "Christendom."* Trans. with an intro. by Walter Lowrie. Boston: Beacon Press.

King, Martin Luther, Jr. 1963: The Ethical Demands of Integration. *Religion and Labor*. May 1963.

Kirkpatrick, Frank G. 1985: From Shackles to Liberation: Religion, the Grimke Sisters and Dissent. In Yvonne Haddad and Ellison Banks Findly, eds., *Women, Religion and Social Change*. Albany: State University of New York Press, 433–55.

Kirkpatrick, Frank G. 1986: *Community: A Trinity of Models*. Washington, DC: Georgetown University Press.

Kirkpatrick, Frank G. 1994: *Together Bound: God, History and the Religious Community*. New York: Oxford University Press.

Knight, Janice. 1994: *Orthodoxies in Massachusetts*. Cambridge, Mass.: Harvard University Press.

Kuttner, Robert. 1997: *Everything for Sale: The Virtue and Limits of Markets*. New York: Alfred A. Knopf.

Kymlicka, Will. 1988: Liberalism and Communitarianism. *Canadian Journal of Philosophy*, 18, 2 (June 1988), 181–203.

Kymlicka, Will. 1994: Communitarianism, Liberalism, and Superliberalism. *Critical Review*, Spring 1994, 263–84.

Lawrence, C.H. 1984: *Medieval Monasticism*. London: Longman.

Leone, Mark P. 1979: *Roots of Modern Mormonism*. Cambridge, Mass.: Harvard University Press.

Littell, Franklin. 1964: *The Origins of Sectarian Protestantism*. New York: Macmillan.

Lockridge, Kenneth. 1970: *A New England Town: The First Hundred Years*. New York: Norton.

Lohfink, Gerhard. 1984: *Jesus and Community: The Social Dimension of the Christian Faith*. Philadelphia: Fortress Press.

MacIntyre, Alasdair. 1981: *After Virtue*. South Bend: University of Notre Dame Press.

Macmurray, John. 1938: *The Clue to History*. London: SCM.

Macmurray, John. 1943: *Constructive Democracy*. London: Faber and Faber.

Macmurray, John. 1962: *Reason and Emotion*. New York: Barnes and Noble.

Macmurray, John. 1991: *Persons in Relation*. Intro. by Frank G. Kirkpatrick. New York: Humanities Press.

Macmurray, John. 1991: *The Self as Agent*. Intro. by Stanley Harrison. New York: Humanities Press.

Macpherson, C.B. 1972: *The Political Theory of Possessive Individualism*. Oxford: Oxford University Press.

Madison, James. 1965: The Federalist Papers, Number 10. In Russel B. Nye and Norman S. Grabo, eds., *American Thought and Writing*, vol. 2. Boston: Houghton Mifflin.

Marx, Karl. 1977: On James Mill. In *Karl Marx: Selected Writings*, ed. David McLellan. Oxford: Oxford University Press.

McGiffert, Michael. 1992: Religion and Profit Do Jump Together. In *Reflections*. New Haven: Yale Divinity School.

McLoughlin, William. 1974: Revivalism. In Edwin S. Gaustad, ed., *The Rise of Adventism: Religion and Society in Mid-Nineteenth Century America*. New York: Harper and Row, 119–53.

McLoughlin, William. 1978: *Revivals, Awakenings, and Reform*. Chicago: University of Chicago Press.

Meeks, Wayne. 1993: *The Origins of Christian Morality*. New Haven: Yale University Press.

Milbank, John. 1997: *The World Made Strange*. Oxford: Blackwell.

Milis, Ludo J.R. 1992: *Angelic Monks and Earthly Men*. Woodbridge, UK: Boydell Press.

Morris, Colin. 1989: *The Papal Monarchy: The Western Church from 1050 to 1250*. Oxford: Clarendon Press.

Mueller, William A. 1965: *Church and State in Luther and Calvin*. Garden City: Anchor Books.

National Conference of Catholic Bishops. 1986: *Economic Justice for All: Pastoral Letter on Catholic Social Teaching and the US Economy*. Washington: United States Catholic Conference.

Niebuhr, H. Richard. 1956: *The Kingdom of God in America*. Hamden: The Shoe String Press.

Niebuhr, H. Richard. 1963: *The Responsible Self*. New York: Harper and Row.

Niebuhr, Reinhold. 1932: *Moral Man and Immoral Society*. New York: Charles Scribner's Sons.

Niebuhr, Reinhold. 1941: *The Nature and Destiny of Man*. New York: Charles Scribner's Sons.

Niebuhr, Reinhold. 1944: *The Children of Light and the Children of Darkness*. New York: Charles Scribner's Sons.

Niebuhr, Reinhold. 1956: *An Interpretation of Christian Ethics*. New York: Meridian Books.

Niebuhr, Reinhold. 1965: *Man's Nature and His Communities*. New York: Charles Scribner's Sons.

Nielsen, Kai. 1982: Capitalism, Socialism, and Justice. In *And Justice for All: New Introductory Essays in Ethics and Public Policy*, eds. Tom Regan and Donald VanDeVeer. Totowa: Rowman and Littlefield, 264–87.

Noyes, George Wallingford, ed. 1971: *Religious Experience of John Humphrey Noyes*. Freeport, NY: Books for Libraries Press.

Noyes, John Humphrey. 1966: *History of American Socialisms*, with a new intro. by Mark Holloway. New York: Dover Publications.

Nozick, Robert. 1974: *Anarchy, State, and Utopia*. New York: Basic Books.

Parker, Charles H. 1998: *The Reformation of Community: Social Welfare and Calvinist Charity in Holland, 1572–1620*. Cambridge: Cambridge University Press.

Parker, Robert Allerton. 1935: *A Yankee Saint: John Humphrey Noyes and the Oneida Community*. New York: G. P. Putnam's Sons.

Parsons, Susan. 1996: *Feminism and Christian Ethics*. Cambridge: Cambridge University Press.

Peck, M. Scott. 1987: *The Different Drum: Community-Making and Peace*. New York: Touchstone Books, Simon & Schuster.

Pemberton, Prentiss L. and Daniel Rush Finn. 1985: *Toward a Christian Economic Ethic*. Minneapolis: Winston Press.

Peters, Edward, ed. 1980: *Heresy and Authority in Medieval Europe*. Philadelphia: University of Pennsylvania Press.

Phillips, Derek. 1993: *Looking Backward: A Critical Appraisal of Communitarian Thought*. Princeton: Princeton University Press.

Rasmussen, Larry L. 1993: *Moral Fragments and Moral Community: A Proposal for Church in Society*. Minneapolis: Fortress Press.

Rauschenbusch, Walter. 1918: *A Theology for the Social Gospel*. New York: Macmillan.

Rauschenbusch, Walter. 1964: *Christianity and the Social Crisis*, ed. Robert D. Cross. New York: Harper Torchbooks.

Rawls, John. 1971: *A Theory of Justice*. Cambridge, Mass.: Harvard University Press.

Rawls, John. 1985: Justice as Fairness: Political Not Metaphysical. *Philosophy and Public Affairs*, 14, 223–51.

Rawls, John. 1988: The Priority of Rights and Ideas of the Good. *Philosophy and Public Affairs*, 17, 251–76.

Redekop, Calvin. 1989: *Mennonite Society*. Baltimore: Johns Hopkins Press.

Robertson, Constance Noyes. 1972: *Oneida Community: The Breakup*. Syracuse: Syracuse University Press.

Rousseau, Philip. 1985: *Pachomius: The Making of a Community in Fourth-Century Egypt*. Berkeley: University of California Press.

Royce, Josiah. 1913: *The Problem of Christianity*, vols. 1 and 2. New York: The Macmillan Company.

Rugoff, Milton. 1989: *America's Gilded Age*. New York: Henry Holt and Co.

Ryan, John A. 1942: The Economic Philosophy of St. Thomas. In Robert E. Brennan, ed., *Essays in Thomism*. New York: Sheed and Ward.

Sandel, Michael. 1992: The Procedural Republic and the Unencumbered Self. In Shlomo Avineri and Avner De-Shalit, eds., *Communitarianism and Individualism*. New York: Oxford University Press, 12–28.

Scroggs, Robin. 1977: *Paul for a New Day*. Philadelphia: Fortress Press.

Scroggs, Robin. 1998: The Bible as Foundational Document. In Paul T. Jersild et al., eds., *Moral Issues and Christian Response*. Forth Worth: Harcourt Brace College Publishers.

Selznick, Philip. 1992: *The Moral Commonwealth: Social Theory and the Promise of Community*. Berkeley: University of California Press.

Shain, Barry Alan. 1994: *The Myth of American Individualism: The Protestant Origins of American Political Thought*. Princeton: Princeton University Press.

Smith, Kenneth L. and Ira G. Zepp, Jr. 1974: *Search for the Beloved Community: The Thinking of Martin Luther King, Jr*. Valley Forge: Judson Press.

Smith, Timothy. 1965: *Revivalism and Social Reform*. New York: Harper and Row.

Smith, Timothy. 1974: Social Reform. In Edwin S. Gaustad, ed., *The Rise of Adventism: Religion and Society in Mid-Nineteenth Century America*. New York: Harper and Row, 18–29.

Sobrino, Jan. 1981: The Witness of the Church in Latin America. In Sergio Torres and John Eagleson, eds., *The Challenge of Basic Christian Communities*, trans. John Drury. Maryknoll: Orbis.

Stein, Stephen J. 1992: *The Shaker Experience in America*. New Haven: Yale University Press.

Stephan, Karen H. and G. Edward Stephan. 1973: Religion and the Survival of Utopian Communities. *Journal for the Scientific Study of Religion*, 12, 89–99.

Sullivan, William M. 1982: *Reconstructing Public Philosophy*. Berkeley: University of California Press.

Taylor, Charles. 1989: Cross-Purposes: The Liberal–Communitarian Debate. In Nancy Rosenblum, ed., *Liberalism and the Moral Life*. Cambridge, Mass.: Harvard University Press.

Taylor, Charles. 1992: Atomism. In Shlomo Avineri and Avner De-Shalit, eds., *Communitarianism and Individualism*. New York: Oxford University Press, 29–50.

Thomas, Lawrence. 1989: *Living Morally*. Philadelphia: Temple University Press.

Thornwell, James Henley. 1969: The Rights and Duties of Masters. In Robert L. Ferm, ed., *Issues in American Protestantism*. Garden City, NY: Doubleday, 189–200.

Tocqueville, Alexis de. 1969: *Democracy in America*, trans. George Lawrence, ed. J.P. Mayer. New York: Doubleday Anchor.

Tonnies, Ferdinand. 1957: *Community and Society (Gemeinschaft und Gesellschaft)*, trans. and ed. Charles P. Loomis. New York: Harper Torchbooks.

Tyler, Alice Felt. 1944: *Freedom's Ferment*. New York: Harper and Row.

Ullman, Walter. 1972: *A Short History of the Papacy in the Middle Ages*. London: Methuen & Co., Ltd.

Universal Declaration of Human Rights. 1948: US Dept. of State, Selected Documents, no. 5.

Vasquez, Manuel A. 1998: *The Brazilian Popular Church and the Crisis of Modernity*. Cambridge: Cambridge University Press.

Wayland, Francis. 1968: The Elements of Political Economy. In William McLoughlin, ed., *The American Evangelicals 1800–1900*. New York: Harper Torchbooks, 101–27.

Weber, Max. 1958: *The Protestant Ethic and the Spirit of Capitalism*. New York: Scribner.

Williams, G. H., ed. 1957: *Spiritual and Anabaptist Writers*. The Library of Christian Classics, vol. 25. Philadelphia: The Westminster Press.

Winthrop, John. 1988: A Modell of Christian Charity. In Robert N. Bellah et al., eds., *Individualism and Commitment in American Life: Readings on the Themes of Habits of the Heart*. New York: Harper and Row.

Wood, Gordon. 1969: *The Creation of the American Republic*. Chapel Hill: University of North Carolina Press.

Wood, Gordon. 1985: "Hellfire Politics." Review of J. P. Diggins, *The Lost Soul of American Politics*, in *New York Review of Books*, Feb.

Wood, Gordon. 1992: *The Radicalism of the American Revolution*. New York: Alfred Knopf.

Woody, J. Melvin. 1998: *Freedom's Embrace*. University Park, Penn.: Pennsylvania University Press.

Wuthnow, Robert. 1994: *Sharing the Journey: Support Groups and America's New Quest for Community*. New York: The Free Press.

Yack, Bernard. 1988: Liberalism and Its Communitarian Critics: Does Liberal
    Practice "Live Down" to Liberal Theory? In Charles H. Reynolds and Ralph
    V. Norman, eds., *Community in America: The Challenge of Habits of the Heart.*
    Berkeley: University of California Press, 147–71.
Young, Iris Marion. 1990: *Justice and the Politics of Difference.* Princeton: Princeton
    University Press.
Zablocki, David. 1971: *The Joyful Community.* Baltimore: Penguin Press.

Index